UNCOVERING
SHAME

UNCOVERING
SHAME

An Approach
Integrating Individuals
and Their Family Systems

James M. Harper, Ph.D.
and
Margaret H. Hoopes, Ph.D.

DEPARTMENT OF FAMILY SCIENCES
BRIGHAM YOUNG UNIVERSITY
PROVO, UTAH

W. W. NORTON & COMPANY • *NEW YORK* • *LONDON*

Library of Congress Cataloging-in-Publication Data

Harper, James M.
Uncovering shame : an approach integrating individuals and their family
systems / by James M. Harper & Margaret H. Hoopes.
p.   cm.
Includes bibliographical references (p.   ) and index.
ISBN 0-393-70101-8
1. Shame.   2. Mentally ill—Family relationships.   3. Family—
Mental health.   I. Hoopes, Margaret M.   II. Title.
RC455.4.S53H37   1990   152.4—dc20   90-36004

W. W. Norton & Company, Inc., 500 Fifth Avenue, New York, N.Y. 10110
W. W. Norton & Company, Ltd., 37 Great Russell Street, London WC1B 3NU

2   3   4   5   6   7   8   9   0

Foreword

THIS IS NOT AN ordinary book. It is path-breaking and pioneering, in keeping with a contemporary trend toward the integration of diverse theories and therapies within the repertoires of therapists. Here we have an exemplary effort to harmonize a number of concepts and approaches from individual psychology within a sophisticated family systems frame of reference. This is not an easy thing to do, either in theory or in practice, and that may be one reason why there are not more books like this one.

Illuminating such concepts as identity, intimacy, dependency, and responsibility, James Harper and Margaret Hoopes bring different perspectives to bear on important matters of development and relationship functioning. A certain synergy accrues from their blend that is more than the sum of its parts. They offer a liberating way of thinking about human behavior and of putting together different pieces of research literature with a pertinent array of theories and practices that causes one to think differently about all the phenomena. For such reasons, both academics and practitioners will find this book thought-provoking.

With shame (vs. guilt) as their centerpiece, the authors discuss a wide array of issues in personality theory, relationship and family theories, and therapeutic change. This strategy works well. Readers should be advised that the authors do not focus narrowly; rather, they educate us anew concerning the major issues in contemporary approaches to mental health. Professionals in all mental health disciplines will benefit from reading this book.

This book underscores the need for interdisciplinary integrations. In this instance, the comprehensiveness of the family perspective is visible along with the penetrating quality of psychological perspectives. The various ways in which these perspectives rise and fall throughout the narrative is an artistic achievement in itself—one that other professionals might well imitate.

Allen E. Bergin, Ph.D.
Professor and Director of
    Clinical Psychology
Brigham Young University

Contents

List of Tables and Figures

TABLES

FIGURES

Preface

FOR US THIS BOOK REPRESENTS an odyssey of approximately 12 years, as we have matured in life and professional experiences and wrestled with the concepts of shame and guilt and their psychological effects in the lives of people. Until recently others with whom we discussed the terms of shame and guilt knew what these terms meant to them, but there was little agreement; in addition, the literature provided little theory and research about how to conceptualize and treat the negative affects of shame and guilt. Our journey is not over; however, the contents of this book carve the path and set the challenge for the testing of these ideas through research and the practice of therapy. We look forward to the enrichment of readers' responses and research as valuable feedback in the second stage of our journey.

This book emphasizes the integration of individual and systems concepts rather than the traditional psychoanalytic approach to shame. Its purposes are to articulate a conceptual model of shame and guilt, to help professionals assess and identify shame-prone individuals and family systems, to describe how people of different sibling positions experience and exhibit shame, and to develop treatment approaches for shame-prone clients in individual, couple, and family therapy. Therapists experience shame-prone clients as among the most challenging cases they treat. One reason is that the underlying dynamics of shame and the behaviors that represent those dynamics are not well understood by most therapists. Therapists' own unresolved shame issues also color the dynamics of shame in therapy.

Clinical examples are used throughout the book. The first part of the book, Chapters 1, 2, and 3, provides definitions and explains the development of shame and guilt. In Chapter 1 the difference between shame as an emotion and shame as an identity is introduced, with healthy vs. unhealthy guilt integrated into this presentation. A review of the literature and a case study fortify this introduction. Chapter 2 introduces the application in families of the affirmation triangle of accountability, intimacy, and dependency as one explanation of the development of shame-prone identities. The third chapter focuses on the relationship between psychological needs, affect, and shame-prone issues, as well as the effects on individual identity when needs are not met with positive affirmations.

The second part of the book, Chapters 4, 5, and 6, describes the effects of various family environments on development of individual, couple, and family identity. The characteristics of healthy families and conditions leading to healthy identities are covered in Chapter 4. Transient shame and healthy guilt mark these families, rather than internalized shame and the use of unhealthy guilt, as is common in the families described in Chapters 5 and 6. Chapter 5 introduces the negative affirmation triangle, as well as the dysfunctional family profile and conditions leading to shaming systems that produce shame-prone identities. The families that produce moderate shame-prone identities are described in Chapter 6. These families have conditions that lead to identities shamed on the intimacy or dependency dimensions. Also in this chapter is a model that integrates the shame conditions produced by these families.

The third part of the book focuses on assessment of shame and guilt. Chapter 7 describes the response patterns of the first four systemic positions in families. Whether families are healthy and affirm each systemic position or are unhealthy shaming systems that negatively affirm these positions affects each of the four systemic positions differently. Knowing these patterns allows the therapist to assess clients from this perspective. Standardized and informal methods and measures of shame-prone individuals, couples, and families are described in Chapter 8. Checklists of shame-prone behaviors for individuals and shaming system, along with shame and guilt concepts applied to the Circumplex Model, provide immediate practical assessment aids for therapists.

The last part of the book is devoted to treatment of shame-prone clients. Chapter 9 focuses on therapists' confronting their own shame. Signals for recognizing feelings of shame and identification of activators of therapist shame are described and integrated with therapists' family-of-origin issues. The treatment map for working through the patterns of unmet needs, issues, and affect of shame-prone clients and systems is presented in Chapter 10. Chapter 11 sets the stage for therapy by describing an approach to working with shame-prone clients and pitfalls and guidelines for therapists. Chapter 12 focuses on the early stage of therapy, with emphasis on client-therapist relationship, assessment goals, therapeutic goals for the client, process goals for the therapist, and interventions and therapeutic strategies. The middle stage of therapy, covered in Chapter 13, integrates the use of the treatment map with interventions and therapeutic strategies to deal with shame-prone patterns, the wounded inner child, and other shame issues to move the client and shaming systems toward wholeness and health. Interventions that target shame-prone feelings, beliefs, and behaviors, using visualizations, metaphors, and affirmation patterns, form the thrust of the chapter. Pitfalls for therapists and guidelines for dealing with the special challenges of client-therapist relationships are also part of this chapter.

The last stage of therapy is covered in Chapter 14. Assisting clients to live with wholeness, adjust to less therapy support and more community support, and manage the termination of some therapy modalities facilitates this last stage of therapy. The last chapter presents a representative therapy case showing assessment, a variety of therapy modalities, the utilization of the team approach, and interventions from each of the three stages of therapy.

Acknowledgments

FIRST OF ALL, we acknowledge our families and friends for their support through the time-consuming process of writing this book. Without that support it is doubtful that we would have finished. Secondly, we acknowledge two mentors of the early '70s, Jerome Bach and Alan Anderson, who introduced us to some shame and guilt concepts. Their ideas and applications challenged our thinking and creativity. Third, we acknowledge the untiring efforts and skills of our secretary, Annette Hoxie, who gleans the errors in our manuscripts, meets our deadlines, and does many behind-the-scenes tasks that are never recognized. We also want to recognize the support of our colleagues and students at Brigham Young University, who have supported us and cheered us on.

We would also like to acknowledge those who read early versions of the manuscript and gave us helpful advice and encouragement to complete the book: Sally Barlow, Raphael Becvar, Cindy Cooley, Leslie Feinauer, and Barbara Fisher.

UNCOVERING
SHAME

SECTION I

Development of Shame and Guilt

CHAPTER 1
"Will I Ever Quit Being Bad?"
The Case of a Shame-Prone Woman

THE DIFFERENCE BETWEEN shame and guilt puzzles most people since the words are often used synonymously. In fact, experiences of guilt and shame are often intertwined. However, differentiating between the two is crucial in understanding the development of personal identity. Shame is an emotion in response to a negative evaluation of one's *self*, whereas guilt is an evaluation of *behavior*. When people recognize that their behavior has violated some standard that has meaning to them, they feel guilty for having done it. Guilt is emotionally healthy and a necessary process of living with others, as long as it is an evaluation of behavior rather than being, leads to changing that behavior, and is not chronically excessive.

In contrast, the feeling of shame does not involve an evaluation of behavior as much as an evaluation of the self. Isolated experiences of shame occur in most people's lives, but when individuals have chronic shame experiences they develop a shame-prone identity. Shame-prone persons interpret every incident as validation of how worthless they are, how bad they are, how unlovable, how incapable of loving and giving to others. All shame-prone people also experience guilt; however, rather than being healthy, this guilt is excessive, chronic, intense, and rarely producing of a change in behavior. When guilt looks pathological, there is always shame underneath. Individuals who are shame-prone use guilt to shame themselves more. Rather than changing behavior for the better, they just keep feeling guilty. Persons with shame-prone identities split off feelings as bad parts of themselves (Ahktar & Byrne, 1983; Grotstein, 1981). They avoid their hidden and lost true self, the feelings of childhood, until depression or some other emotional or mental disorder confronts them (Miller, 1981).

Therapists often recognize symptoms of unhealthy guilt in their clients, but when guilt becomes the focus of therapy the more basic problem of shame-proneness remains uncovered. It appears to be the nature of people to hide their feelings of shame, and shame-prone clients go to great lengths to keep their shame embedded in other symptoms and dynamics. The following case illustrates the mix of shame and unhealthy guilt that is typical of many clients.

When Marilyn* called to make her first therapy appointment, she wanted to be sure that I knew that she had seen several different therapists, including some psychiatrists. She emphasized that she had tried many different kinds of medications for her depression, but none of them and none of the other therapists had been helpful. I wondered, if all of these other therapists had failed, how could I be successful with her? I responded by asking Marilyn how she thought I might fail her also. There was stunned silence on the other end of the phone. I asked if she was still there, to which minimal responses were given. Confused and frustrated, I wondered what type of client this woman really was. What was I getting myself into?

Before Marilyn arrived for her first appointment, I conjectured what she might be like. She must be very fragile, I thought. It will be difficult to get her to talk and she will probably try to manipulate me. Because she had barely been able to talk to me on the phone, I assumed that she must not function very well in everyday life. If making an appointment had been that difficult, what was the therapy process itself going to be like? I envisioned a woman unable to handle most of the daily stressors in life, a person incapable of handling most aspects of her life.

When Marilyn arrived for her first appointment, I quickly decided how wrong I had been. She was an attractive, well-groomed young woman who looked me in the eyes as she offered a firm handshake. Seeing her sitting in one of my chairs with her legs crossed, I had no difficulty imagining her as the very successful businesswoman she said she was. She reported that her involvement with several consulting firms in Chicago had led to consultation with several nationally based corporations. She had graduated with a master's degree in business administration at the top of her class. She had applied to many prestigious doctoral programs in business, and it appeared likely that she would be accepted at every one of them with offers of significant financial support. I marveled at her intellect and accomplishments.

When I commented on her accomplishments and her intellectual brightness, the mood of the session quickly changed. She was silent, just as she had been on the phone. I was puzzled. I had said something that would normally be positively affirming to a client. Yet she appeared very distressed by what I had said. She never again looked at me directly in that

*Like the other clients in this book, "Marilyn" is a composite of many clients we have seen. Any resemblance to an actual person is coincidental.

first session. She spent most of the time with her eyes glued to her hands in her lap, slouched just enough so that her long hair angled forward, hiding most of her face and especially her eyes. I asked her what I said that appeared to have upset her, and she became even more withdrawn and silent. I puzzled again. The air in the room seemed heavy and I felt burdened by unidentified expectations. How could a woman who appeared so bright and intelligent a few minutes ago, a woman who had been a consultant to several national companies, a woman applying to some of the most prestigious doctoral programs in the country—how could such a woman switch before my eyes into this withdrawn, suspicious, hidden person? After a long silence and in a subdued voice, Marilyn told me that all anyone appreciated in her was her I.Q. and what she could do.

The following dialogue is taken from the early part of the first session with Marilyn, after the shift in her demeanor.

Therapist: (pleasantly) How long have you lived in this area?
Marilyn: (with a quick look and a suspicious voice) Why do you want to know?
Therapist: I was just curious as to what brought you to (name of city)?
Marilyn: What do you mean by that?
Therapist: Well, I just wanted to know.
(long period of silence)
Therapist: What brings you to therapy, Marilyn?
Marilyn: As I told you over the telephone, I have been to many different therapists over the last seven years. I have tried many different kinds of medication, and none of it has helped. I am weary of fighting my depression, so I thought I would try one more time. Other people get help. Why can't I?
Therapist: So tell me what you would like to have happen in therapy at this time.
Marilyn: (quickly, in a rather terse, hard tone) What do you mean by that?
Therapist: I would just like to know what your expectations about our relationship are . . .
Marilyn: (interrupting) What do you mean, *my* expectations?
Therapist: (calmly and rationally) People usually have some notion of what they hope to accomplish by coming to a therapist.
Marilyn: So you think I have preconceived notions?
Therapist: I just assume that you probably thought about what coming here today would be like, and I was curious about what you thought. What is it that you are feeling here with me now?
Marilyn: (quietly, with a small lessening of stress in her posture) I don't know. Everything inside of me just gets so confusing.
Therapist: (in the same quiet tone) Your feelings get all jumbled up inside and they seem hard to sort out.

Marilyn: (in a very defensive tone, with more rigidity in her posture) What
      do you mean?
Therapist: (calmly) I'm hoping to better understand how you feel.
Marilyn: (defensively) Why?
Therapist: Because I care . . .
Marilyn: (interrupting) How can you care—you haven't even met me be-
      fore today.
Therapist: (firmly and compassionately) I am still interested in how you
      feel.
Marilyn: Isn't there something you're not telling me?
Therapist: Well, no, I don't think so. I am just trying to understand you
      better (leaning slightly forward and looking at her intently).
Marilyn: What do you mean by that? (a quick look at the therapist and then
      dropping her head)
Therapist: I'd like to get to know you if I am going to be your therapist.
Marilyn: What do you mean, "get to know me"? (a slight raise to her voice)

Marilyn seemed incapacitated by my simple attempts to join with her.
At times throughout the initial session she responded to my questions, but
at other times she seemed unreachable. After the mood of the session
changed when I commented on her accomplishments, Marilyn avoided eye
contact with me by averting her eyes to other targets or by staring at the
floor. As the session progressed and she appeared to get more defensive,
she leaned farther forward, so that her hair covered her face. She grabbed
hold of her body and held herself tightly.

When I asked normal "chit chat" types of questions, Marilyn asked why
I wanted to know. She seemed to be suspicious of everything I asked, and
her questions indicated that she was constantly trying to second guess
what I was thinking. She wanted to know what was behind everything I
said and did. She ascribed motives not only to what I said but also to what I
was thinking, and all of the motives she ascribed to me put her in negative
light. It was as if she had decided that she was flawed at her basic core.
Based on her knowledge of this flaw she assumed that everyone else felt
the same way. She suspected rather quickly that I thought negatively of
her; if I would only tell the truth, it would confirm what she already felt.
Marilyn acted as if I already felt she was a bad person and adopted a
defensive stance toward everything I did or said, including a friendly greet-
ing like "hello." Marilyn had internalized her parents' attitudes of her,
especially her feelings, as bad. As an adult she now projected her "bad me"
part on everyone that had contact with her. These introjection and splitting processes in which children lose touch with their emotions and real
self, and as adults project on to others, are described in more detail by
object relations theorists (Fairbairn, 1963; Masterson, 1985; Masterson &
Klein, 1989; Miller, 1981; Scharff & Scharff, 1987).

When I met Marilyn the first time I was not focused on the possibility that she was shame-prone. Little did I know about the amount of shame Marilyn carried as part of her identity. Nor did I speculate at that moment that Marilyn based her identity on an accumulation of the shame she had experienced in her family.

As I had time to think about our interaction, I guessed that I had come too close to uncovering my client's shame. The external facial signs, her nonverbal behavior, her shift in her presentation of herself—all were typical symptoms of being shame-prone. Her emotional demeanor was that of unexpected exposure and then expectations of more exposure. It was as though, by asking seemingly benign questions, I had exposed Marilyn's bad self to view. Experiencing her reactions to me, I was aware of feeling exposed myself and wanting to hide. For some reason her suspicious and questioning style was threatening to me. I knew I was irritated; after all, I was simply trying to help her feel at ease, to make some connection between the two of us that would be the beginning of a trusting therapeutic relationship. But my anger was really a reaction to her questioning what she thought were my underlying, devious intentions and motives. I realized that I felt shamed, as if I had done something wrong. Marilyn's shame had somehow reminded me of times when I felt shamed and now I, as a therapist, was feeling shamed by the behavior of my client.

SHAME AS EMOTION

According to Tompkins (1987, 1984, 1982, 1963, 1962), shame is one of nine innate affects and is related primarily to a feeling of inferiority in individuals, families, and groups. The judging behavior of other people, established standards, and cultural mores, whether implicit or explicit, provide the context for shameful experiences. Other words used to describe this same feeling include humiliation, embarrassment, discouragement, and sometimes shyness. When one feels shame, the simultaneous facial display includes lowering the eyelids, decreasing the tone of all facial muscles, lowering the head via a reduction in tension of the neck muscles, or a tilting of the head in one direction (Kaufman, 1989; Tompkins, 1987). Internally, the person wants to disappear, be someone else, erase the present, and back up time to undo what is shameful.

Everyone has experienced shame. Yet there is a vast difference between a person having a shameful experience and a person having a shame-prone identity. In fact, some degree of shameful experience is unavoidable and even helpful when people relate to each other, but shame-proneness is always devastating. Marilyn, in the above example, exhibited a shame-prone identity, and the therapist experienced shame as an emotional reaction to her.

When shame is experienced as a transient emotion it provides certain adaptive functions in families and other groups (Bradshaw, 1988; Izard, 1977; Kaufman, 1989). Children's early experiences of shame usually occur within their families, when their parents, siblings, and other adults react negatively to something they have done. Reading both verbal and nonverbal behavior from others, children are overwhelmed with a feeling of worthlessness, of not being accepted, of humiliation. Through this process they learn from the reactions of people that they have done something wrong or inappropriate for that situation and the people involved. By exposure to the family system and the guidelines provided by someone, usually their parents, they are persuaded to conform to certain standards regarding group identity and behavior. When they do not conform, they often feel guilty as well as shamed. The emotional experience of shame teaches us that we have limits and boundaries, as do other people (Bradshaw, 1988; Friesen, 1979).

The shaming process is not always intentional. For example, the courtship process encourages a couple toward emotional closeness, self-disclosure, and sexual connectedness in the context of privacy, a sharing only appropriate in that relationship and not meant to be shared with the "public," even one's children. In the process of encouraging these generational boundaries, parents teach their children that their marital relationship differs from their relationship with their children. Initially, this may be experienced by children as their having done something wrong and consequently being punished. Regardless of how the parents maintain the boundaries, the child may experience this as shame. Although painful to children, these types of incidents and others accompanied by momentary feelings of shame can provide the impetus for constructive self-evaluation, leading to confidence in a child's identity, to the development of beliefs and attitudes that match the identity, and to more effective behavior. Thus, shame experiences contribute to our forming and knowing who we are (Lynd, 1958). As an example of this kind of influence, Friesen (1979) cites the example of Eskimo children, who through a shaming process learn not to step on thin ice. Parents, older siblings, and extended family members laugh and make fun of the Eskimo child as soon as a foot enters water. Schneider (1977) refers to the same idea when he says that shame is a controlling and limiting affect which sustains the personal and social ordering of the world.

Shame Continuum: The Difference Between
Shame as an Emotion and Shame-prone Identity

When does shame become unhealthy? Shame is the emotional experience or feeling of painful embarrassment or humiliation that includes a sense of being insufficient as a person (Fossum & Mason, 1986). The ability to feel shame is present from birth, but developing a shame-prone identity takes time. To understand the difference between shame as a transitory affect and proneness to shame, one must understand that proneness to shame involves the formation of a negative personal identity. Those who experience shame as a transitory affect develop healthy identities.

Because they live in a consistently shaming environment, individuals who are shame-prone believe that they are flawed as people. When they expressed normal needs such as the need to be dependent, to be intimate, their parents were inconvenienced by their needs and even expressed rage in response. Children cannot sort out their parents' feelings of anger, rage, sadness, and fear from themselves. To them such reactions over a period of time can only mean that they are bad as people and must split off the bad parts of themselves (Miller, 1981). At the very core of their existence they know that they are bad. In any context they believe that others think they are bad because they believe it themselves. They even negate and disqualify feedback from others that offers any alternative to their being bad. Shame as emotion is almost always present when shame-prone people relate to others.

Table 1.1 contains the shame continuum, illustrating the differences between transitory shame experiences that assist in developing healthy identities and chronic, recurring shame experiences that lead to shame-prone identities. The headings down the right side describe several characteristics of experience: (1) the internal experience of self, (2) the range and quality of the emotional expression, (3) the beliefs people develop about themselves as a result of their shame experiences, (4) the social behaviors which they are most likely to display, and (5) the use of guilt. The continuum across the top ranges from healthy identity formation on the left to shame-prone identity on the right, with an intermediate area in between. Three categories (healthy, shamed on issues in specific contexts, and shame-prone) are identified along the continuum in order to contrast and compare the five characteristics down the right side at various places along the continuum. In reality, people in intermediate areas of the continuum may lean more toward the shame-prone end or more toward the healthy identity end.

Healthy Identities

As described in Table 1.1, people on the healthy identity end of the continuum still occasionally experience shame as an emotion. However, they do not make shame a part of their internalized identity. Their overall internal experience of self is good. The passing shame experience helps such people recognize the limits of self and prevents them from becoming self-aggrandizing or arrogant (Bradshaw, 1988).

TABLE 1.1
Shame Continuum and Identity

	Healthy Identity	Intermediate	Shame-Prone Identity
	Experiences shame as an emotion, but not as part of an internalized identity	Has some aspects of healthy identity; depending on situations, experiences shame as part of identity	Shame is part of identity; experiences shame as more than an emotion; shame confirms identity; it is better to be bad than to be nothing
Internal Experience of Self	Core is good; Self has limits	Some aspects of self are flawed in some contexts; some aspects of self are good in some contexts	Self is disgusting; flawed at very core
Emotional System	Wide range of affect; not paralyzed by intensity of emotion; emotion is integrated with intellect	Experience is at times entirely emotional; at times emotion and intellect can be integrated; may be blocked to feeling certain emotions or may get stuck in specific emotion	Experience is mostly emotional or totally blocked to emotion; very limited range of affects; can be stuck in intensity of specific emotions, e.g., fear, rage, or humiliation

Beliefs	"I am a good person." "I sometimes behave in ways I do not like, but I can change my behavior." "Others will like me if they will take the time to get to know me."	"I am bad, but maybe I can still change" (this belief is situational). "There are people in the world who will not victimize me if I keep searching for them."	"If others discover how bad I am, they will abandon me." "Others will eventually victimize me." "When others offer positive feedback, I believe they do not know me well enough. If they really knew me, they would see me as bad."
Social Behavior	Warm, self-disclosing, can have close friends	Sometimes sets up situations so that others will victimize them, but can also be "with" others in the right contexts; somewhat closed and guarded; can have close friends	Sets up context so that the tendency of others is to do things "to them" (victimize them) or do things "for them" (totally take care of them); closed, guarded, suspicious; close friendships tend to be dysfunctional; discounts all positive information
Use of Guilt	Feels guilt, and it is healthy because focus is on changing behavior rather than on the self being bad	Uses guilt to shame self in certain contexts	Excessive guilt that is used to shame self or total lack of guilt (sociopathic)

In terms of the emotional system, people with healthy identities experience a wide range of emotions, including elation, joy, and surprise as well as fear, sadness, humiliation, and anger. These emotions change and pass with time; one of them is not characteristic of the majority of a person's experience. In people with healthy identities, the intensity of any one affect is not paralyzing, and such people are able to connect emotional experiences with cognitive, more rational explanations.

The beliefs about self on the healthy end of the continuum are positive. These people believe they are good people. They are not perfect, but they recognize that they are capable of changing behaviors they do not like. For a healthy individual, the issue is not one of goodness or badness as a person; rather, it involves an evaluation of behavior as being good or bad. Bad behavior is something that can be changed, whereas a "bad" person is more difficult to change. Capable of disclosing a great deal of personal information in relationships, these people also display warmth in their interactions and have a capacity for meaningful intimacy with others.

Healthy Use of Guilt.   People with healthy identities still feel guilt when their behavior violates standards that are significant to them. No one is totally exempt from guilt (Freedman & Strean, 1986). In fact, guilt is a necessary and healthy experience when it does not lead to shaming (Zuk & Zuk, 1987). Guilt is necessary because it helps people be accountable to a set of standards for their behavior. Healthy guilt helps preserve order, maintain mutual dependency, and establish meaning and values in human relationships.

The feeling of healthy guilt can be intense and accompanied by extreme remorse. But the duration of the feeling is limited, and over time a sense of relief is felt as new learning occurs and relationships are mended.

In the healthy guilting process, the focus is on repair and growth. People can identify an actual behavior or attitude that they desire to change and anticipate an opportunity to change it. The person who experiences healthy guilt says, "I have behaved badly, and I can correct my behavior. In fact, one of the reasons I can change my behavior is that I am basically a good person." Such people change their behavior, restore any harm done to others, request forgiveness if necessary, and let go of the guilty feeling. The guilt is not pervasive or in excess, but occurs only when people desire to change some behavior that has violated their values or the values of someone with whom they have a meaningful and accountable relationship.

Shame-prone Identities

The other end of the continuum in Table 1.1 represents people who have shame-prone identities. These individuals experience the results of shaming experiences as a total part of their identity. Shame is much more pervasive for such people, and being shame-prone is more than just experiencing the emotion of shame. Proneness to shame means that cumulative experiences through life have confirmed that the basic core of the individual is defective, at least from a phenomenological perspective. Since it is impossible to throw out one's core, being "bad" as a person is better than having no identity at all. Therefore, shame-prone people interpret all of their experience through "shame-colored" glasses and even recreate experiences in relationships that shame them, thereby reaffirming their shame-prone identities. Shame-prone people's internal experience of self is that of disgust and defectiveness.

Shame-prone people usually operate out of totally emotional experience. They have difficulty integrating feeling with thinking; as a consequence they have little awareness of many of their emotions. Yet many act out of emotional experience rather than cognition. Such individuals have difficulty experiencing a wide range of affect. They appear to be stuck in the intensity of one specific emotion. For example, they may appear to be angry with everything and everybody. Such an angry individual might have difficulty expressing hurt, fear, sadness, joy, or satisfaction. It appears to others as though anger pervades every aspect of his or her experience. In contrast, another shame-prone person may be stuck in fear. To others this person would appear irrational and even paranoid. Such a person might have difficulty expressing anger or hurt.

The belief of the shame-prone individual is, "I am bad regardless of what I do, even if what I do appears good." So when others offer praise and encouragement, a shame-prone person believes these people are lying, that they do not yet have enough information, or that they are stupid. Shame-prone individuals believe that if other people just get enough information about them as a person, those others will recognize their badness. Consequently, shame-prone persons expect others to victimize them. It is as though shame-prone people have a perceptual filter that recognizes only experiences that are shaming. In this way their world is consistent and matches their beliefs about self. As paradoxical as it seems, a person who confirms the shame-prone person's "badness" has more credibility than one who proclaims the "goodness" of that person.

In relationships with other people, shame-prone persons are either victims or victimizers and may alternate between the two roles. The distinctions among doing something *to*, something *for*, or something *with* a shame-prone person are important in understanding interpersonal relationships. "Doing something to" describes the process of victimizing. Shame-prone people expect others to do something to them. However, if that is not what actually happens, then shame-prone people expect to become totally and inappropriately dependent on people, which is the "doing something for me" idea. Because intimacy and mutual sharing are incompatible with hiding and covering their core of shame, these people have difficulty thinking in terms of "doing something with" others. They must guard against others' discovering their defective, flawed personal core of self. Consequently, most relationships they develop are dysfunctional, either abusive or dependently enmeshed or both.

Unhealthy Uses of Guilt.   Guilt becomes unhealthy when people use it as a shaming mechanism. Shame-prone people almost always use guilt as a means to keep the shame-prone identity consistent and intact (Nathanson, 1987b). When guilt is used in this way, no possibility of redemption appears to exist. Shame-prone people believe they are bad even when they change the undesired behavior or attitude. Regardless of what they do, they will remain bad. Rather than focusing on repair, the shame-prone person centers on being bad, and guilt is used to affirm the shame. "See the terrible thing I have done; I am bad," is the internal belief that affirms the shame-prone identity.

There are three characteristics of unhealthy guilt. First, as identified in Table 1.1, guilt is used to excess. Shame-prone people may use guilt about anything and everything to maintain and affirm the consistent sense that they are bad. Second, rather than being time-limited, feelings of guilt may last a lifetime or, in an intergenerational sense, several lifetimes. The guilt is used to perpetuate the shame-prone identity, which in turn perpetuates the guilt, which never goes away. Third, the focus is on the "bad behavior," confirming once again the "bad self." Repair seems impossible (Fossum & Mason, 1986).

For the shame-prone person, one other possibility exists, that of no guilt whatsoever. People can behave badly against their own set of standards or against the standards of someone to whom they desire to be appropriately accountable. Yet they may feel no guilt whatsoever. Antisocial personality disorders, narcissistic personality disorders, and conduct disorders include descriptions of symptoms related to feeling no guilt.

Lacking feelings of guilt when it would be appropriate to change some behavior can be just as unhealthy as using excessive guilt to confirm proneness to shame. A person with a shame-prone identity who experiences no guilt will exploit people in relationships and appear irresponsible. The underlying belief of such persons is, "I am bad anyway, so what does it matter if I violate the standards of others."

Healthy/Shame-Prone Identities

The middle ground of the shame continuum in Table 1.1 represents people who have some aspects of healthy identity but also experience proneness to shame depending on the situations in which they find themselves. In fact, all of the descriptors, i.e., internal experience of self, emotional system, beliefs, social behavior, and use of guilt, become contextual

entity. In
1 because
o wear in
. When I
. Marilyn
1 her life
be some-
The list
ange and
ess, addi-
l to have
cused on
uld neu-

ntagion
Her be-
I asked
e inter-
rapists.
transi-
initial
ternal-
myself,

middle of the continuum. In certain situa-
to be totally shame-prone; yet in different
be quite healthy.
almost anything. Thoughtful and unhurried,
to make adjustments and corrections with
home. His parents valued his ability to fix
praise. However, people were puzzled as to
s personal appearance. Most of the time his
he looked unkempt and unwashed. If he was
ned ill at ease and out of place. This behavior
child he was ugly; no matter what he did, his
e wrong shirt on, he should smile more often,
way.

ntermediate area is also contextual. At times
a healthy way to lead to behavior change and
such people use guilt to emphasize how bad
no hope that changing their behavior would

f Marilyn: Is She Shame-Prone?

al characteristics of the shame-prone person in
had a difficult time maintaining eye contact. It
could be discovered through her eyes. It also
to hide. She seemed to want to disappear into
he maneuvered to cover her face. The questions
his behavior in Marilyn, even though there was
t would appear to an outsider to be shaming.
d unwillingness to disclose even the least bit of
her suspiciousness of my motives and intentions

ter in
amily
esting
eople
the

was
time,
ernal
her
o at-

saw
l re-
hole
lth,

er shame. She was even suspicious of attempts to
er. Her emphasis on the number of professionals
nsequent failures of therapy and medication was
even was affirmed by shaming experiences. Her
might encourage a therapist to do things to her,
or comment to her about her lack of eye contact,
the face of her suspiciousness. Some therapists
to take care of her, e.g., buy into her seeming
ropriately in a session, be extremely empathic and
her dependency, make assurances, etc. Either set
experienced by Marilyn as shaming because of its
orld view. She knew that if I ever really did get to
cover her defects. Therefore, she guarded against
he first contact.

Excessive guilt was used to affirm Marilyn's shame-prone
later sessions she told me that every decision was a moral decis
it involved being right or wrong. Even deciding which clothe
the morning appeared to her to involve moral and ethical issu
challenged her beliefs about this, she, of course, felt more sham
had catalogued almost everything she felt she had done wron
and often spent time thinking about the long list. She longed
one else. To her, everyone she knew was better than she w
confirmed her defective core. Rather than encouraging her to
grow, contemplating the list served to create emptiness, hopeles
tional guardedness, and wishes to escape. In fact, Marilyn seer
the capacity to feel guilty about almost anything. It was as if she
whatever would maintain her shame. By focusing on guilt she
tralize her accomplishments and abilities and deny her lovablen

On the other hand, I experienced what Tompkins calls affec
in response to Marilyn's shame-prone behavior (Tompkins, 198
havior confirmed that I might not be good enough. Every quest
was met with defensiveness and suspicion. Her responses cou
preted to mean that I too would fail, just like all of her other
Although therapists' sense of their own limitations can lead to
tory shame; this is not necessarily dysfunctional in and of itself.
session with Marilyn is a good example of the differences betwe
ized shame as exhibited by Marilyn and transitory shame as fel
her therapist.

Shaming Dynamics in Marilyn's Family

Proneness to shame develops within the context of family a
other meaningful relationships. Later chapters discuss the sham
system in greater depth, but Marilyn's family is particularly
because to outsiders it would seem to be well functioning. O
inside the family could understand, experience, and particip
shaming process that was characteristic of the family.

The process of the first several sessions of therapy with M
similar to the description at the beginning of the chapter.
however, Marilyn began to disclose some information about h
world, and she was willing to give a great deal of information
family. Eventually, an invitation was extended to her entire fa
tend several therapy sessions, which they did with some relucta

Most people who associated with members of Marilyn's
them as quite healthy and functional. Mom and dad were bo
spected in their work and social circles. The image the family
presented to the outside world was one of competence, modera

warmth, and love. However, Marilyn reported her experience in her family very differently. To her the family was stifling, intrusive, distant, emotionally intense, burdensome, and unpredictable.

Marilyn's parents' marriage was conflictual as Marilyn was growing up, but her parents had spent two years in therapy and were doing better than when they entered therapy. They reported that Marilyn was and always had been a source of contention between them. Mom was critical of Marilyn as she was growing up. Dad usually defended Marilyn when mom was openly critical, but after the face-to-face confrontation had passed, dad usually tried to suggest that maybe Marilyn needed to be different, as mom suggested. There were many arguments between mom and dad about other things, and Marilyn always felt that she was responsible for their conflict, regardless of whether their argument was about her or not. When Marilyn was in high school, the conflict between them pushed mom and dad so far apart that mom refused to go with her husband to social events with colleagues from his work setting. Dad often asked Marilyn to go with him to these social events, and out of guilt Marilyn went. Mom didn't keep them from going together. In fact, Marilyn later perceived that it was convenient for mom to have Marilyn appease dad by attending these events. Very uncomfortable with the fact that colleagues often mistook her for her father's young wife, Marilyn was never at ease. She felt uncomfortable explaining that she was not his wife, but his daughter. Compelled to lie about why her mother wasn't able to be there and to cover for both her dad and mom so that no one knew why they were not attending the social event together, she was shamed and helplessly angry.

Marilyn reported that during her youth, two to sixteen years of age, her mother was totally unpredictable. While marital and individual therapy had helped her mother in the last few years, during Marilyn's childhood it was not uncommon for her mother to have episodes of rage, crying, and sometimes depression. Marilyn described one incident in which her mother took all of the dishes out of the kitchen cupboards and threw them on the floor, smashing every one. It was Marilyn's job in the family to cover for her mother during mom's hysterical tirades. When people at church asked about her mother or when someone came to the door, it was Marilyn who protected her mother and kept these people from knowing what was really happening.

Dad's response to mom's emotional outbursts usually included getting all the children shuffled off to their rooms. After such an episode, Marilyn would believe that she hadn't done what her dad wanted her to do. She would sit in her room and obsessively go over and over all of the details of the incident and think of different ways she could have responded. When she later talked with her father, he always referred to her mother's condition and never to the quality of Marilyn's performance. With no response or thanks from her mother and no qualitative criticism from her father,

Marilyn believed that she did not do things the way her parents wanted her to do them. The anger, despair, and worthlessness grew within her as she pretended to fill the role of a dutiful, accomplished daughter.

As the children grew older, Marilyn's parents would often leave for an extended period following these intense emotional outbursts. According to Marilyn, it was impossible to predict when her mother would flip into prolonged rage, crying, or total isolation and sadness. Consequently, the children could never predict when or for how long they would be without their parents. Of course, with both parents gone Marilyn's responsibilities were multiplied.

When Marilyn began to date, both father and mother were intrusively interested in her experience. Dad tried to teach her how to flirt with her dates. When she came home, it seemed to her that he expected a detailed account of her conversation with her date. Mom was also concerned that Marilyn be feminine and gave her instructions on how to behave. Irritated and confused by all of this sudden and persistent attention and overconcern with her dating relationships, Marilyn avoided giving information to either parent. She operated in secret as much as possible, trying to keep her parents from knowing what was going on. If they didn't know they couldn't be critical. The message Marilyn received from all of this was that she couldn't be a woman or date appropriately, another instance of not being able to do something right.

On one occasion during her adolescence when Marilyn was upset, puzzled, and worried, she talked to a friend about her mother's unpredictable hysteria. At church Marilyn's friend's mother inquired of Marilyn's father how his wife was doing. Marilyn received the brunt of her father's anger for talking to someone outside the family about mom's problems. When mom found out what Marilyn had done, she threw a tantrum and left the house. Dad followed to try to find her. Later that night he called Marilyn to tell her that they were at a motel two hours away and would be there for a few days. Five days later mom and dad returned home. The incident was never mentioned again. The pressure to keep the "secret" was overpowering.

Whenever Marilyn returned from visiting the neighbors' homes, both mom and dad wanted to know what she had talked about with the neighbors. They wanted to make sure that she had not talked about the family or anyone in the family while she was visiting.

In terms of sibling relationships within the family, Marilyn had a great deal of conflict with her sister, Neva, the second child. Neva was a coy, flirtatious young woman, much as dad had tried to coach Marilyn into being. The conflict between the two of them often centered on dating and recreational activity. Neva often instructed Marilyn on how to gain the attention of young men. Marilyn found her sister's advice disgusting and resented trying to manipulate men into attending to her.

Randy, the third child in the family, seemed a complete mystery to her.

Their relationship was distant; they ignored or, at most, tolerated each other. To Marilyn, he seemed detached from the family as, early in his life, he plunged into activity in several sports. Although Marilyn felt very responsible for her siblings, she often felt guilty because she didn't like them.

By the time the family members came to therapy, many of the dynamics described above were no longer occurring. Mom and dad had spent two years in marital therapy and resolved many of their issues. Mom's unpredictable emotional outbursts had disappeared. Yet, whenever Marilyn went home to visit her family, she felt totally incapacitated. Her feelings of "badness" intensified. She constantly anticipated how they would respond to her and prepared to defend herself. Obviously, visiting her family was not a pleasant experience for her.

Not everyone in Marilyn's family was shame-prone, but the family system itself was shaming. Why Marilyn internalized the shame when her siblings did not will be discussed in later chapters; for now it is enough to realize that all individuals within the family do not have to be shame-prone for the system to be shaming. However, it is common to find more than one shame-prone person in the same family. In Marilyn's case, her mother was prone to shame as well, and in family therapy we discovered that her sister was also.

CHAPTER 2
Individual Affirmation and Family Dynamics

THE MOSAIC OF FAMILY events and processes combined with the personalities of family members influences the quality of the home environment. Parents' values, experiences, personal psychological needs, couple needs, and goals set the stage for the quality of parent-child interactions. The quality of these interactions and the overall quality of the family environment shape the identities of the children. How parents meet their children's needs and their own needs to a large extent determines whether children experience transitory shame and healthy guilt or develop shame-prone identities.

In this chapter we paint a picture of how healthy identities are formed. We describe an affirmation triangle and draw some implications for how it influences patterns of transitory and shame-prone behaviors. Healthy guilt is integrated in the affirmation process through the application of parental accountability.

THE AFFIRMATION TRIANGLE

The development of healthy, as opposed to shame-prone, identities in family members is related to three important processes in the family system: accountability, dependency, and intimacy. These three dimensions are dynamic processes that affect the quality of affirmation in the family. Together they make up the affirmation triangle, as shown in Figure 2.1. Although these three processes do not function in isolation from one another, it is possible to have one or two of them operating without the other(s), e.g., accountability without dependency or intimacy, or intimacy without accountability or dependency. Children learn many things from the interaction of these three dimensions, including attitudes about

FIGURE 2.1
Affirmation Triangle

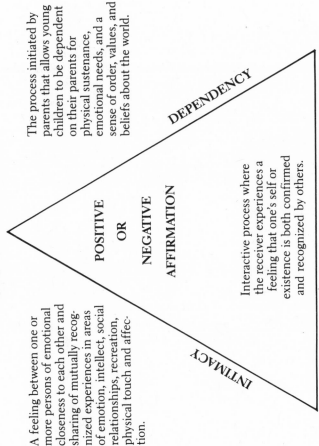

AFFIRMATION TRIANGLE

DEPENDENCY

The process initiated by
parents that allows young
children to be dependent
on their parents for
physical sustenance,
emotional needs, and a
sense of order, values, and
beliefs about the world.

POSITIVE

OR

NEGATIVE

AFFIRMATION

Interactive process where
the receiver experiences a
feeling that one's self or
existence is both confirmed
and recognized by others.

A feeling between one or
more persons of emotional
closeness to each other and
sharing of mutually recognized experiences in areas
of emotion, intellect, social
relationships, recreation,
physical touch and affec-
tion.

INTIMACY

ACCOUNTABILITY

The process in which individual family
members feel obliged to account for their
own behavior to themselves or to others
according to values and standards — to be
accountable *to* another and to be accountable
for another.

change, beliefs about self, others, and the world, spirituality, and the nature of boundaries that govern appropriate social exchange.

What Is Affirmation?

Affirmation is an interactive process where the receiver experiences a feeling that one's self or existence is confirmed and recognized both by others and by the environment. It is the process of demonstrating and acknowledging that from the perception of the affirmer something is true, a reality for him or her (DiOrio, 1986; Elkins, 1978; Glover, 1988). Affirmation can be either positive or negative for the one affirming and the receiver. The receiver does not necessarily receive the affirmation in the same way that it is given; consequently, there may be a disparity between meaning intended and meaning received. When repeated, congruent messages are sent by parents that the family is accountable and will provide appropriate dependency and intimacy, children are affirmed as unique, valuable people. The accumulation of these positive affirmations creates a sustained feeling that one's very core as a person is good, of intrinsic value just because the self exists.

If the accumulation of affirmation triangle experience is more negative than positive, individuals feel that their very core is bad, flawed in some way, disgusting to others, and deserving of shaming responses from the environment. Such negative experience is still affirming because the experience confirms that whatever one's basic core is exists, even though that core is bad in some way. Family members, especially children, will be negatively affirmed when mutual accountability is absent, physical and emotional needs go unmet, and family members feel distant, share little with each other, and have difficulty being affectionate. Such children develop shame-prone identities.

What Is Accountability?

Accountability is the process by which individual family members feel obliged to account for their own behavior to themselves or to others according to values and standards (Semin, 1983; Shotter, 1984). Accountability has two aspects—being accountable *to* another and being accountable *for* another. Being accountable to someone means feeling responsible for one's behaviors to that other person. For example, if children are given directions about how to clean their rooms, they are accountable to the parents for the quality of their room cleaning. Being accountable for others means feeling obliged to help them meet their needs. When parents recognize their children's need to eat and prepare the food for them, they are accountable for them. When children and parents are accountable to and for each other, they are mutually accountable.

By being accountable, parents set standards of acceptable conduct and enforce them, and they affirm the worth of their children. When both parents and children willingly live by the same standards and values, they are mutually accountable. When mutual accountability is present in a family:

- It is a two-way, implicitly understood part of parent-child relationships.
- Parents expect children to obey family rules.
- Children expect parents to obey rules.
- Children expect parents to set appropriate limits.
- The degree and kind of accountability shift as children grow older.

When children are young, parents own the responsibility for expecting children to live up to the parents' values and standards. As children grow older, parents expect children to begin to set some of their own limits and standards. Mutual accountability is felt by family members even when children are adults and have families of their own. At first, accountability is experienced by children as an expectation to which they must conform because of the power of parents. As children grow older, they experience the process of accounting as the importance of conforming to rules. As they grow even older, accountability is experienced as an obligation or loyalty to the relationship with parents. And even later, standards are internalized and accountability is experienced as responsibility to be true to one's own expectations and standards. The degree and kind of accountability vary within families across time and between families, with some family systems having little accountability and others expecting too much accounting from family members and in too harsh or rigid ways.

What Children Learn from Accountability

Although much of children's positive affirmation comes from the simultaneous interplay of combinations of intimacy, dependency, and accountability, children also learn specific things from the dimension of accountability. It is through the accountability dimension and the perceived power of their parents that children learn the importance of complying to standards and the necessity of maintaining social order through rules. Such attitudes are related to initial levels of moral development and are important developmental precursors for higher levels of moral development later in life (Kohlberg, 1984, 1983; Kohlberg, Levine, & Hewer, 1981). When the enforcement of rules is harsh, individuals often stay at these lower levels of moral development and base their moral decisions on factors related to the power of authority figures to punish or disapprove of them (Damon, 1988; Kurtines & Gewirtz, 1987).

When parents are accountable and expect mutual accountability in the family, children learn:

- to perceive and sense a predictable order in the world, beginning with their families;
- to accept that the order in the world is rule-governed;
- to generalize to other systems what they learn about order in the family system as they grow older;
- to predict others' responses to their behavior;
- to control social responses by controlling their own behavior;
- to respect and adhere to their own values, beliefs, feelings about and behavior toward authority.

When only accountability is present and intimacy and dependency are lacking, children learn:

- to survive in a world they perceive as a frightening place with harsh rules to which they must always conform;
- to function through blind conformity and fear of authority.

When mutual and appropriate accountability is not present, children learn:

- to fear authority because parents' expectations about children's accountability are rigid and high and enforced by harsh discipline;
- to disregard authority in other systems.

Children raised in such conditions, and later as adults, will be distrustful of anyone in authority. Outwardly, these children may appear extremely rebellious or may avoid interaction with people in power. Regardless of which explicit form the behavior takes, fear of authority is the core issue.

When accountability is low or absent in families, children tend:

- to be impulsive and lean toward extreme individuality, totally ignoring family loyalty;
- to have poor self-discipline, because the family has not required them to be accountable, which makes it even harder for them to account for themselves.

How Accountability Affects Guilt.   Accountability is the dimension that most influences guilt in family members. Parents who are accountable to and for their children foster a climate that encourages children to recognize mistakes and change their behavior. This type of guilt is healthy because the emphasis is on bad behavior that can be changed rather than on "bad me." If shame accompanies healthy guilt, it is transitory and passes. When accountability is absent, family members learn to be irresponsible and appear to lack guilt responses when their behavior has violated some standard and hurt others. When accountability is present but expectations are unreachable and harshly enforced, family members feel excessively guilty. Such guilt usually shames individuals so that, rather than being able to focus on changing behavior, they focus on feeling bad inside. If such processes are chronic and repetitive in families, the excessive guilt turns to internalized shame.

What Is Dependency?

Dependency is the condition of being dependent, of needing assistance to survive. Children are born dependent upon adults to care for them because they have needs that they cannot initially meet for themselves. It is also the process initiated by parents that allows young children to be dependent on them for physical sustenance, emotional needs, and a sense of order, values, and beliefs about the world (Birtchnell, 1988; Phillipson, Bernard, & Strang, 1986). If family members can depend on each other to meet physical, emotional, and psychological needs, the family works as a unit to provide security. When appropriate dependency is provided, a parent is accepting of a child's dependent status. Parents recognize their children's needs and freely accept these needs within the context in which they occur. There is a greater need for dependency of children upon parents when children are young. As children grow older, it is appropriate for them to develop independence from their parents by meeting many of their own needs or getting them met elsewhere. They also learn to be interdependent as they accept increasing responsibility for their own decisions and actions. By accepting the family values and rules and incorporating them into their behavior, they become interdependent with their parents and other family members.

When parents do not or cannot accept a child's need for dependency, the child experiences separateness but not individuation. Such children grow up being distant and isolated from others, distrustful of people and their environment, and lacking confidence in their own power and ability. The provision of dependency in early childhood is necessary in order for children to develop healthy identity during adolescence (Goodrich, 1984). When parents accept the need for a child to be dependent on them, they foster the conditions for that child to be a unique, valued person who can separate appropriately as he or she grows older. In such a relationship, children receive respect and acceptance for whatever they experience emotionally. When parents allow dependency, children:

- feel safe as parents supply their physical and emotional needs;
- follow and trust parental guidance as parents accept responsibility for establishing and enforcing their values and beliefs;
- own and accept their emotional experiences;
- know that to feel is good when parents teach and demonstrate this concept;
- learn to differentiate feeling from acting;
- move toward responsible independent behavior as their parents respect the changing needs for dependency as their children age;
- accept that they are little and need their parents and others.

In adolescence, children strive to become independent of parents and families. In later adulthood, children can appropriately become interdependent with parents, as they give to one another without coercion or guilt. As adult children individuate, they can meet some of their parents' needs, and parents can meet some of their children's needs, but both maintain their separate identities. Individuation with appropriate separateness can be maintained.

The existence of dependency in families varies from family to family, as do parents' and children's feelings about dependency. In families where parents allow dependency and meet physical and emotional needs of children, this process contributes to the development of healthy identities. In other families, if the parents are conflicted about, threatened by, or chronically feel inconvenienced by their children's need for dependency, children believe that they are a nuisance, which leads to their feeling worthless. They experience feelings of doubt about their identity, worth, and value as people.

What Children Learn from Dependency

From appropriate dependency with parents, children learn:

- to perceive a set of moral values or standards in parents on whom they can depend;
- to later internalize their own set of moral values and standards;
- to balance individuality with obligation to the family group and later to other systems in which they will be involved;
- to begin to develop spirituality that serves them later in their lives.

Spirituality is the ability of persons to trust and have faith in someone or some power greater than themselves (Bradshaw, 1988; Van Kaam, 1987).

Strength, a sense of power, and metaphysical help are gained through people's personal spirituality (Nelson, 1988). This spiritual strength is an outcome of acceptance by children that they are unique and separate from their parents and that they have the right and obligation to own their own beliefs. Negative affirmation leading to shame-proneness blocks people's potential for spirituality (Van Kaam, 1987). On the other hand, appropriate dependency relationships in the family, leading to positive affirmation, foster spiritual awakening (Bradshaw, 1988; Larranaga, 1987). When children are young, they do not have an internalized set of personal or moral standards that governs their social relationships or their obligations to themselves. It is important that parents of young children clearly own their own values and standards, with the expectation that their children will live in accordance with parental values. Young children accept the sense and order that clear parental values create as part of the dependency relationship. Not only do they eat and sleep at home, but children are also nurtured by parental expectations, by knowing that they are a part of the family and that they belong.

When the dimension of dependency is present in the family, children learn to resolve any issues with authority early through processes learned in their homes with their parents. When it is missing, children may be fearful of authority and/or rebellious in the home, at school, and any place where they perceive authority over them. Learning that parents, the first authority figures, are dependable and can be counted on allows children to generalize positive attitudes and behavior to other authority figures later in life.

Out of dependency also grows implicit rules for how to relate to other people. If appropriate dependency is present in the family, family members trust other people and move into relationships with others quite easily. When it is lacking, family members come to mistrust others, feeling that they cannot be counted on and that they are usually unhelpful.

Adults with dependency issues prefer to be alone and seek to do things by themselves, although they constantly long for some relationship in which they can be totally dependent and "little" again (Ponizovsky & Rotenberg, 1987). At the same time, they fear personal abandonment so much that they cannot take the risk involved in forming close relationships. Unfortunately, their fears of being abandoned are often confirmed, as others feel inconvenienced by and afraid of their "emotional neediness," their desire to be totally "taken care of." Their apparent "littleness" frightens others, who then unintentionally withdraw, thus confirming their "flawed core" and exacerbating their abandonment issues (Greenway & Greenway, 1985).

What Is Intimacy?

Intimacy is defined as a feeling of emotional closeness between persons (Harper & Elliott, 1988; Waring, 1988, 1981). When family members feel emotionally close to each other and share mutually recognized experiences in areas of emotion, intellect, social relationships, recreation, and physical touch and affection, they are intimate (Schaefer & Olson, 1981). As a process intimacy assists in teaching family members that they are valued and that they belong in the family. Like accountability and dependency, the degree of intimacy varies from family to family. The presence of intimacy in a family communicates to family members:

- that they are valued and loved for who they are rather than for what they do;
- that intimacy is a normal and appropriate way of communicating and meeting one's needs.

What Children Learn from Intimacy

From the dimension of intimacy in family systems, children learn:

- implicit and explicit rules for affection in relationships, for touch and physical expression;
- ability to both give and receive affection in the family and in relationships outside the family;
- implicit and explicit rules for the expression of feelings;
- trust in what they feel and validation of their emotional experiences;
- ability to share their feelings with others and acknowledge the feelings of others;
- conflict resolution in relationships.

When the dimension of intimacy is lacking, family members learn:

- that their own feelings are not to be trusted;
- to be afraid of the expression and recognition of others' feelings.

The ability to share and acknowledge feelings is a direct consequence of the presence of intimacy processes in families (Derlega & Chaiken, 1975). The presence of intimacy also encourages family members to live according to standards and values out of closeness and caring from others. The ability to feel close to family members, as well as to feel that family members can be counted on when they are needed, allows individuals to set their own limits and thus feel confidence and satisfaction in controlling their own behavior (Miller, 1986).

How to handle conflict in relationships grows out of intimacy in families (Frey, Holley, & L'Abate, 1979). When family members can express emotions, both positive and negative, their potential for working through conflict with others is enhanced. Successful resolution of conflict almost always involves individuals' expressing feelings in appropriate ways. When intimacy is present, individuals can express even intense feelings with the confidence that others love and care about them and will not abandon or turn on them because of their expression of emotion. Knowing that one is loved, even in the presence of another's anger, lowers defensiveness and promotes the ability to hear what is being communicated.

No one or no family is perfect in accepting intimate behaviors or in initiating them, since everyone is constantly interacting in new situations requiring new interpretations of relationships. Proximity, space, and touch are easily observed information about the quality of intimacy. Because touch can be both positively affirming and shaming, touch behaviors provide valuable clues about the family, intimate relationships, and individuals. People's ability to initiate and accept touch provides some clues as to whether they are experiencing transitory shame or are shame-prone. Four descriptive conditions postulated by Hoopes (1974) provide another method of examining shame-prone behaviors (Table 2.1).

Parents who are comfortable with touch, who can both initiate and accept touch (category 1), foster the same kind of affectionate behavior in their children. This ability to both initiate and accept touch contributes to healthy identity development when the individuals involved are sensitive to each other and always appropriate. People who fall into category 2 can initiate and accept touch, only situationally. This category includes people who do not touch in public or stop hugging and holding their children when they reach a specific age. Although family members learn these rules about when and where to touch, the reasons for having the rules are rarely discussed. When such conditions of physical touch are combined with other shaming behaviors, children may assume that there is something wrong with them.

Categories 3 and 4 are most likely to contribute to shaming experiences and to shame-prone identities. People in category 3 control their touch behavior and that of others as well. Some of them can initiate touch but have difficulty receiving it. They are very passive receivers or may even pull away. Others show the opposite response. They can accept touch, but they cannot initiate it. The acceptance is passive, at times barely perceptible. People in category 3 feel that they must always control situations that involve physical contact.

An inability to initiate or accept touch is typical of people in category 4. Fear, very little experience with touch, and lack of trust set the stage for the characteristics of category 4. Although these people may shake hands and touch someone in a work or play situation, their physical contact is awkward and seems forced. Other people in this condition do touch, but inappropriately. Much of the touch is brutalizing, e.g., beatings, sexual

TABLE 2.1
Conditions of Touch Behaviors

Condition	Initiation	Acceptance	Response	Distinguishing Characteristics
1	Can and does as a natural part of communication	Can and does	Responds promptly and appropriately for the other person — verbally and nonverbally (smile), but usually with touch.	Experiences a great deal of freedom in communicating by touch.
2	Can if situationally prompted	Can if situationally prompted	Usually responds situationally; falls into a pattern: fighting, sexual behavior, handshake.	Freedom limited situationally
3a	Can in some instances	Cannot if initiated by the other	Avoids, ignores, and pulls away from an initiator.	Touch very controlled, no trust, insecure
3b	Cannot	Can	1. Passive acceptance 2. Responds verbally or nonverbally without touching (smile, nod of head) 3. Touch response in reply or replication of touch (squeezing back in a hand squeeze, pat on the arm)	Insecure, no trust
4a	Cannot	Cannot	1. Ignores 2. Avoids 3. Denies	No control, no trust
4b	Can but it is inappropriate	Can but it is inappropriate	1. Overreacts 2. Misinterprets the message	No control, no trust

assaults, or inappropriate sexual contact. Some of it is a nuisance, e.g., hanging on, touching incessantly like tapping on the arm.

Rarely are mothers and fathers identical in their ability to initiate and respond to touch. Children learn to interact with each parent. Whatever message is strongest may have the most influence. It is not unusual for boys in a family to hug their mothers with a great deal of affection and transmit affection to their fathers through a handshake or a roughhouse game. If touch messages are integrated with messages that teach children to like themselves and to trust others, the touch behavior may be accepted and integrated. Behaviors in categories 1, 2, and appropriate touch from category 3 may create transitory shame but not internalized shame, depending on whether other shaming behaviors are present in the family. However, children with one or both parents in category 4 will very likely fear touch, think there is something wrong with themselves, and feel very little worth.

The Interaction of Intimacy, Accountability, and Dependency

When all three dimensions—intimacy, accountability, and dependency—are present in families, children learn:

- to control their lives by making changes when they choose to do so;
- to be loving, nurturing adults;
- to accept mistakes as correctable and not as a statement that they are bad;
- to know that they are loved and that their parents are there for them;
- to depend on their parents to help them change and be accountable to standards and values;
- to accept that changing behavior and attitudes is possible and even desirable as a normal part of adapting to the requirements of family living;
- to take risks and not be afraid of making mistakes, since mistakes are seen as one way of learning;
- to recognize the world as a place that can be trusted in general;
- to rely on other people;
- to be more forgiving of mistakes in others and more accepting of feelings and attitudes in themselves, because interpersonal irresponsibility by others is seen as momentary and not the constant state of things;
- to accept a full range of emotional experience as desirable and nonthreatening;

- to appreciate both emotional and rational abilities and seek to integrate the two;
- to own their feelings and accept responsibility for how they are expressed;
- to develop a personal sense of ethics and spirituality;
- to set appropriate boundaries both in terms of order in relationships and in terms of interpersonal relating;
- to differentiate context, personal feelings, and beliefs and cognitions to regulate the setting of appropriate physical boundaries of touch and affection;
- to respect implicit rules about the flow of information, people, and things in and out of the family;
- to preserve the unique identity of the family;
- to depend on something or someone higher or more powerful than themselves in their relationships with parents.

If parents are intimate and dependable and require accountability in firm but not harsh ways, children learn that people with power and authority can be trusted (Larranaga, 1987). As children grow older, the dynamics of dependency and accountability change in accordance with the needs of the child. High levels of moral development are nurtured by the expectation that children will be accountable to rules that are first negotiated with parents, and eventually by the expectation that older children will be accountable to their own internalized set of values and standards (Boyce, 1974; Reimer, Paolitto, & Hersh, 1983). Such conditions allow people to trust powers beyond themselves, to have faith in deity, and to develop a metaphysical sense of one's ability to communicate through prayer or other means with powers beyond oneself.

In this area dependency and accountability become intertwined. As children grow into adolescence, they question the values and standards of their parents and seek to establish a different type of dependency relationship with parents. Adolescents want to be independent from parents but still need to feel that they can fall back on parents' values and standards at times. Consequently, parents need to be supportive and dependable even for adolescents. It is the very questioning of parental moral values that leads to individuals' developing their own internalized set of standards. Children's ethics and values are largely external to them, that is, they are the values and ethics of their parents. As adolescents question the values of their parents, they essentially choose what best fits for them and make these values their own (Windmiller, Lambert, & Turiel, 1980). When parents have unresolved dependency issues and cannot tolerate others' being dependent on them, moral and social development becomes stuck. Their children search for ethical and moral values even as adults but have difficulty sensing any internal set of personal ethics.

The dimension of dependency also ingrains in children motivation based on loyalty and indebtedness to others (Metzner, 1985). Children learn that they must balance individuality with obligation to the family group and later to other systems in which they will be involved (Goodrich, 1984).

Accountability without dependency motivates children to live up to family standards because of power and authority alone. When dependency is also involved, children are motivated as much or more by the relationship as they are by power and authority. As children grow older, it is particularly important for them to be motivated by their relationship loyalty to parents, as parental power and authority decrease.

When some degree of intimacy and dependency is present along with accountability, children learn:

- eventually to develop the capacity to be self-disciplined;
- to develop informed compliance to rules rather than blind compliance or rebellion.

WHAT CHILDREN LEARN FROM
FAMILY STRUCTURE

Family structure is a term to describe how families are organized. Dynamics of family structure include subunits of the family (e.g., the marital relationship, parent-child relationships, intergenerational relationships, triangles) and the nature of the boundaries that keep the family's particular type of organization intact (Becvar & Becvar, 1988).

Marital Relationship

In functional families the boundary of the marital relationship is clear and children are not pulled into a triangle to help resolve marital conflict (Umbarger, 1983). Marital partners look to themselves and each other for the resolution of their differences and send clear messages to children that some activities and conversations are unique to the marital relationship. When the marital bond is strong in this way, children generally benefit (Umbarger, 1983).

In dysfunctional families, the structure is often such that individual family members get brought into others' conflict (Aponte & VanDeusen, 1981). When marital partners are upset with each other, children often get involved, as each parent tries to pull a child to his or her side. Similar triangling can occur in parent-child or sibling relationships, as one sibling becomes the scapegoat and thereby relieves the tension between a parent and another child or between two other siblings. When chronic triangling occurs, negative affirmation results for one or more of the family members involved. Over time this negative affirmation will develop into a shame-prone identification.

Parentification

In another type of dysfunctional family organization, parents feel inadequate in their role and in fulfilling the demands that the dependency of young children presents. These individuals usually grew up in families where intimacy and dependency needs were not met and their parents were not accountable and consistent in setting standards and living values (Boszormenyi-Nagy & Spark, 1984; Boszormeny-Nagy & Ulrich, 1981). Now as parents they expect their children to take care of them. The dependency roles get reversed. Children may even be given major responsibilities that would normally be more appropriate for the parent, such as fixing meals, cleaning house, caring for younger children, etc. This kind of relationship organization does not allow the dependency needs of the children to be met. Consequently, children are negatively affirmed and more prone to shame when they have dependency needs. They tend to grow up feeling inadequate to fulfill demands present in adult relationships. The cycle often repeats itself when they have children who they hope will meet their unfulfilled dependency needs (Kramer, 1985).

Relationships Outside the Family

The nature of relationship boundaries in families combines with the dynamics of intimacy, accountability, and dependency to inform family members how to relate to each other and to people in systems outside the family—friends, community leaders, teachers, bosses, colleagues, neighbors (Kramer, 1985).

What Difference Does Family Membership Make?

Influence of Parents. If the dimensions of accountability, dependency, intimacy, and family structure all influence how individuals in the family feel affirmed, what happens when one parent provides these dimensions leading to positive affirmation of the child but the other parent does not? The other parent may, by withholding what is needed or by substituting demanding, abusive, or childish behaviors, negatively affirm the children. The power of one parent can unbalance the direction of the affirming messages (Lidz & Fleck, 1985). The interaction is complex and influenced by many factors.

The optimal family environment is one in which both parents can provide dependency, be intimate, and expect accountability, and in which there is a strong marital relationship with little triangling. When only one parent provides dependency, intimacy, and accountability, family members will have less healthy identities than if these dimensions existed in relationships with both parents.

In most cases, however, the incongruency created when one parent provides one or all three of these dimensions and the other does not leads to children's receiving confusing messages about who they are and how much they are valued. For example, suppose a father provided accountability. He expected his children to adopt certain standards of behavior, he had a method of enforcing the standards, and he accepted some of the emotional dependency of his children on him. It was difficult, however, for father to be affectionate and intimate with the children. On the other hand, mother was intimate and allowed dependency but she did not expect accountability. Rather, she saw her warmth, physical affection, and willingness to be emotionally available to the children as a buffer against father's expectations. Children in this family quickly learn to triangle, to align with one parent against the other (Umbarger, 1983). The marital bond is likely to become weaker over time, with more fights between parents over how to raise their children. These children will receive more negative affirmation than children provided intimacy, dependency, and accountability by both parents, but they will not have the degree of proneness to shame as children who receive no intimacy, accountability, or dependency from either parent.

Single-Parent Families. The absence of one parent in single-parent families does not directly in and of itself affect affirmation processes in these families. After the death of a parent, children can still have healthy identities when the remaining parent provides intimacy, dependency, and accountability. In cases of divorce, the same is true. When these dimensions are provided, children will receive positive affirmation. In some cases, however, divorced parents seek to sabotage each other's relationship with the children (Cashmore, 1985; Kehle, 1987; Roddy, 1984). Even when one parent attempts to provide intimacy, accountability, and dependency, the children will be less positively affirmed when the other parent sees the development of such relationships as threatening. In many single-parent families the custodial parent, often a mother, is carrying a heavy financial responsibility and works full-time (Ryan, 1981). The added load of household tasks leaves little emotional energy to meet children's needs. In this way, the nature of single-parent families can indirectly affect the provision of intimacy, accountability, and dependency. There is a greater tendency for children to be parentified in these circumstances, as single parents turn to their children for inappropriate emotional support and management of many household tasks.

Stepfamilies.   The ideal dimensions of intimacy, dependency, and accountability are slightly different in stepfamilies (Beer, 1988; Visher & Visher, 1988). It is still essential that biological parents provide intimacy, appropriate dependency, and accountability, but stepparents need to be aware that a push for too much closeness with a stepchild can aggravate loyalty issues to biological parents and create conflict for the child (Einstein & Albert, 1986). In terms of accountability and discipline, biological and stepparents need to be in agreement about both parents' requiring children to be accountable. When parents present a "united front," accountability is provided for children and the tendency to triangle recedes (Burgoyne & Clark, 1984). In terms of dependency, stepparents need to realize that a child may have concerns around becoming too dependent on a stepparent. Yet stepchildren do need to know that a stepparent can be counted on to be there when needed. The establishment of such an attitude by stepparents for stepchildren is more important and affirming than the child's actual decision to become dependent on the stepparent (Bradley, 1982; Hyde, 1981).

In cases of foster placement or death of parents, both biological parents may be absent for a child. What is crucial in such situations is that children are provided with an environment and people who provide dependency, intimacy, and accountability. Moving from family to family, as is often the case with foster children or with orphans, usually increases negative affirmation, and such children are more prone to shame.

Extended Families.   Members of the extended family can have tremendous impact on children. Grandparents who promote accountability, intimacy, and appropriate dependency do much to promote positive affirmation in grandchildren. Family members typically model implicit rules and patterns of the extended family. When grandparents, aunts, and uncles seek to provide intimacy, accountability, and appropriate dependency with each other and with the children in all nuclear families, all extended family members are more likely to have healthy identities and to be able to experience shame without being unhealthily bound by it.

DEVELOPMENTAL STAGES AND AFFIRMATION

Individuals' needs for dependency, intimacy, and accountability and their effect on affirmation change over the life cycle. As discussed earlier, the dependency that an infant requires is very different from that needed by an adolescent. Because this need differs at each developmental stage, we use the term *appropriate* dependency. The modifier "appropriate" means that the dependency process is appropriate for the age and developmental tasks of family members. If families do not adapt to accommodate the developmental changes in family members, dysfunction usually results (Carter & McGoldrick, 1989; Falicov, 1988).

All three processes—intimacy, accountability, and dependency—need to change over family members' life cycles to accommodate individual developmental changes. The accountability required of infants should be very different from what is required of school-aged children, which in turn should be different from what is required of adolescents. In terms of intimacy, as children grow older they become more capable of sharing deep feelings, intellectual experiences, and social and recreational interests with parents.

The nature and sources of affirmation also change as family members grow older. For young children, the primary source of affirmation is their family; in fact, these early experiences with family members plant the seeds of negative or positive affirmation, leading in turn to shame-prone or healthy identities. Early experiences with the family also set a frame of reference for individual family members. This frame of reference encompasses expectations about how others in the world feel about them and will treat them. As children mature, peers and teachers become sources of affirmation, but the frame of reference gained in interaction with the family serves as a filter, a set of lenses through which individuals view affirmation processes from these sources. When individuals become shame-prone, they construe experiences and other people as shaming even when others may not see it that way. Thus, the family remains a basic source of affirmation even as family members move out into the world.

Adolescents gain much of their affirmation, negative and positive, from their peers. If adolescents are already prone to shame, they usually associate with shame-prone peers and seek experiences that end up being shameful. The cycle is completed, and the experience is consistent with their frame of reference—shame. Shame-prone individuals seek consistency with their frame of reference more than they do rewards. Because of this process, shame-prone people often appear to others to be self-defeating and even masochistic. Observing adolescents and their shaming experience, other family members often become even more shaming and respond with ridicule, because they also feel humiliated by the seeming failure of their adolescent family member. In this way shame can be contagious, and it is possible for every member of a given family to have a shame-prone identity.

Adult family members receive affirmation from many sources, including work, social relationships, recreational pursuits, spouses, parents, adult brothers and sisters, etc. However, the power of the family to affirm, either negatively or positively, remains. Differentiating from parents is a difficult task. Williamson (1982a, 1982b, 1981) claims that most adults do not complete this process until the fourth decade of life. To do this individuals must develop a sense of their personal power and resolve childhood feelings of obligation and defenselessness. Shame-prone individuals have great difficulty differentiating from their parents because they have rarely been positively affirmed as having personal worth, let alone personal power.

Much of what has been called "midlife crisis" involves shame and unresolved issues of personal power. As adults, shame-prone individuals continue to be involved with people and in experiences that are shaming. Consequently, they do not know how to positively affirm others.

MORE ABOUT MARILYN'S FAMILY

Typically, the three dimensions that characterize shaming family systems are lack of nurturance leading to decreased intimacy, little or intermittent acceptance of dependency needs appropriate to the ages of family members involved, and little demonstration of mutual accountability between parents and their children. This may or may not be true for each child in the family, but it is true for anyone who becomes shame-prone.

Rather than being isolated separate processes in families, intimacy, dependency, and accountability interact and fluctuate over time. Families may have high levels of intimacy but little dependency or accountability; others may have high levels of dependency and accountability but little intimacy. The patterns of these processes determine how individuals become shame-prone and what their symptoms will be.

In the case introduced in Chapter 1, Marilyn's family provided little intimacy or dependency for Marilyn. Neither her father nor her mother was affectionate with her. Her mother was unwilling to accept the dependency relationship demanded by Marilyn as a baby. Early in Marilyn's life, and especially when she was a teenager, her father focused on moving her into a "substitute spouse" role to meet his needs. The parents' messages to Marilyn were that they needed to depend on her. Her parents' inability to allow Marilyn to become increasingly independent as she grew into adolescence is a symptom of the inappropriate dependency issues in the family. It is little wonder that Marilyn was confused about her worth. The fact that she was never able to be dependent on either parent was coupled with the lack of intimacy in all her family relationships and both were linked to Marilyn's proneness to shame.

In contrast to the lack of appropriate dependency and intimacy, the expectation that Marilyn be accountable to her parents was quite high. Marilyn had many demands placed on her by her parents. The fact that many of her parents' expectations were chaotically imposed and even unrealistic is irrelevant to the outcome. There was an extreme, almost radical demand that Marilyn be accountable to and for both her mother and father, as well as her siblings. Marilyn was given a huge job. She was asked:

- to guard the family secrets,
- to achieve in school,
- to obey a set of rather rigid rules, and
- to adopt her parents' versions of gender-appropriate behavior for their happiness.

On the other hand, the failure of the parents to meet Marilyn's need for dependence and intimacy blocked all possibility of mutual accountability. This process of extreme, almost harsh, demands for Marilyn to be accountable was related to how Marilyn later used excessive guilt to further maintain her shame-prone identity.

CHAPTER 3
Patterns of Needs, Emotions, and Issues of Transitory Shame

THE FIRST CHAPTER established the difference between internalized shame (shame-proneness) and shame as emotion (transitory shame). People with healthy identities may experience intense shame as emotion, but it fades with time. Those who accumulate shaming experiences as evidence of being flawed to the core of their beings develop shame-prone identities. This chapter builds on the affirmation triangle by examining patterns of affect and interpersonal issues that arise when intimacy, dependency, and other basic needs do not get met.

INDIVIDUAL IDENTITY, A SENSE OF BEING

Every family creates a home environment that is both unique and typical in comparison to other families. Within this home environment children develop a sense of being somebody. This sense of being, which is both personal and unique, becomes the person's identity. Out of that sense of being numerous questions are generated: "Who am I?" "How do I belong in this family?" "Am I unique and separate from the family?" "How do I make a contribution to this family group?" Based on the internal and external evaluations of their identity, individuals develop beliefs and questions about their self-worth, e.g., "I am valuable," "I am lovable," "I am OK," "I am bad," "I am capable," "I am hopeless," "I am pretty," "I am ugly." To a great extent, how the children in a family experience shame and guilt shapes the beliefs and feelings they have about themselves. In the early years personal identity develops out of the experiences in which children feel valued and evaluated by family members, particularly their parents (Fischer, 1985).

The quality of the home environment reflects the kind and amount of shame and guilt experienced by all family members. Whether or not children internalize shame is specifically related to how accountable parents are as they accept the dependency needs of their children and regulate intimacy in family relationships.

AFFIRMATION AND PSYCHOLOGICAL NEEDS

Children develop a sense of who they are through the quality of the interaction with their parents. It is assumed that when family members are accountable in meeting dependency and intimacy needs, other psychological needs also get met. However, it is helpful to identify what other needs interact with intimacy and dependency in shaping children's identities. These include the needs to be productive, to make sense and order out of the world, to be accepted as unique and valuable, and to have choices in making life changes. If family members are to have healthy identities, a family environment must be able to meet all of these needs most of the time (Cohen, 1988). When the needs represented by the affirmation triangle are met most of the time, the foundation for meeting the rest of the needs is firm, and ultimately family members will be fulfilled in their need to belong to the group.

It is not reasonable to expect that children's needs can be met all of the time, even in functional families. Part of growth and maturity is learning to adapt when others do not instantly gratify our needs. When needs go unmet in a particular situation, even individuals with healthy identity experience shame, but the shame is transitory.

RELATIONSHIP BETWEEN UNMET NEEDS AND AFFECT/PSYCHOLOGICAL ISSUES

When individuals' psychological needs go unmet in any particular situation, they experience certain emotions and issues (Donohew, Sypher, & Higgins, 1988; Heise, 1979). Table 3.1 identifies patterns of needs and associated affects and issues. This table represents how people with healthy identities respond when they experience transitory shame. A map representing patterns for shame-prone people is presented in Chapter 10.

Psychological Needs

Out of many needs seven are thought to influence the development of people's identities (Scheff, 1985). The column on the left side of Table 3.1 identifies these seven basic needs. The last, *wholeness*, the need to be whole or healthy, is often talked about by people in recovery from addiction

TABLE 3.1
Identification of Psychological Needs and
Connected Affect and Interpersonal Issues

Psychological Need	Affect When Need Is Not Met	Interpersonal Issue When Need Is Not Met
Intimacy	Nonspecific rage	Insufficiency
Productivity	Anger/hurt	Rejection
Dependency	Humiliation	Worthlessness
Sense and Order	Fear	Abandonment
Uniqueness	Terror	Emptiness
To have choices	Grief	Loss

Psychological Need	Affect When Need Is Met	Interpersonal State When Need Is Met
Wholeness	Joy	Acceptance

as the need to be "regular." It represents a healthy mature acceptance of one's life and circumstances. Whole adults are also accountable in that they meet the needs of their children, at least enough of the time for their children to develop adequate coping skills and healthy identities. This state of wholeness cannot be reached without the other six needs being met and the growth that accrues from struggles to have them met. The remaining six basic needs are:

1. to be *intimate*;
2. to be *productive*;
3. to be *dependent* and accepted by one's parents;
4. to make *sense and order* out of one's world;
5. to be recognized and valued as *unique* by parents and other family members;
6. to experience and welcome *choices* as part of making changes.

Affirmation sets the stage for meeting the six needs. Accountability is closely related to sense and order and to productivity. Dependency and intimacy help meet individuals' needs to feel unique and to risk making choices in their life. When these first six needs are met with some regularity, or when individuals recognize the loss, experience a release of the feelings, and accept the loss, they can then be *whole* and *healthy*.

Affect Experienced When Needs Cannot Be Met

The second column in Table 3.1 lists emotions experienced by even healthy or shame-prone individuals when their needs go unmet in a partic-ular context (De Rivera, 1977; Kemper, 1987). With the exception of joy, people experience these emotions in response to a disruption or a conflict in maintaining psychological needs over time. Joy is experienced in re-sponse to psychological needs being met. Not all of the feelings are experi-enced in every situation. Sometimes more than one feeling is experienced. For example, a person may oscillate back and forth between anger and hurt and then experience humiliation and later fear. The affects can be thought of as layered, meaning that many of them may be experienced in relation to one given event. Healthy individuals eventually recognize these feelings and accept them as part of the context of the moment. When asked to do so, they can acknowledge the full range of emotions. They may feel shamed, unloved, unacceptable, miserable, and hopeless at that moment, but such feelings are passing. Other experiences confirm them as valuable and loved so that they do not internalize the shame as a permanent part of their identity. In contrast, shame-prone individuals may be blocked to all of the feelings or they may be focused on highly exaggerated reactions, usual-ly to one emotion.

Interpersonal Issues Experienced When Needs Are Not Met

Interpersonal issues related to both the affect and unmet needs are identified in the far right column of Table 3.1. These interpersonal issues are experienced cognitively. They may occur almost simultaneously with the affect; alternatively, a person may become polarized into the emotional experience or rationally into the issue. Defenses develop around these interactions of affect and unmet psychological needs, as people defend temporally against the projected issue. Later in the chapter we will give examples of how the dynamics work.

PATTERNS OF UNMET NEEDS, AFFECT, AND INTERPERSONAL ISSUES

The patterns of needs, affect, and interpersonal issues provide a map for understanding experiences related to transitory shame. This map is not the territory; that is, the patterns exist in this linear form only on the map. In reality, the interactions are dynamic, integrated from one pattern of needs/affect/issues to another, and holistic. Even people who are not shame-prone may experience all seven levels of the need/affect/issue patterns in response to a particular situation.

Wholeness, Joy, Acceptance Pattern

The last pattern in Table 3.1 represents *wholeness,* health for every individual, the ability to function adequately in the world with predominantly positive feelings. As children experience having most of their needs met, they feel *joy.* Interpersonally they accept parental decisions, disappointments, and struggles along with successes and positive interactions. Each time children work through one or more of the other need/affect/issue patterns, they usually experience joy and acceptance. They feel the joy of having their needs met or of releasing fear and pain. Accepting what is and "letting go" of the situation, as they let go of transitory shame, moves them to a sense of wholeness for the moment.

Intimacy, Nonspecific Rage, and Insufficiency Pattern

When the need for *intimacy* is not met, the affect of *nonspecific rage* and the interpersonal issue of *insufficiency* ("I'm not good enough") are experienced (Gaylin, 1984). Children's emotional, physical, and cognitive intimacy needs are insistent and persistent, changing as they move through various stages of development. Not knowing when or if they can be intimate with a parent can be shaming to the child.

Unconsciously children harbor all the incidents of failure by parents and other adults to allow and welcome them in intimate encounters. Times when intimacy needs are met positively affirm children. Times when intimacy needs are not met, e.g., the times of being brushed aside, discounted, or pushed away, create feelings of frustration and unexplained rage. At these times individuals feel *insufficient,* unacceptable, and overwhelmed by *nonspecific rage.* The rage is *nonspecific* because it is never consciously acknowledged or labeled. Tantrums displayed in public places by well-behaved, loved, and cared-for children are examples of this rage. Mom or dad says no to something the child wants or corrects some behavior, and the rage flies. The child is out of control, the magnitude of the rage apparently unrelated to the "no" or the correction.

For example, a child who wants to be held and cuddled by her mother will experience *nonspecific rage* when her mother brushes her aside because she is nursing her younger sister. The interpersonal issue for that child is *insufficiency.* She receives a message that someone else is more important than she is at this moment. It is not likely that she will rationalize in this situation. Nor will she be able to label her feeling as anger at being thwarted in her attempt to be intimate. Likewise, her mother cannot or does not label the rage for her child. Provided this situation does not occur frequently, the child's feeling of not being enough will be transitory shame. If such occasions are more the norm than the exception, the child will internalize shame.

Productivity, Anger/Hurt, and Rejection Pattern

The psychological need to be *productive* and positively affirmed for *productivity* sparks the dynamics in this pattern. In functional families, where children receive some recognition for their implicit and explicit role assignments, they tend to view themselves as *productive*. Recognition and acceptance by parents for products and results aid children's development of positive views of their capabilities. When the need to be productive is thwarted by some specific situation, individuals experience *anger and/or hurt*, along with *rejection* (Averill, 1982). Failure to be perfect in their attempts at being *productive* in their families may be perceived by children as *rejection* because they do not receive confirmation and positive affirmation from their parents. Parental criticism adds to children's perception of rejection, and they think, "I can't do anything right!" Some of the anger and hurt is toward parents, as children sense, often erroneously, that they have not received enough support. *Any* parental reaction may be seen as confirmation that they are unacceptable as a person, adding to their experience of shame as well as their fear of rejection. Some individuals defend against rejection by projecting *anger*, which hides the underlying hurt.

Dependency, Humiliation, and Worthlessness Pattern

When the need to be *dependent* goes unmet, individuals respond with *humiliation* and *worthlessness*. Much has been written about dependency in the preceding chapter; here we will simply describe how dependency interacts within the need/affect/issue pattern. Being small and incapable of taking care of themselves, children have a need to be *dependent* upon their parents for material goods, emotional support, and information about how to live. Functional parents are fairly consistent in meeting most of their children's needs. They give positive and honest messages to their children, such as, "We love you. We are happy to do things for you. What we have is yours too. You are being unreasonable with your demands. We love you, but if we give you all you want there is not enough for the rest of us."

Messages of caring, sharing, and accountability permeate the functional family. Values are owned by parents and taught to children to guide them through challenges in their lives. With parents who are accountable for themselves and their beliefs, children learn to model parental behavior and feel good about themselves. However, there are times and situations when every parent is unwilling, incapable, or insensitive in allowing children to be *dependent*. Children then feel confused, angry, and at times hurt. Beneath the anger at not being allowed to be dependent on their parents is a sense of *worthlessness* connected with a feeling of *humiliation*. Because of their implied "badness," children at that moment may feel neglected and unworthy of parental care.

The following example illustrates the interaction of several need/affect/ interpersonal issue patterns in response to a particular situation. Bob, 14 years old, experienced a number of situations that accumulated into feelings of failing or not being acceptably productive, which translated into transitory shame. First, he received a B in math on an important test instead of his usual A. Second, his dad asked him to clean out the garage and organize everything that was stored there. He completed the job three days earlier, but his dad had said nothing about it. Third, the coach announced who would be on the school basketball team, and he had only made the second team. Fourth, he came home to discuss how he was feeling about these events with his mom and found a note indicating that his dinner was in the oven and that she and his father would be home by seven. He was rageful as he stormed around the house. Although he did not verbalize his feelings, he felt rejected by his teacher, his coach, and his parents. Convinced that he was worthless and humiliated by his failures, he fantasied about running away from home and upsetting his parents in some way.

His need for intimacy was not met because his mother was not home. His need for positive affirmation for his "products" was not met. His father had not given him any feedback about the garage, he had "failed" a math test (at least in his mind), and the coach had overlooked him for someone else. He perceived himself as inadequate in three areas—math, the basketball team, and at home. The anger and humiliation he experienced plunged him into a feeling of worthlessness. He felt shamed. (We will return to Bob's story later.)

Sense and Order, Fear, and Abandonment Pattern

Beginning at birth, children seek to make *sense and order* of their environment. Curiosity is natural in meeting this need as children grow bigger and stronger, with increased mental faculties. Beginning with their parents, adults are essential to children as they try to figure out their world and how it works. Most people have experienced the incessant questions of children seeking understanding. "What holds the sky up? Who made rocks? Why did you say that? What does 'end' mean? How can I get big like you?" This same curiosity functions as children try to understand their relationships with their parents, siblings, and others. They want to know who they are, if there is a God, the role of government, etc.

Parents often feel impatient and frustrated by children's clamor to have their questions answered, by the seemingly never ending need to know everything. When parents do not or cannot help children make *sense and order* of the world and provide some kind of structure for a particular situation, children experience the world at that moment as crazy. They become *fearful*. Other need/affect/interpersonal issue patterns often add to the fear.

Such was the case with Bob. The unexpectedness of his mother's absence when he thought he really needed her threw him into a panic. He felt terrible, alone and afraid, *abandoned*. He also believed he was "insufficient," "rejected," and "worthless." All of these beliefs intensified as he experienced rage, anger, and humiliation. Although he had come home on other occasions and found a note explaining his parents' absence, this time was different. The accumulation of events set the stage for his experiencing transitory shame.

Uniqueness, Terror, and Emptiness Pattern

Within each child is a desire to be *unique* and separate. At the same time, children want adults to accept them by being intimate and by allowing them to be dependent. Having these needs met creates a sense of belonging. When parents say to their children, implicitly and explicitly, "You are special, one of a kind, and valued for who you are and how you serve the family," children know they are unique and valued. Setting boundaries for themselves and their children is one way parents demonstrate the separateness of family members and their rights as unique people.

Even emotionally healthy children can experience the *terror* and *emptiness* associated with the unmet need for uniqueness. However, in healthy individuals it only happens occasionally, when unusual events cause unforeseen and unpredictable circumstances.

Bob's situation continues to illustrate this pattern. Sonia, Bob's mother, did not go out to dinner with her husband. An old friend from college was in town and asked her out. She called her husband, Russ, who said, "Go ahead, I'll be home by seven." She thought she, too, would be home by that time, so she wrote the note indicating that they would both be home. When Sonia met her friend at 5:30 p.m., three other college friends were with her. She had seen none of them for 12 years. Dinner was fun with everyone reminiscing, laughing, and having a great time. Shortly after seven she noticed the time. Thinking that her husband would be home with Bob, she stayed longer. She intended to break away and call home, but she was too involved.

In the meantime, Russ had an emergency call just as he was preparing to leave work. He figured that Bob would be okay until his mother arrived. Neither parent returned home at the time planned, and neither one called home, an unusual happening in this family. Bob felt terrible. It was 7:30 and neither one of his parents was home. He needed them. His emotions were on a rampage, and he was not thinking calmly. He went from *anger* with them to *terror*, convinced that they had left him permanently. He was immobilized. "Maybe they have been killed in an accident," he thought. He felt *empty*, hollow, and hopeless. He called his dad's office, but no one answered.

Choice, Grief, Loss Pattern

People have a need to make their own *choices* or at least know that they have choices that could make a difference in their lives and/or the lives of others. When this need is not met, issues of *loss* and feelings of *grief* arise. The losses, real and imagined, focus on unmet psychological needs, broken dreams, lost relationships, and attempts at success in their lives (LaGrand, 1988).

Within each individual is the intent to grow, to change on many levels, e.g., physical, emotional, cognitive, social, personal, interpersonal, and spiritual (Luthman & Kirschenbaum, 1974; Satir, 1972). At the root of personal change is the will or agency of a person, the need to make choices, to take charge of one's life. Everyone is endowed with this right to make choices, although control by others, such as parents and other adults, sometimes limits the possibilities. In functional families parents recognize this right and do not make all decisions for their children. They tutor their children in making choices by establishing rules supported by personal adult values. Mistakes are viewed as mis-takes with consequences, as part of normal interaction and growth.

Choices for children affect three areas—personal, interpersonal (including family relationships), and societal (including anything outside the home). The psychological need is integrated with all other needs, especially the need to be a unique, separate, valued individual. On a personal level, choices fuel all activities that are self-motivated and self-originated. When children make choices and the results are manifest, they feel that they are in control.

The issue of who is in control pervades childhood, adolescence, and adulthood, with children being introduced early to adult power and family rules. When parents meet their children's dependency needs, they make choices that are appropriate for their children. Shifting choices to the domain of the child is usually gradual and age appropriate. Most children experience the sometimes tyranny of people bigger than they are, whether parents, siblings, teachers, or peers. In the family, there may be power struggles. A 16-year-old, for example, may want to choose when she will come home from a party, while her mother may feel a curfew is appropriate. All other psychological needs are integrated into these power struggles on some level, sometimes explicitly, but more often implicitly. For the 16-year-old, having the right to choose is enmeshed with the need to be recognized as a unique individual, capable of making wise choices. This need may be more important than the time she comes home. However, the power struggle focuses on the rule and the right of the parent to enforce the rule.

When the child's need to have a choice meets resistance, the child experiences a sense of loss. The loss may be experienced at a deep level as losing part of oneself or part of one's childhood or a relationship. Whatever the loss, the emotional reaction is grief.

Bob experienced everything as being out of his control. He studied for the test, he did what his dad asked him to do, and he played the best he could for the coach. His parents gave him no prior notice about their being gone, and he had no way to reach them. The loss he experienced in not being able to contact them was powerful. In his distraught state, he had them gone forever. Although he was 14 years old, he felt about four, terrified and impotent. The grieving would come later, as he worked his way through all the other need/affect/issue patterns.

The depth of grieving in transitory shame is very different from that experienced by shame-prone individuals. Transitory grief is situational and can be assessed consciously and fairly rapidly. For shame-prone individuals, on the other hand, grief is rooted in many situations and intertwined with a deep belief of unworthiness.

Bob and the Pattern of Wholeness, Joy, Acceptance

When Bob's parents arrived home, they were both concerned to find Bob so intensely emotional. At first he was furious with them. They listened to his raving and at one point his mother held him. He was then able to talk about other events that had happened during the day. He expressed his hurt and anger over not making first string on the basketball team and doing more poorly on a test than he had hoped to do. His parents listened and empathized. When they heard how he had anticipated being able to tell them how rotten his day had been, they apologized for not being there. Dad pointed out how much he appreciated Bob's sharing his feelings and acknowledged Bob's contribution to the family and to dad's life. They even laughed a bit at the irony of their circumstances.

The situation ended with Bob sitting between mom and dad, each with an arm around him. Together they discussed ways Bob might respond to the events of the day. Bob's transitory shame began to lift as he worked through each of the patterns of unmet needs and consequent feelings and issues. His parents' ability to listen to and acknowledge his feelings, accompanied by his own ability to share and explore his reactions, restored his sense of his own goodness. He felt joy in who he was and in belonging to a loving family. He felt whole again.

SECTION II
Shame and Family Systems

CHAPTER 4

The Family's Contribution to the Development of Healthy Individual Identity

ALL PEOPLE ARE AFFECTED by their family systems and other complex societal systems (Constantine, 1986). Individuals, families, and society interact to provide the quality of life we experience (Lusterman, 1985). Some people immediately feel shame or guilt when they think of their families, while others deny that there was anything wrong with their families when there was, and others have few shameful memories of their families. This chapter discusses the concept of identity in healthy family systems. Some of the conditions necessary for children to develop healthy identities are integrated with the influences of the family including the marital/parental subsystem, the sibling subsystem, the extended family, and individuals and systems outside the family.

FAMILY IDENTITY

Family members have separate and unique identities; in addition, the family as a unit develops an identity (Reiss, 1981). Family identity is the shared composite of what family members believe and feel about themselves as a family. The development of this identity begins with the courtship of two people and is influenced by the family of origin identities which both partners bring to the relationship (Kerr & Bowen, 1988). As children are added to the family, their personal identities, the history of all experiences for individuals and the family, current experiences, and feedback from outside individuals, extended family, community and agencies all shape the family identity. The family may ask: "Who are we as a family?" "Are we respected and valued as a family by others?" "Does this family exist as a separate unique entity, separate from all others?" "What do other people think of us?" "Are we worthwhile?" "Are we productive?" A family's identity can be healthy, shamed on specific issues or contexts, or totally shame-prone.

The quantity and quality of affirming processes, as well as shame and guilt, in the family contribute to the quality of the family identity and are predictive of whether members will develop shame-prone identities. Such variables determine whether family members feel good or bad as a family and whether the family as a whole looks good or bad to others. Both implicit and explicit feelings contribute to the family identity.

Much has been written about how individuals develop images to mask who they really are (Hultberg, 1988; Sidoli, 1988; Wurmser, 1981). Not trusting others to deal fairly if they discover personal weaknesses, people develop an image to secure their safety in interpersonal situations. Families do the same thing by projecting a family image in interaction with others, including extended family, friends, peers, and community.

Types of Family Identities

By combining two dimensions—how a family feels about itself and how a family looks to others—types of family identities can be identified, as shown in Figure 4.1. The characteristics of each type are related to shame and guilt processes.

Families that look good and feel good develop healthy family and individual identities. The context and conditions for this type of identity development are described in this chapter. Families that look bad and feel bad are described in Chapter 5 as families with totally shame-prone identities. Families that look bad and feel good, or look good and feel bad, are described in Chapter 6 as families that are shame-prone in relation to specific issues or contexts.

	Feels Good	*Feels Bad*
Looks Good	Healthy family and individual identities	Shame-prone in specific circumstances
Looks Bad	Shame-prone in specific circumstances	Totally shame-prone

FIGURE 4.1
Types of Family Identities

Families With Healthy Identities

A family that feels good about itself and also looks good to others has a positive identity. Consequently, shame-prone individuals are rarely developed in these families. However, family members do participate in shaming and guilting processes resulting in transitory shame and healthy guilt. Families that feel good have intrafamily experiences that produce positive results.

Families that Feel Good. The following characteristics describe families that share a mutual feeling of goodness:

- Experience a sense of pride in the family and in family members through processes of trust, loyalty, and respect.
- Perceive themselves as a loving, close family, with combinations of appropriate emotional, physical, and intellectual intimacy.
- Experience unity as a family, unique and separate from others.
- Experience feelings of worthiness, of deserving and receiving abundance.
- Experience being in control, being actors in their environment.
- Experience the ability to adapt to changes, to what cannot be changed, and to losses.
- Experience openness to family information and information from outside the family. Communication and negotiation are a way of life.
- Experience feelings of security and safety. The family and most family members are perceived as accountable and dependable.
- Experience family values and standards as explicit and congruent. Questioning and experimentation regarding rules governed by these values and standards are expected and accepted.
- Feel the positive influence of spirituality.

Families that Look Good. For these families the family public image seems to be mostly congruent with what is happening within the family. Because they do not view themselves as perfect, they often accept feedback from others as verification and learning for the family. The following are characteristics of families that look good to others:

- Appear to progress with common goals and purposes.
- Seem to deal well with crises, stress, and outside demands.
- Appear to be a unique entity with family members bonded, happy and supportive of one another.
- Appear to have talents and capabilities to share with others outside the family.
- Interact with others freely and openly.

CHARACTERISTICS OF FUNCTIONAL
FAMILIES

Functional families are those that have structural, attitudinal, and behavioral patterns within the system that promote the achievement of consensual goals and that shift appropriately with stress and growth within the environment (Olson, Sprenkle, & Russell, 1979). To accomplish this families develop many patterns and behaviors.

After a thorough review of the theoretical and empirical literature Fisher and Sprenkle (1978) developed a list of items that described healthy functioning families. This list was verified by a sample of marriage and family therapists and later confirmed by a sample of nonclinical parents and teenagers (Fisher, Giblin, & Hoopes, 1982). These items, divided into three subheadings, identify many of the aspects of family functioning. Cohesion, the emotional bonding of families, included emotional attraction, differentiation, mature dependency, supportiveness, loyalty, psychological safety, reliability, family identification, physical caretaking, and pleasurable interaction. Adaptability, the family's ability to change, included flexibility, leadership, assertiveness, negotiation, rules, roles, and the ability to receive and utilize feedback. Communication, the means through which family members develop patterns of adaptability and cohesion, was described by 17 items subdivided into listener, sender, and general skills.

When families are functional they tend to positively affirm all family members. It is not likely that this occurs all of the time, but it occurs often enough that family members know that they are valued and loved (Epstein, Bishop, & Baldwin, 1982). Although dysfunctional families may positively affirm family members in some situations, negative affirmations are more common and have a negative effect on individual and family identities.

The quality of family functioning is affected by forces within the family and from the society in which it is embedded. Stages of development for individuals and the family guarantee change in individuals and situations, stress in interactions within and without the family, and demands to meet the growing and changing needs. How well a family responds to change, stress, and demands reflects the functionality of the family system (McCubbin & Patterson, 1982). As an entity in its own right, any given family is a mystery, difficult to understand. Why are siblings so different within the same family? Why do some families seem competent and adaptive to problems for many years and then suddenly, or so it seems, fall apart? Or the reverse happens. Some families or members within seem to continually have difficulties, until something happens and everything falls in place. Suffice it to say that families are complex and not easily described.

In families that look good and feel good the quality of family functioning is nonpathological. Adequate coping strategies and interpersonal skills manage the resolution of developmental and life crisis (Boss, 1980). Having

healthy personalities, family members utilize variability and resourceful-
ness in solving personal and family problems (Pearlin & Schooler, 1983).

Families that develop healthy identities are functional families with
many of the following general characteristics:

- Intimacy and dependency needs are met with accountability and
  positive affirmations are dominant.
- The quality of the marital/parental relationship, parent-child, sib-
  ling and extended family relationships influence positive affirma-
  tion of individual identities (Bensman, 1979).
- They have a family structure that allows for shared power (Olson,
  McCubbin, Barnes, Larsen, Muxen, & Wilson, 1983).
- They practice appreciation and promotion of individuality among
  members.
- They have demonstrated the ability to deal realistically with separa-
  tion and loss (Eisenstadt, 1989).
- A warm, expressive feeling tone is exhibited (Olson, Sprenkle, &
  Russell, 1979).
- They demonstrate an acceptance of the passage of time and inevi-
  tability of change (children growing up and becoming as powerful
  or more powerful than their parents, the eventual waning abilities
  of the parents, the inevitability of death) (Lewis, Beavers, Gossett,
  & Phillips, 1976).
- Useful amounts and quality of information from outside the family
  are allowed to stimulate and guarantee a dynamic process (Luthman & Kirschenbaum, 1974).
- They utilize coping skills to resolve problems created by internal
  and external stress and to recover or adapt from trauma (McCubbin, Cauble, & Patterson, 1982).
- Implicit and explicit rules and boundaries are congruent with family and community standards and values.
- There are meaningful and appropriate intimate relationships (Harper & Elliott, 1988).
- Individual and family needs are recognized and accepted, with appropriate strategies for meeting them by the family and by key
  family members.
- A financial balance between need and income exists.

THE STEVENS FAMILY

The Stevens family is one that looks good to others and feels good to
those who live within it. Kathy and her brother, Chad, live with their
parents, Kent and Laura Stevens, who love their children and enjoy family
activities, whether they be work or play. Kent is a respected lawyer in a

local firm and Laura owns a popular specialty shop. As ninth and seventh graders respectively, Kathy and Chad attend the same school. They are capable students, energetic and active in a number of their interests. Although often going in many different directions, the children and parents feel supported in their activities and appear to have little difficulty asking for what they need from each other. Crises and problems interact with the challenges of the family's daily activities.

Recently Laura received a call from the police station indicating that Chad had been detained. The police urged one parent to come down there as soon as possible. Kent was out of town on business and was returning that night. Somewhat amazed, mystified, and horrified, Laura dashed to the police station. Before she was allowed to see her son, a police officer told her that Chad and three other boys had been caught in a stolen car that was being driven in a dangerous fashion by one of the other boys. Open beer cans were found in the car and all of the boys had been drinking. Before reading about Laura's interaction with Chad, let us examine some of the conditions in the Stevens family environment that are related to the development of healthy individual identities.

FAMILY CONDITIONS LEADING TO
HEALTHY IDENTITIES

Certain conditions in the family system promote interactions, feelings, and outcomes that positively affirm family members.

- *The family creates a context for each person to be a separate, unique, valued individual* (Kerr & Bowen, 1988).

By affirming Kathy's and Chad's right to be separate, their parents signal that each of them is uniquely different from his or her sibling and parents. This acceptance and respect for uniqueness and differences must be reflected in the marital relationship or the children will get mixed messages. Family members affirm each other by accepting differences, by acknowledging specific contributions to the family, and by recognizing personality characteristics, personal talents, skills, ambitions, and progress in school, work, community, or at home.

In the Stevens' home Laura and Kent notice different things about their children and affirm them in different ways. Kent often initiates conversation about their performance at school and talks with them about their struggles as well as their accomplishments. Although Laura does not initiate the same type of discussion, she responds to her children's requests for help on school assignments. She always takes time to review their grade reports in great detail and comments appropriately. Her comments about what the children contribute, e.g., Chad's sense of humor, Kathy's willingness to prepare meals, seem to be natural for Laura. When parents indicate to a child or a spouse that he or she makes unique and specific contributions to the family, they affirm that person as being valuable. This assists all family members in feeling that they belong to the family, while recognizing their identities as separate and unique.

- *Errors or mistakes by family members are seen as correctable incidents rather than opportunities to label children or parents as bad* (Zuk & Zuk, 1987).

Although the Stevens look good to others and feel good, they have their share of problems and faults. For example, children and parents sometimes speak unkindly to each other; they judge harshly without enough information; they fail to show up when and where they promised; they may lie to each other; and they sometimes use each other's property without permission. Kent and Laura teach their children that mistakes are inevitable. They expect each person in the family to make restitution of some sort when mistakes are made. Defensiveness and denial sometimes slow acceptance of mistakes by both parents and children. Eventually, however, they are recognized. Consequently, although family members sometimes feel shame or guilt, they have not developed shame-prone identities. Even though they are sometimes disobedient, careless, and are forgetful, they still feel loved and accepted as worthwhile members of the family. This has helped Kathy and Chad to develop healthy identities.

- *Children know that they are loved, valued, and supported by their parents* (Olson et al., 1983).

When children are affirmed by parents who love, value, and support them, they believe in themselves. Parents and siblings may show their love and support intermittently and in a variety of ways, but family members "get it." Kent and Laura are affectionate with their children and with each other. Family members share a variety of feelings and ideas with each other. Lately the children do not share as readily as in the past, but Laura and Kent interpret this as a product of their being teenagers. They do not make a big issue of it.

Kent rarely expresses his love verbally, but he is quick with a hug or a pat on some part of the anatomy in passing and he gives easily read eye messages. In addition to verbal messages, Laura often expresses tender feelings for her family intermixed with written instructions. Both Kent and Laura attend as many of Kathy's and Chad's functions as possible. They have devoted many hours to assisting their children in finding supplies and ferreting out resources for class projects. Family squabbles and disagreements are over rather quickly with anger and disputes forgotten. Kathy and Chad share their feelings and opinions freely, knowing that they are accepted and loved.

- *The potential for one or more close relationships in the family is guaranteed and unconditional* (Olson, Sprenkle, & Russell, 1979).

This environmental condition is closely related with the preceding three. Kathy and Chad know from experience that no matter how many mistakes they make, no matter how upset their parents and sibling may be with them, no matter what is required of them to make restitution, they are loved and accepted. They know that Laura's and Kent's feelings of disappointment, anger, and sadness are somehow a reflection of how much concern they have for them. Openness, vulnerability, listening, and fairness by at least one of their parents when Chad and Kathy have failed to do something or have done something they know they shouldn't set the stage for unconditional love and acceptance. With most of their needs for intimacy and dependency being met by their parents, Kathy and Chad participate in intimate relationships that are not conditional. As they get more and more involved with meaningful and important relationships with their peers, they are secure in their relationships with each other.

- *Values, including standards and expectations, are clearly identified and owned by parents and other significant adults* (Schulman & Melker, 1985).

Clear values encourage children's accountability and independence. Children are socialized by their parents' value systems, including their standards and expectations. Kent's and Laura's values are embedded in such things as the rules for behavior in the home, in their attitudes toward authority, in the standards for personal appearance and speech that they model, in the expectations about how Kathy and Chad should behave, and in what they expect Kathy and Chad to do to prepare for their adult lives. These messages, as well as contrasting ones, are given implicitly and explicitly by parents, extended family, and other important adult figures, e.g., teachers, neighbors, peers, and religious leaders. In this type of family, parents claim their value systems and send explicit messages to their children and others that they own these values and live by them.

Although parents may have different values from one another in some areas, they demonstrate in their interactions respect and acceptance of the other's point of view. Thus, children know what to expect from each of their parents and know that they can depend on them. When parents supply an appropriate level of congruence and negotiation and are consistently accountable for the values they espouse, they encourage the development of independence and internalization of values as their children mature (Boyce & Jensen, 1978).

Chad and Kathy have the possibility of being accountable individuals because their parents own their values and accept and believe them, even though these values may or may not match what is expected at school or in the community. Each year, as Kathy and Chad grow older, Laura and Kent expect that their children will become less and less dependent on them and develop as unique and independent individuals who espouse their own set of internalized values. They foster this evolution by openly discussing their expectations and by sharing their own struggles as teenagers in selecting their values. Frequent discussions with their parents about differences in values, rather than secrecy and hypocrisy, encourage Chad and Kathy to at least evaluate what they do and think, even though they may not share everything with their parents. Involvement in exploring values and standards, rather than expecting blind conformity to the parents' values, provides a context for responsibility and accountability for parents and children. Through this involvement Kathy and Chad are still dependent and accountable to their parents, but in a way more appropriate for an adolescent stage of development. Laura and Kent, with personal struggles around "how much" and "how soon" their children can be independent, expect and trust their children to develop an internalized, self-regulated set of standards that may be the same as the parents' or different, but nevertheless separate and owned by each of the children.

- *Values, including standards and expectations, when consistently enforced by one or both parents, foster guilt rather than shaming experiences* (Lindsay-Hartz, 1984).

The consequences for breaking rules or for inappropriate behavior were usually clearly explained to the children, and either Laura or Kent consistently and fairly administered the consequences. Kent seemed to be the softer of the two, but the children learned early that it was not easy or acceptable to work one parent against the other. If this happened family conferences occurred quickly between the parents and the involved child. Parental unity and evenhanded consequences were very evident. Because Kent and Laura were explicit about what they expected of their children, grandparents and other adults in the children's lives usually aligned with the parental values and supported the family members in ways that were congruent and acceptable. The inconsistencies were infrequent enough that Kathy and Chad benefited from their interaction with the extended family and other adults in their lives.

If children know what is expected of them and do not follow through, they feel guilty. Healthy guilt is the recognition people have when they have failed to meet the expectations of someone with whom they have a significant relationship and to whom they feel accountable (Stierlin, 1974a). For example, Chad knows that it is his job to cut the lawn, trim it, and dispose of the clippings. His father has been very explicit about how to care for the lawn and how to clean all tools and return them to their proper place. One Saturday as Chad was finishing the lawn he realized that he could not trim the last side of the lawn and get to his Little League baseball game on time. He dropped everything right where he was, changed his clothes, grabbed his glove, jumped on his bicycle, and raced for the playing field. Before long his parents drove up to watch the game. When he saw them Chad remembered the tools that he left in the grass and his unfinished job. Guilt washed over him as he thought, "Am I going to get it when I get home!"

Rather than focusing attention on the self, healthy guilt emphasizes *action* (e.g., the failure by Chad to finish the job as expected and to put the tools in their designated space) and *cognition* (e.g., the thoughts of what would happen to him when Chad returned home after his father saw what he had done). In contrast, shame guards the boundaries of self, by labeling and blaming the self (Nathanson, 1987b). Guilt cannot occur as early as shame because it requires the development of cognition, whereas the process that leads to shame-proneness can begin at birth because it has to do with innate affect (Nathanson, 1987b).

In the guilting process, children learn to feel secure in knowing that they are accountable to someone for what they do. Parents (or some other adult) can be trusted to set consistent limits. Children experience comfort and security in such a "dependency" relationship because others, usually parents, are willing and confident in their responsibility to provide for the well-being of their children (Phillipson, Bernard, & Strang, 1986). This sense of accountability is reciprocal: The child feels responsible to someone who in turn feels responsible for the child in a very personal way. Using Chad as an example, let us review the guilting process.

Recognition of Wrongdoing.   The guilting process began with recognition by Chad that when he did not complete the job and put the tools away he failed to meet the expectations of his father, to whom he felt accountable.

Knowledge of Penalties and Rewards.   Chad knew clearly that the penalty for not doing what was expected of him was that he would lose a privilege for the week. He also knew that his father would be displeased. The rewards were that he and his father would take pride in a job well done. He knew that neither the rewards nor penalty were so extreme that he would have to give up his integrity, his sense of being a worthwhile person.

Feelings of Remorse and Sorrow. Having not met these expectations, Chad experienced a feeling of sorrow and wished that he had done things differently. These feelings were mixed with feelings of shame because he did not do as well as he could.

Recognition of Strain on Relationships. Chad realized that because of his actions there was stress in his relationship with his father. Possibly his father would be angry with him and not trust him as much as he had. But more than that, Chad knew that his father would be disappointed by his careless behavior. Chad began to feel very sorry that he had not taken enough time to do what was expected of him.

Expectations for Repair. Chad knew that his father expected that he would finish the job with the grass and clean and oil the tools before putting them away. Apologizing and talking with his father was also part of what Chad would do. Having been through similar situations with his father and mother, he knew what was expected of him. For a moment he felt anxious and somewhat angry. "Why couldn't they just understand!" He also knew that by finishing the job he would feel better about himself and he could then talk with his father about how he felt.

Having Choices and Consequences. Chad knew that he had a choice about what actions to take, even though there would always be consequences. As he thought about what to do, he remained whole, a worthwhile person, even in the face of making a wrong decision.

As a result of his actions Chad felt guilt, healthy guilt. Guilted people recognize: that they have value as human beings; that they have the right and capability to maintain a separate existence and be consistently affirmed; that errors are to be dealt with as something to be corrected, not as evidence of flaws in their character; that they have the potential, but not the necessity, for a close relationship with one or more significant others that is not conditional upon each act or decision. Under these conditions people can experience real closeness. No matter what happens—criticism, anger, disappointment, disapproval—they know that they are loved, supported, and valued. They know that they need not be suspicious of compliments. Genuine intimacy is possible because the interpersonal bond is always intact, regardless of the amount of healthy guilt experienced (Kaufman, 1989). They know that the values they are expected to adopt are clearly owned and consistently enforced by those significant others in their lives with whom they have developed reciprocal accountability. They know that those expectations represent a personal commitment to their wellbeing.

• *Children feel safe as a consequence of learning that it is healthy and useful to have significant adults who can be depended on to meet their needs* (Phillipson, Bernard, & Strang, 1986).

Kent's and Laura's acceptance of Chad's and Kathy's various dependency needs has provided healthy affirmation that they are unique and valued individuals. At the same time the parents' consistent expectations for acceptable performance have produced healthy guilt experiences. If both intimacy with affirmation and dependency with accountability are present between children and parents, children will feel guilty when they do something wrong. This is healthy guilt. Although they may feel very bad about what they have done, they will not feel internalized shame.

• *As parents enforce family rules, they teach children the importance of the hierarchical nature of the parent-child relationship and also affirm the child's right to be dependent* (Haley, 1987).

The enforcement of family rules emphasizes that the parents are the adults and that they are in charge. This emphasis points to a hierarchical boundary between children and their parents and acknowledges the parents' acceptance of their children's dependency needs. By recognizing the boundary, parents state that they are responsible and accountable for their children. As children become successively less dependent on their parents, rules change to fit the developmental stage of the children (McGoldrick & Carter, 1982). Within the marital relationship roles are often interchangeable, reflecting choice and desire rather than dependence on the other person. Thus, parents model interdependent behavior.

When parental and child roles and boundaries are clear, accountability is not blurred. Parents are not manipulating their children to assume responsibility for them, so dysfunctional patterns such as parentification of a child are absent (Boszormenyi-Nagy & Spark, 1984).

FAMILY SYSTEM DYNAMICS

Family system dynamics influence the development of healthy identity. Variations of behavior, interactions, and personal preferences foster unique family and individual characteristics without deleting wholesome influences. Sometimes children from within the same family vary in whether they show shame-proneness or healthy guilt. However, children in families that look good and feel good rarely develop shame-prone identities, even though children and parents have shameful experiences and feel guilted at times. One or both parents consistently affirm their children, although to varying degrees. The behavior of one parent complements the behavior of the other. These families have many crises, but their coping skills are adequate in most instances to deal with each other and with others outside the family (McCubbin & Patterson, 1982). The children develop healthy identities.

Marital/Parental Systems

The quality of the marital/parental system reflects joint responsibility, accountability, and acceptance for their children, as well as nurturance for each other and other family members.

Marital relationships in family systems that foster healthy identity development have the following characteristics.

- Spouses are interdependent, independent, and sometimes dependent, usually appropriate in all three areas.
- Each spouse shares joint responsibility and accountability for dependency and intimacy needs for the children, and nurturance for each other and other family members.
- Each spouse exhibits a healthy personality and is quite capable of independent thinking and acting.
- Spouses accept growth, development, and change as a natural part of life.
- Spouses have the skill to negotiate personal projects, disagreements, differences in desires and values, and other conflicts, and to attend to intimacy needs and other parameters of the coupleship.
- Boundaries established jointly guarantee individual freedom and also privacy from the children.
- Spouses have a mutual respect for each other, share intimacy, and forgive and forget mistakes.
- Spouses demonstrate love by expressing their differences through honesty, accessibility, and accountability.
- Pain, momentary doubts, misunderstandings, and feelings mix with negotiation, listening, and adjustments.

Parent-child relationships in family systems that foster healthy identity development have the following characteristics.

- Parents are united in parenting their children with fairly consistent disciplinary actions as well as love and support for the children and themselves.
- Parental response is consistent, therefore predictable by the children and the other spouse.
- Parents are comfortable and consistent with their values and standards and they teach their children acceptable values and behavior.

- Parents accept the dependency of their children and support it through explanation, direct teaching, specified disciplinary consequences, and appropriate intimate behavior.
- Parents are consistent and beneficient to everyone, as the family and individuals move through developmental stages and day-to-day problems.
- Parents affirm their children for what they contribute to the family and for their own endeavors.
- Parents allow their children to be close and valued even when they have made mistakes.
- Boundaries for intimacy and privacy blend with respect for individual needs and expectations.
- Rules for behavior are consistent with the values espoused by the parents.
- Modifications of rules occur as the children assume more responsibility for their own behavior.

Because Kent and Laura comfortably owned their own values, messages to their children started with, "I expect . . . ," "I believe . . . ," or "Your mother and I have this family rule because. . . ." These and similar phrases indicated that the parent(s) clearly expected their children to conform to a set of standards that they accepted.

As Chad and Kathy became more involved with peers and outside interests, Kent and Laura discussed with them their expectations for their behavior and emphasized the complexity of relationships as they approached differing stages of development. They openly discussed their need to have their children involved with them, individually and with the family. As distressing incidents occurred, Kent and Laura sought understanding of their own feelings and at times inconsistent behaviors.

Let us return to Chad's situation after being picked up by a policeman in a stolen car. Chad was probably more frightened, shamed, and overwhelmed with guilt than he had ever been in his life. Knowing that the officer would eventually tell his mother that there were open beer cans in the car, he was afraid of what his parents would think of him and what the consequences would be. His parents had long ago asked him not to experiment with alcohol or drugs. As he walked into the room where his mother was and looked at her anguished face, he hesitated a moment. She opened her arms and he rushed into them; feeling that he was safe, he then began to tell her the story. Acting on dares from one another, the boys first cut classes, then *borrowed* one boy's uncle's car. Finding a six-pack of beer in the car, they decided to drink it. Chad knew that everything he had done was against family values and rules, yet a part of him wanted to defend himself and what he had done. They hadn't meant any harm to anyone. One thing had led to another without careful thought.

Laura listened as she held her young son close to her. Then she held him away from her and indicated that she was taking him home and that they would talk about the incident and the consequences for his behavior as a family. This incident provided Kent and Laura another opportunity to explore and discuss values, rules, laws, and accountability with Chad rather than to demand blind conformity to their beliefs and values. Chad was still dependent and accountable to his parents, but now he was also accountable to the community and faced consequences imposed by someone other than his parents. He and his parents faced a different situation, with all family members embarrassed by the incident and uncertain about what to do and say.

Kathy was shocked, embarrassed, and confused by her anger, while at the same time she wanted to help Chad. Laura and Kent felt guilty, wondering where they had failed their son. The parents assumed that Chad had internalized a self-regulated set of standards that matched their own and were confused by his behavior. The level of healthy functioning in the family fostered communication and sharing of feelings as Chad's situation was resolved within the family, with the police, and with the school.

Sibling Systems

The quality of the sibling system reflects the quality of other family functions. Sibling interaction often replicates the patterns learned from interaction with parents.

- Older siblings accept accountability and dependency for and to the younger siblings in keeping with the values and modeling exhibited by their parents.
- Siblings recognize their differences and accept their separateness from one another.
- Siblings feel emotionally close and are affectionate, but they also are able to be autonomous.
- Conflicts are resolved through negotiation and problem-solving.

Extended Family Systems

When two people join together in marriage or any other form of a committed relationship, they bring both of their families of origin into a new system (Kramer, 1985). The relationships created by this union are multigenerational with siblings, in-laws, aunts, uncles, grandparents and great-grandparents extending as far as the nuclear family chooses. Some basic assumptions about these levels of family connections will be helpful in understanding the dynamics of healthy family systems.

- Individuals are influenced by, and also influence, the three-plus generational system within which they are born and live.
- A three-plus generational family system has all the characteristics of any multiperson ecosystem, but it is more complex.
- Because multigenerational systems are developmental in nature, individuals, the marital system, the nuclear family, other subsystems, and the larger multigenerational system constantly move through stages of change and development.
- The multigenerational system's patterns and influences are stored, transmitted, transformed, and manifested within the multigenerational system. This phenomenon is designated as intergenerational transmission.
- Nuclear families are influenced by two multigenerational systems: the nuclear and extended families of the husband and of the wife.
- Multigenerational issues are transmitted and appear within certain contexts. Consequently, issues can remain hidden and be transmitted at unconscious levels until the appropriate context is presented in which these issues are called forth.
- Multigenerational systems have boundaries that are hierarchical in nature, which influence individual and system development as well as intergenerational transmissions.
- Multigenerational systems develop functional and dysfunctional patterns based on the legacy from previous generations and the "here and now" happenings within individuals, subsystems, the three-plus generational system, and societal contexts. These patterns can serve functional or dysfunctional purposes in the marital, family, or extended family systems (Hoopes, 1987).

The influence and quality of extended family relationships are regulated by the quality of the various family environments within the larger system. If the nuclear family has a healthy identity and a large proportion of the extended family is healthy, the following descriptions apply.

- The often complicated and varied quality of interaction between individuals and families is generally positive.
- Extended family members, grandparents, siblings, aunts and uncles respect the boundaries, values, and standards of the nuclear family.
- The nuclear family is successful in establishing itself as a separate independent entity.
- The nuclear family clearly indicates that it is an involved, caring, contributing part of the extended family.
- The nuclear family allows for differences in other members and families.
- Some families throughout the extended family system contain

shame-prone individuals and shaming systems, but there is enough health to support families.
- The secrets, myths, and feuds within the extended family have very little effect on the nuclear family (Pillari, 1986).

Laura's family tended to take for granted that Laura would be involved in all their family gatherings. As the oldest sibling, she sometimes assumed too much responsibility for their pain and personal problems. With Kent's understanding and help she gradually established methods of integrating and supporting her family without such emotional and physical costs.

Kent's family lived in another state and tended to lose track of each other. As a team, Laura and Kent made special efforts to stay in touch with everyone and encourage visits. Because they were clear with their children about their values and expectations for their family, the extended family also knew what to expect from Kent, Laura, and their children. Generally, they honored and respected them, although there were misunderstandings, misbehaviors by children, and complications that had to be recognized and resolved.

Friends, Neighbors, Work, and Community Relationships

Families with healthy identities interact with friends, neighbors, colleagues, and others in community settings. These relationships are important for their development and growth. From Little League participation to running for school board, families belong or feel estranged according to the quality of friendships developed and the outcomes of services delivered or received. Some of the characteristics that mark healthy families are:

- They are good neighbors by offering support and help when neighbors need it.
- Friends are valued and their home is open to them.
- The respect that they show each other is reflected in how they interact with friends, work colleagues, teachers, and other individuals in the community.
- The children are taught to be friendly and to respect people and their property.
- Parents participate in their children's activities in the community, neighborhood, school, church, and other contexts.
- Neither family members nor the family as a whole has difficulty in interpersonal relationships and in other social contexts, including work.

Let us return to the Stevens family to examine family members' interactions with others. Much more concerned with school and community issues than Kent, Laura volunteered for projects and committees. Kent, on the other hand, showed up to help a neighbor move or to put in a garden. The children were involved in sports and drama activities with full support of their parents. They belong to their community and neighborhood.

CHAPTER 5

Family Systems With Shame-Prone Identities

INDIVIDUALS WHO ARE shame-prone generally belong to families that are also shame-prone. This chapter describes shame-prone family systems and their effects on individuals' identities. These individuals may vary in the amount of shame-prone symptoms they exhibit, but usually they can identify that family conditions were "bad."

TOTALLY SHAME-PRONE FAMILIES

This family type is one in which family members feel bad and look bad to outsiders. Families that look bad to others and feel bad to those who live within them are very dysfunctional. Unhealthy guilt and shaming incidents proliferate this environment (Evans, 1987). Nothing ever seems to go right for the family or family members. The fact that they know it and believe that everyone else does too is doubly shaming and hopeless (Nathanson, 1987c). Some of these families have active scapegoats, allowing them to pretend to be a capable family, but at some level, as individuals and as a family, they know they are not. To those on the outside, these families look bad in some or all of the following ways.

- Appear to have very few common goals and purposes. These families seem to be unable to formulate and work toward goals and purposes.
- Seem continually to be dealing with crises, stress, and outside demands in a haphazard, ineffective way.
- Appear to be unhappy people going in many directions or so enmeshed that little gets done—very codependent.
- Appear to have few talents and capabilities to cope with what goes on inside the family.

- Very little interaction with others unless the situation is low-risk and routine.

Those inside the family *feel bad* in all or some of the following ways.

- Experience false pride in the family and in family members with little genuine trust, loyalty, and respect.
- May perceive themselves as a loving, close family, although intimacy is confusing and sometimes inappropriate. Some family members may experience combinations of emotional, physical, and intellectual intimacy, e.g., parents and/or siblings may be inappropriately sexual with family members, or even abusive, and suicidal.
- Experience the family, themselves, and other family members as bad. Others are good; they are bad.
- Experience feelings of unworthiness, not deserving and not receiving abundance. They operate from survival beliefs; therefore, they accumulate as much as they can—money, favors, etc.
- Experience being out of control most of the time, always the victim with many excuses.
- Experience stress and practice deception as they pretend to be able to adapt to changes and losses.
- Experience too much dependence on family information, and distrust information coming from outside the family. Communication ranges from mediocre to bad and negotiation is lacking.
- Experience lack of feelings of security and safety. Undefined fear and anger are common in the family. The family and some family members are perceived as not being accountable and dependable.

CHARACTERISTICS OF DYSFUNCTIONAL FAMILIES

Families with shame-prone identities are dysfunctional. Patterns of structural, attitudinal, and behavior within the marital and family systems fail to meet the needs and goals of both the system and the individuals. The patterns do not allow for continued growth of individuals, of the marriage, or of other family relationships. In addition, one or both of the spouses and one or more of the children may exhibit symptomatic behavior. Thus, the level of family functioning in families that look bad and feel bad is often pathological. For many family interactions the lack of adequate coping strategies, interpersonal skills, and healthy identities contribute to the failure to resolve developmental and life crisis (Falicov, 1988). With family members experiencing shame and unhealthy guilt, individual and family problems escalate, accumulate, and block resolution and feelings of value and appreciation for one another.

Families that develop a shame-prone identity have many of the following general characteristics:

- They are pathological.
- Coping strategies and conflict resolution skills are inadequate (Lavee, McCubbin, & Olson, 1987).
- Some or all family members have unhealthy personalities.
- Intimacy, dependency, and other needs are usually not met, with negative affirmations dominant (Carnes, 1989).
- The quality of the marital/parental relationship, parent-child relationships, sibling relationships, and extended family relationships influence negative affirmation of identities as members experience shame and guilt.
- Such family systems are either chaotically or rigidly disengaged. The use of space, time, and energy is such that family members are always distancing from each other (Olson, Sprenkle, & Russell, 1979).
- One or more adults bring to the nuclear family unresolved issues from their family of origin, e.g., unresolved emotional illness of their parents, incest, addictions, codependency, cult practices, parentification, and money or property conflicts (Kerr & Bowen, 1988).
- Chronic illness and/or disability, e.g., cancer, AIDS, multiple sclerosis, amputations, strokes, may be present.
- Uncontrollable trauma, e.g., rape, murder, loss of home by fire or flood, stock market collapse, has been experienced (Potter & Ronald, 1987).

The total family affect is often that of anger, hurt, and discouragement, and the meanings that family members derive from the family interaction are:

- that the world is hopeless;
- that change does not matter if one is basically flawed ("bad" people can't initiate "good" change);
- that the world and especially people are black and white, right and wrong, good and bad;
- that others are necessary to one's existence but cannot be depended upon.

THE NEGATIVE AFFIRMATION
TRIANGLE

Negative affirmations in dysfunctional families far outweigh the positive ones (Jacob, 1987). However, parents and siblings have some personal strengths that translate into specific situational and contextual positive affirmations for some of the family members, some of the time. The predominance of negative affirmations guarantees that many of the needs of children and adults will not be met. Such things as lack of healthy food, shelter and education, few coping skills and strategies, low intimacy, scant training to be productive, and inadequate medical and dental care contribute to negative affirmation. Individuals do not get strong messages that they are valued, contributing members of the family. Lack of feelings of belonging, of being safe and secure, predominates in shame-prone families.

Intimacy

The following are characteristic of families who chronically fail to meet intimacy needs:

- Intimacy is inappropriate (e.g., enmeshed) or nonexistent.
- Members emotionally overreact or suppress feelings (Coleman, 1982).
- Relationships are distant or enmeshed (Olson, Sprenkle, & Russell, 1979).
- Boundaries are rigid or changing all of the time, with insensitivity to other's boundaries.
- Little genuine affection is given or received. Touch needs are not met.
- Expression of feelings is gushy, inappropriate to maintain a safe context, or lacking.
- There is minimal sharing of intimate thoughts, goals, wants, dreams, and needs.
- Incongruence and lack of emotional safety threaten stability and sense of order.

Dependency

When dependency needs are not met, the following conditions exist in dysfunctional families:

- Members are emotionally needy because they cannot be dependent.
- Members are fearful of their own and others' emotions. No role models are present for dealing with emotions.
- There is a loss of connection to "higher power"—spirituality.
- Authority issues are reflected in rebellious and/or passive-aggressive behavior.
- Victim, martyr roles are frequently practiced.

- Abandonment issues are present.
- Disorganization and instability are common in family life.

Accountability

When parents and other influential adults in children's lives fail to be accountable with some regularity, the following conditions exist in dysfunctional families:

- Rules are harsh and rigid, permissive, or lacking.
- Parents are unable to account to others and have problems with authority figures.
- Children are unable to be accountable for themselves and exhibit undisciplined and passive-aggressive behavior.
- Behavior is incongruent with values and standards of self, family, organizations, and society.
- Life is disorderly, undisciplined, impulsive, or highly controlled.

FAMILY CONDITIONS LEADING TO THE FORMATION OF SHAME-PRONE IDENTITIES

The case that follows illustrates the family conditions that lead to shame-prone identities. This case is a synthesis of people whom both of the authors have seen professionally. It became obvious during the first therapy session that Carol possessed a shame-prone identity based on deficits in both dependency and intimacy.

A Shame-Prone Individual and Her Family

Carol was an attractive young woman, 24 years old, who was raising a son, age 7, by herself. She reported she had fallen in love with a boy a year older than herself when she was 17. She loved him because he was the first boy to pay attention to her. He did almost everything for her. In fact, he was more like a parent than a boyfriend. She tried to be all the ways he wanted her to be. She never asserted her wants because of her constant fear that he would abandon her. She just wanted to be taken care of, and he seemed to be the person in her life most willing to care for her. She was sexual with him because she did not want to lose him. She knew that if he ever discovered her true "inner core" he surely would abandon her.

When she discovered that she was pregnant, he was the first person she told. He immediately turned on her, accusing her of trying to trap him, blaming her for not protecting herself from getting pregnant. As she sobbed, he slapped her hard several times and left. She never saw him again.

When Carol told her parents she was pregnant, they were furious. Her father beat her, and her mother withdrew almost totally. As Carol remembered it, her mother never said anything about the pregnancy after that. In fact, her mother basically stopped interacting with her in any way except for the most superfluous conversations. Her father contacted a social service agency for unwed mothers. He told Carol to get into the car one day and then drove her to the agency. He did not discuss it with her beforehand.

Carol lived several states away with foster parents during her pregnancy. She decided to keep the baby, despite her parents' objections, but she did return to live with her parents following the birth of her son, mostly because she was incapable of sustaining herself financially. Two months after the birth of her son, her parents arranged to have her evaluated by a psychiatrist. Carol was diagnosed as an inadequate personality and kept in an inpatient hospital for several months while her mother cared for her son. Following her dismissal from the hospital, Carol found a job as a waitress and eventually left her parents' home with her son. She did not tell her parents she was leaving and moved to an apartment far across the city, where she hoped they could not find her.

At the time I started to see her, Carol had been in therapy for two and a half years with another therapist. That therapist had referred Carol to me because she felt stuck and reported that therapy was not moving anywhere.

Carol had been on welfare for almost three years. She had failed to keep any job for more than a few months, and her son was having many academic and behavioral problems in school. Her parents knew where she was living and had frequent association with Carol and her son, but Carol reported that they were mostly controlling and interfering. Shortly after my second therapy session with Carol, her mother called to inform me that Carol was very sick, had been diagnosed as an inadequate personality by another psychiatrist, and needed to be hospitalized. The real purpose of the call was to convince me to hospitalize Carol. When I refused, she called me several demeaning names and hung up.

Conditions Typical of Shame-Prone Families

The following descriptions are characteristic of these shaming family systems.

- *Parents treat other family members as extensions of themselves and often treat children as possessions rather than people. The formation of separate and unique identities with their own personal needs is seen as a threat to the system* (Kerr & Bowen, 1988).

Marriages in these families usually begin with implicit expectations by both husband and wife that the other spouse will "take care of me." Both partners have often been shamed in their families of origin and are searching for the parenting they never received (Boszormenyi-Nagy & Ulrich, 1981). Because each partner's demands for "getting taken care of" are overwhelming to the other, the marriage becomes a disappointment to both. As children are born, each parent looks to the children to "take care of" his or her neediness. When children make their own demands to be taken care of, parents sense that their expectations won't be met and turn on the children. Parents usually feel rageful and resentful toward the children because the children are incapable of filling the emotional emptiness of the parents (Potter & Ronald, 1987). Under such circumstances differences of opinion, feeling, personality, and activity become threatening. Children are expected to do what parents want. Parents seek to live their lives through their children, often pushing them to do the activities and experience the feelings that the parents dreamed of doing but felt incapable of accomplishing. This no-win game aggravates the disappointment and consequent rage of the parents and becomes shaming to both the parent and child. For parents, it is simply another way of affirming their shamed identity. The children learn that they must be bad because of the disastrous consequences of asserting any feeling, thought, or action that originates within them (Naiditch, 1987).

When Carol was born, both her father and mother looked to her and her older brother for the fulfillment of their damaged dreams. But the demands of having a second young infant who cried when needs went unmet further threatened Carol's mother. Her mother developed a deep sense of offense and accompanying rage toward Carol almost as soon as they brought her home from the hospital. Carol's needs for dependency were too overwhelming to a mother who desired to be totally dependent on a parent herself. Her mother's rage, sense of abandonment, and terror at being all alone further compounded Carol's negatively affirmed identity. Carol's mother reported having difficulty cuddling and being affectionate toward Carol just a few days following her birth. She had tolerated her son's demands by relying on her husband a great deal.

Carol's father was a stern man, deeply disappointed by his wife's inability to soothe his own battered emotional system. Carol felt that her father owned her. For as long as she could remember he had treated her like a possession to do with what he wished. She always sensed that he wanted something from her, but she couldn't ever figure out what it was.

- *Errors or mistakes set the stage for demeaning and humiliation by other family members. The attack is personalized and the individual who made the mistake experiences a sense of "personal badness"* (Stierlin, 1974a).

It seemed to Carol that she had never been able to please either of her parents. Her father's angry outbursts and harsh discipline confused her. She could never predict how he would respond. She was afraid of him and did not want to have him touch her or be near her. While she craved affection and caring from someone, she also felt she did not deserve to be treated nicely.

When her father made sexual advances toward her, she was terrified. Her sense of being filthy and bad intensified over the years that the incestuous relationship continued. After sexual encounters her father often turned on her emotionally, calling her his "tempting little bitch." He told her that she needed to stop being a temptation to him, that it was her fault for being too seductive.

As she entered puberty, Carol attempted to hide her femaleness in demeaning clothes, lack of personal care, and "tomboyish" activity. Her father responded with ridicule, telling her how ugly she was, and pushing her to clean up, take care of her hair, and wear different clothes. Carol felt she was somehow flawed. Her behavior eventually became disconnected from her sense of self so that, regardless of how good her behavior was, she felt bad at the core.

- *Children question whether they are loved. They feel of little value to other family members and they expect nonsupport* (Naiditch, 1987).

Neither of Carol's parents helped Carol feel of value. She felt like an inconvenience to her mother and a possession of her father. But even though her father and mother both seemed to need something from her, they were incapable of helping her feel valued as a person. Carol soon learned not to expect her parents to come through for her. Although she often felt alone, she had discovered that hoping her parents would be dependable and then being disappointed was more painful than feeling alone. At least being alone was predictable and reliable.

Rare is the situation where only one parent is shaming. Usually shame finds shame, so that both parents are shame-based (Bradshaw, 1988; Fossom & Mason, 1986). However, the form of shaming that each parent exhibits may be different. In Carol's family the father was much more verbally expressive. He was verbally demeaning, physical with Carol in inappropriate ways, and treated her as he did his possessions. Carol's mother, on the other hand, withdrew and kept great emotional distance between her and Carol.

There are a small percentage of families in which only one parent is shaming. In these families children still feel negatively affirmed because of the incongruence between parents, but the sense of negative affirmation may not be as intense as when both parents are shaming. When one parent is shame-prone, the intensity with which children will feel "damaged at the inner core" depends on the systemic position of both the shame-based parent and the children. Chapter 7 explains more about shame and systemic position.

> • *Children raised in this family environment will have shame-prone identities. However, the intensity of their shame and the way they exhibit their proneness to shame will vary according to the systemic position of parents and children* (Hoopes & Harper, 1987).

Carol was born into a system with two parents and an older brother. Her systemic position was typical of a second child. Second children are often keenly attuned to their mother's unresolved needs and issues, as explained in Chapter 7. She implicitly sensed any affect present in the family system but was unaware that the emotions had their source in other family members rather than in herself. She usually felt crazy because of the emotional overload, since there were no outward, observable reasons for the emotional roller coaster she experienced. The shame-proneness of second children is intensified by the incongruities between the explicit and implicit processes in the family; in other words, the underlying mood and meanings of other family members do not match what they say and do (Hoopes & Harper, 1987). Such children's shame-proneness is especially intensified when their mother is shame-prone, as these children will often act out mother's unresolved needs. In a sense they become an alter for their mothers. Because of the melding of emotional experience with other family members and because they intuitively sense the implicit, boundaries are a problem for children in Carol's systemic position, that of a second child (Hoopes & Harper, 1987). That fact that Carol's father treated her like a possession further intensified her problems with interpersonal boundaries.

At the time Carol started therapy with me, she had been involved in many inappropriate sexual relationships. She had difficulty asserting any personal boundaries when it came to sexual advances by men. She felt that what she did for men was to be sexual. Her identity received temporary affirmation by being able to provide something for men, but that sense was soon overshadowed by her "badness."

Carol's older brother was also shame-based. Being the first child in the family, he exhibited symptoms of shame-proneness differently from Carol. He was more verbal and cognitive in his shamed state. Carol usually seemed histrionic and was always confused by a jumbled set of emotions. Carl, her brother, was very verbal and seemed to get tied in cognitive dilemmas that he could not unravel. For example, he constantly questioned the meaning behind other people's words. He would go on for long periods of time about semantics of words. He focused primarily on rational, explicit information, while Carol focused on the implicit, underlying feelings in interpersonal situations. Carl was much more attuned to the unresolved issues of his father, whereas Carol was tuned into her mother. Because both parents were shame-based, both children were shame-based as well. Had Carol's mother not been shame-based, Carol's intensity of shame would have been reduced but Carl would have remained more shame-prone because of his "tuning into his father" and his father's verbal abuse.

- *Any sense of intimacy in family relationships is threatening and creates anxiety for parents and other family members* (Feldman, 1979).

Carol learned that her parents' love for her was very conditional. When she sometimes could soothe the pain of her parents' emotional void, she received at least some semblance of positive interaction with them. However, most of the time her parents were distant and disengaged. Members of such families are usually afraid of their own emotional experience and that of others.

Intimacy involves too much sharing for people who feel so vulnerable and constantly risk exposing their damaged inner core when they get too close in relationships. The family system constantly regulates closeness, so that the shame feelings of all family members are hidden and protected. Sharing of ideas and feelings is avoided because the risk of abandonment and rejection is too great.

- *Values, including standards and expectations, are never clearly identified or owned by parents and other significant adults. Standards are not consistently enforced; when they are, the enforcement is harsh and accompanied by physical force and an intensity of emotion that is inappropriate for the situation.*

Even though Carol sensed that both of her parents wanted something from both her and her brother, it was never clear to her exactly what they wanted. Her mother never interacted enough with her to set any expectations. She only reacted with rage when Carol upset or inconvenienced her and ignored Carol the rest of the time. Father seemed to have many expectations, but they were often contradictory and the enforcement was harsh.

Neither parent owned any standards that he or she set for Carol and Carl. Their mother often threatened them with being punished by God if they didn't behave, and their father told them that if they didn't behave he would tell the neighbors and other relatives how bad they were. This strategy didn't affect Carol as much as it did Carl. Carol said Carl would often beg his parents not to tell anyone. Because of his systemic position, he was much more concerned about getting approval from people, whereas Carol was more concerned about just having an emotional "place."

The message both got from parents is that they were "bad" kids who inconvenienced everyone. Mother told them that if other people knew how bad they were, Carol and Carl would immediately be rejected. They both learned early in life that mom would totally disengage from them and father would physically hurt them whenever they exhibited any needs that placed demands on parents.

Carol knew she was accountable to both mom and dad in some way. She just couldn't ever figure out for what. It appeared to her that dad's rules were arbitrary and constantly changing, depending on what was convenient for him at the moment. Consequences for behavior were never explained. Mom didn't seem to care about accountability. She preferred not to be responsible to other people and didn't seem to care whether they were accountable to her or not.

When the expectations seem high and enforcement is harsh, children learn to be excessively guilty in unhealthy ways (Weigel, 1974). When they make a mistake, the situation is used to further affirm the shamed personal core. Changing the behavior will not make any difference because the personal core will still be bad. So even though such people feel excessively guilty, they appear to others to do little about it in terms of changing behavior. Rather they may talk about how bad they feel that they behaved in certain ways and what "awful, bad" people they are. Such was the case of Carol and Carl because of the harshness and unpredictability of their father's discipline and expectations.

If, however, their father had been more like their mother and could care less whether children were accountable to standards as long as they didn't inconvenience her, Carol and Carl would appear sociopathic, with little regard for rules, standards, or other's rights and needs. The lack of accountability would still affirm their shame-prone identities because they would feel so out of control, and as they violated the rights of others, others would do things "to" them that would affirm their badness. Whereas healthy guilt emphasizes action and cognition (e.g., thinking through consequences of behavior for self and others), shame emphasizes a lack of personal worth accompanied by high intensity of emotion or no emotion at all, particularly a sense of total badness and doom.

In the shaming process, wrong behavior and self are the same. When punishment is given, it affirms the shame-based identity of the person receiving it. If rewards are ever offered, shame-prone individuals are suspicious. Rewards are seen as undeserved and inconsistent with a shame-based person's expectations. Rather than experiencing a sense of sorrow for what one has done, only a feeling of being bad is present.

People who are shame-based set up shaming processes in relationships with others (Wright, 1987). For example, even though Carol resented the intrusiveness of her parents, she constantly made choices that flaunted her badness in her parent's eyes. When she and her son were invited to her parents' home for dinner, Carol made certain she dressed poorly and looked terrible. She told her father about her worst behavior, expecting to hook his anger. The shaming that followed affirmed Carol's identity. It was as if it were better to be consistently and negatively affirmed than to have any praise and positive interaction with her parents.

Carol felt she could not be repaired no matter how hard she tried. Although she constantly apologized to everyone for the ways in which she behaved, she never did anything to change her behavior. To her there was no hope of fixing her "flaw."

- *Children feel insecure and learn that others cannot be counted on to meet personal needs because the family environment seems like such an unpredictable place* (Carnes, 1989).

Shame-based persons are distrustful (Bradshaw, 1988). They expect people to shame them and search for information in their environment that shames them. If they cannot find such information, they will distort their perception of the environment and people in it to match their expectations. They exhibit a great insecurity because they are constantly trying to hide their shame from others. Shame-based people constantly fear being found out, uncovered as it were. They guard against it constantly (Fischer, 1985).

Because they fear that others will abandon them if they are "discovered," they are insecure around all people. They cannot be themselves and must portray a false image that will mask their shame. When Carol came to her first therapy session, she expected me to chastise her. When I responded empathically to her circumstances, she became even more pathetic in appearance and story. When that didn't elicit any chastisement from me, she became rageful, accusing me of not being honest and straight with her.

As she came for subsequent sessions I noticed that she first surveyed the waiting room to see if anyone else was there. If others were there, she often waited in the hall, trying to avoid letting anyone see her.

- *When parents enforce family rules, they teach children to be afraid of power and authority. The need for dependency is denied by other family members' inability to accept having anyone depend on them. Parents often expect their children to meet the parents' unfulfilled dependency needs* (Nathanson, 1987a).

The harsh enforcement of family rules in shaming families teaches children that adults should be feared. The hierarchical boundary between children and their parents that exists in healthy families is reversed in the shaming system. Parents try to ignore or deny their children's dependency needs and hold out a hope that instead they may be dependent on their children. By reversing the roles, parents state that they feel little and incapable and cannot be accountable for their children. Because parental and child roles and boundaries are unclear, accountability is blurred. As parents manipulate their children to assume responsibility for them, parentification occurs (Boszormenyi-Nagy & Spark, 1984).

FAMILY DYNAMICS

In addition to structure in families, specific events can foster proneness to shame. Such things as unresolved losses, addictions, codependency, and affairs are usually shaming to individuals and families.

Marital/Parental Systems

In shaming families, the marital and parental relationships are typical two-person systems that shame people and the ones with whom they interact.

Marital Relationships. Some or all of the conditions described below are typical of these systems.

- Spouses are confused or in conflict about responsibility, accountability, and acceptance for their children.
- Spouses tend to be codependent (Wegscheider-Cruse & Cruse, 1989).
- Spouses fail to adequately nurture each other and other family members (Patton & Waring, 1984).
- Each spouse exhibits some unhealthy personality characteristics and is sometimes incapable of independent thinking and acting (Nathanson, 1987c).
- Spouses are frightened by growth, development, and change, especially in their spouses (Luthman & Kirschenbaum, 1974).
- Spouses rarely negotiate personal projects, disagreements, differences in desires and values, conflict, intimacy needs, and other parameters of the coupleship; they sometimes sabotage each other in these areas.
- Confusion about boundaries or lack of boundaries sabotages individual freedom and privacy as a couple and from the children (Fossom & Mason, 1986).
- Spouses mistrust each other in some areas, intimacy is conditional and contextual, and they badger each other about mistakes.
- Spouses demonstrate love based on their terms and needs; they bargain and manipulate in an attempt to get their needs met; they

rarely are honest, accessible, and accountable (Fossom & Mason, 1986).

- Pain, momentary doubts, misunderstandings, and feelings serve to confuse attempts to negotiate, listen, and adjust to the other's needs (Nathanson, 1987c).

Parent-Child Relationships.   Parent-child relationships in shaming families are characterized by the following:

- Parents communicate, implicitly and explicitly, that fulfilling children's needs for dependency and intimacy is an imposition (Elbow, 1982).
- Parents are unsure of or in conflict about their own standards and values.
- Parents are often very conflicted about having children and usually overwhelmed by both their roles as parents and the social demands that society places on them.
- Parents neither nurture nor provide socialization needs for children.
- Discipline is mostly inconsistent and often alternates from being overly harsh and physical for what the situation requires to appearing totally apathetic about any behavior of children (Boss & Sheppard, 1988).
- Spouses are rarely united in parenting their children and tend to abdicate or contend about disciplinary actions (Nathanson, 1987c).
- Parents may love each other and their children, but they demonstrate the love inconsistently, with mixed messages and abuse.
- Parental response to their children is inconsistent; therefore, parents appear unpredictable and unreasonable to the children and their spouse.
- Parents are inconsistent and uncomfortable with their stated values and standards and those of society; therefore, their children learn few acceptable values and standards of behavior from them.
- Parents do not accommodate and adjust to their children's developmental stages and day-to-day problems (Carter & McGoldrick, 1989).
- Parents fail to affirm their children for what they contribute to the family and for their own endeavors (Naiditch, 1987).
- Parents send mixed messages to their children about being close and valued.
- Parents emphasize mistakes made by everyone in the family.
- Boundaries for intimacy and privacy are nonexistent or confusing and inconsistent, sending messages of disrespect for individual needs and expectations (Fossom & Mason, 1986).

- Rules for behavior can be harsh and rigid and are rarely backed by parental standards and values.
- Modifications of rules may not occur as the children assume more responsibility for their own behavior.
- Children and spouses are often abused or neglected (Boss & Sheppard, 1988).
- Abandonment and punishment are expected and seen as deserved because such children believe that their basic, core impulses are bad.
- Power in relationships in confusing, and parent-child exchanges are often rigid one-up/one-down exchanges, or parents act totally powerless by assuming no responsibility to or for anyone in the family, including each other (Nathanson, 1987a).

These children receive a message that their needs are basically bad. For young children, perception of self and perception of needs are not separate. For infants, they are their needs. Shame-prone individuals learn at a very early age that their needs are bad, wrong, and excessive.

If infants' needs for attention, for caring, for expressing feelings and desires, are not met in ways that affirm children's existence and value, they try to get their needs met by anything that draws a reaction of any kind from the system. Such children believe that, since the need for attention is bad anyway, it is of little concern that they disrupt others by acting on such a need. Such individuals learn to expect this distorted consistency in their relationships with others and form a mental template through which they view the world and construe its meanings to fit their conception of "bad self." As these children grow older, they have difficulty relating to anyone who does not behave in ways that confirm the "bad me" conception (Kaufman, 1989, 1985).

Such shame-prone individuals lack the security of an interpersonal bond and the safety of a reciprocal accountability (Kaufman, 1989). Left with a sense of inferiority to survive on their own, they feel incapable of managing the demands that the world places on them. The following consequences result from the interaction in parent-child relationships:

- Children conclude that genuine intimacy is an illusion never to be experienced (Carnes, 1989).
- Children's sexual identity and sexual feelings are confusing (Carnes, 1989).

Their underlying belief is that they do not deserve closeness; if others really got close, others would discover they were bad. However, it is important to maintain the illusion of a hope of closeness because of a belief that the demands of living cannot be managed by oneself. Such individuals engage in interpersonal behaviors designed to insulate themselves from the sense of outrage, terror, and worthlessness by keeping others at a safe distance. This condition requires behaviors that maintain the delicate balance between keeping others distant enough so they cannot discover the "fatal flaw" and keeping others from "going away" and abandoning.

Sibling Relationships

The following descriptions are often characteristics of sibling relationships in shame-prone families.

- Relationships often reflect the codependency of the marital relationship.
- Older siblings sometimes take the role of a parent and accept the responsibility for younger siblings, sacrificing their own childhood.
- Relationships are characterized by either extreme enmeshment or exploitation.

If the relationships are enmeshed, children act as if they cannot function on their own without the other sibling present. Both act as if they can never be whole as individuals, but maybe together two halves can make a whole. If the sibling relationships are exploitive, children are abused by each other, sexual boundaries are disregarded, and the sibling relationships function to confirm the "bad me" image of each family member.

Extended Family Relationships

Proneness to shame can be transmitted from one generation to another in the multigenerational family system (Bradshaw, 1988). When parents are raised in a shame-prone family, their children are more prone to shame. Individuals who develop a shame-prone identity when they are young are almost always shaming to their own children unless they have received outside help to work through the shame. Shame-prone parents find it very difficult to provide intimacy, dependency, and accountability needs to their children. Needy, shame-based parents feel further shamed by their children's needs and their reactions to those needs. Their children are shamed by the lack of intimacy, accountability, and dependency in the system and are likely to marry other shame-prone people and to repeat the process all over again.

When the extended family is predominantly shame-prone, the following conditions are typical.

- Families throughout the extended family system contain shame-prone individuals and shaming systems.
- Grandparents, parents, aunts and uncles, cousins and their families exhibit psychopathology.
- Secrets, myths, and feuds populate the complicated and varied interactions among individuals and families (Bagarozzi & Anderson, 1989; Pillari, 1986).
- Some extended family members, grandparents, siblings, aunts and uncles ignore the boundaries, values, and standards of the nuclear family.
- Individuals and sometimes whole families are ignored, ostracized, or forgotten.
- The nuclear family and individuals within it are unsuccessful in establishing themselves as separate independent entities (Fossom & Mason, 1986).
- The nuclear family fails to be an involved, contributing part of the extended family because of its own shame and that of the extended family system.

Friends, Neighbors, Work, and Community Relationships

People from shame-prone systems often have difficulty with friends, neighbors, colleagues, supervisors at work, or other relationships outside the family system. The following characteristics describe these relationships with outside systems.

- They often have difficulty in interpersonal relationships and other social contexts, including work.
- Neighborly help ranges from helpful to none at all, combined with paranoia, exclusiveness, insensitivity, and unpredictable behavior.
- In the early stages of work or school, relationship formation may appear to be functioning normally, but they always expect others to shame them and, in fact, they will set others up to shame them.
- Family members are paranoid and look for rejection and judgment in everything others do and say.
- Interpersonal relationships with others are often abusive and exploitive, with the shame-prone person either receiving the abuse or dishing it out.

Shame-prone people tend to form relationships with other shame-prone people (Bradshaw, 1988; Fossom & Mason, 1986). Such people continually defend themselves from allowing others to discover the basic flaws. They both feel bad and worthless but cannot let the other know how they feel. They often lash out with outrage at the potential for abandoning them that they see the other person as having, and yet both partners will stay in such relationships "at all costs."

This tendency to stay in relationships that are unhealthy perplexes outsiders who do not understand that a bad relationship is better than abandonment. In the consistency of shame-prone persons' belief systems they deserve the suffering and abuse that the relationship produces because they are "bad to the core." But because they cannot manage in the world alone, they must maintain the relationship to defend against abandonment. The cycle perpetuates itself all the time, affirming the mental template of "personal badness."

- Children learn to be frightened of people and consequently show them or their property little genuine respect.
- Parents rarely participate in their children's activities in the community, neighborhood, school, church, and other areas.

Grief for Personal and Family Losses

Divorce, death of significant people in our lives, significant people moving away, and the termination of a meaningful relationship are examples of losses. Severe illness, accidents, catastrophic events such as earthquake or fire—events that change how we live—represent different kinds of losses. Broken dreams, aging, "what would have beens" represent still other types of losses (Simos, 1979; Weenolsen, 1988). Losses are experienced daily in our lives, with some having more impact than others. The loss itself may not produce shame-prone identities, but if the relationship system is shame-prone, the grieving process is either avoided or excessively long (Scharff & Scharff, 1987).

Divorce, a failure of the primary dyad in a family, is a family event that affects the quality of affirmation within the family. Regardless of the reasons for divorce, spouses experience a sense of failure and loss (Mowatt, 1987). For children the loss of daily contact with one parent is coupled with the belief that they might be responsible for causing the breakup (Vivekananda & Nicholson, 1987). The sense of failure and the concern about who's responsible for the failure create feelings of shame in both parents and children. The concern about how relatives, neighbors, and others will react to the news of the divorce adds to a sense of being watched and wanting to hide. Divorce does not have to lead to the development of shame-prone identity, even though the emotion of shame may be present, but when spouses or children have already developed identities based on shame experience the divorce will be more shaming to all involved.

Death of a loved one is not usually shaming to the remaining family members unless they are already shame-prone. In functional families, individuals are more apt to feel guilt. Guilt for being alive and for not dying first is a common feeling of surviving spouses. Children sometimes feel guilty for not doing more for parents and siblings before they died, for not telling them that they love them, for not doing some specific thing they had intended to do (Kalish, 1981; Scharff & Scharff, 1987).

When one or more family members are already prone to shame, they may experience a variety of traumas, including death, as shaming. Such individuals wonder whether they are somehow responsible for the death and whether they are being punished by the death for being bad. Perhaps they believe God views them as undeserving of the presence of their loved one. When shame is present, families have difficulty fully experiencing grief. Shame-prone individuals and shaming families are emotionally closed by nature and do not express emotions freely. Crying is often seen as a weakness and exposure of personal flaws and so crying is hidden, covered up in the guise of strength. Because grieving does not take place, families are incapacitated by their decreased ability to function appropriately (Scharff & Scharff, 1987). This in turn shames individual family members even more. Yet no one in the family can express a sense of failure, inadequacy, and grief because of fears of being further shamed or abandoned.

Severe illness and disabilities among family members can also create feelings of shame, which will aggravate any existing shame-based identity in family members (Hauser, 1988). The individual with illness experiences the loss of previous abilities and health. If he or she feels that his/her personal core is already flawed, the inability to be whole physically further adds to the sense of being flawed. Other family members sometimes feel ashamed of their reactions to the illness, which vary from sadness to anger at the inconvenience and burden they feel. When personal feelings are already feared because their source is the central flawed core, the increased intensity of feelings of sadness and anger created by the illness leads to further intensified shame and the consequent increased need to hide and cover such feelings.

Addictive Systems

The term addictive system applies to individuals, relationships, families, organizations, and society. An addictive system calls forth addictive behaviors and addictive processes. It is costly in that it minimizes choices in terms of the roles individuals may take and directions they may pursue. The characteristics of an addictive system limit the information coming in and going out, so that the system tends to be more exclusive and stagnant than an open system (Schaef, 1987).

Recently addiction is being defined broadly to include addictions other than just substance abuse. Peele and Brodsky (1975) defined addiction as a person's attachment to a sensation, an object, or another person to the degree that the addict is unable to appreciate or deal with other things in his environment or in himself and becomes increasingly dependent on that experience as his only source of gratification. Schaef (1987) defined an addiction as anything that people do not want to give up, that people lie about, and that people seem to have no power over. Two categories for addiction are substances, e.g., drugs, alcohol, nicotine, caffeine, sugar, and behavioral patterns, e.g., relationships, spending, gambling, work, sex, religion, television, food, exercise, a relationship, and power. Almost any substance or pattern can become an addiction (Schaef, 1987).

Addicts are very common in society, with many of them having multiple addictions and all of them shame-prone to some degree. In our society denial is rampant, leading to suppression and compulsive behavior, the ideal setting for addiction. The interaction is circular, with people trained in addictive family systems moving into societal systems practicing shaming and guilting processes learned in the home (Nathanson, 1987c). Then they take the shame accumulated from interactions outside of the home back into the home. Some symptoms of addiction in individuals, families, and society are:

- They are unaware of internal processes, thoughts, and feelings.
- They act out of distortion and denial.
- Sensory input is distorted when received and processed incorrectly.
- Relationships are dysfunctional because they manipulate others and do not know how to be intimate.
- They tend to be dependent and look for others to fix them or society.
- They are shamed by what they look like, by what they hear people saying to them, by their own behavior, and by their apparent lack of self-worth.
- Excessive guilt may accompany feelings of powerlessness.
- They live from one crisis to another.
- They are self-centered.
- They are dishonest.

Carnes (1989) has indicated that every addictive system is a shame-based system. Two basic core beliefs developed in the family of origin dramatize the shame: "I am a bad, unworthy person!" and "No one would love me as I am!" However, everyone who is shame-prone is not an addict. According to Carnes, a third core belief makes the difference. This belief develops out of how the family handles dependency issues. When these issues are not resolved, children conclude that no one is going to help them survive. Out of a survival mentality, they develop the belief, "My needs are never going to be met if I have to depend on others!" The addiction develops out of a need for a nurturing source that they can depend on to soothe and medicate the pain, the isolation, and the hopelessness.

This need is supported by the fourth core belief. The addict believes that "my addiction is my most important need." Based on the beliefs and resultant addictive behaviors, sex, alcohol, a relationship, or any other addiction becomes more important than family, friends, work and values (Carnes, 1989).

The fifth core belief that develops from the obsessive behavior and the accompanying shame is "I am bad because the addiction is my most important need!" Every person in addictive and codependency systems experiences shame because of low self-worth. Because the compulsive behavior does not match their basic values, they also experience excessive guilt, which leads to more shame (Carnes, 1989).

Codependency Systems

Another process that accompanies addiction and affects the individual, family, and society is codependency. This is a terrifying, confusing condition that is shaming to those who seem to fit the diagnostic patterns. Beattie (1989) wrote of it as a condition when people are tormented by other people's behaviors. Codependents seem to be responsible for the whole world in an attempt to medicate their pain with control of others. Codependency is part of every addictive system, as well as other dysfunctional family systems. Wegscheider-Cruse and Cruse (1989) define codependency as "a reversible brain disorder that results from a selection of distorted and disabling relationships with substances, persons, institutions, and rigid beliefs" (p. 5). Codependency exists in the brain as a toxic agent of obsession with a belief or a concept (Wegscheider-Cruse, 1989). People become dependent by enmeshment with the toxic agent. If not treated, codependency can result in medical problems, decreased self-worth, and relationship and societal problems. Codependents are often adult children of dysfunctional families who continue the caretaking learned in their family of origin. Children who come from families who did not manifest addictions but who had severe trauma may also be codependent (Whitfield, 1987). Some characteristics of codependent people are:

- They feel shamed by distorted beliefs about their appearance and self-worth.
- They are martyrs and victims. They suffer a great deal.
- They find worth only in serving others. They become chronic caretakers, often developing into workaholics. They feel guilty about not doing enough for others or for having something others do not.

- They are servers and volunteers—to the point of exhaustion.
- They may exhibit compulsive behaviors much like other addicts—e.g., overeating, bulimia, anorexia, workaholism, nicotine and caffeine addiction.
- They appear to be gullible. They want to believe what they are told so that they can go on doing what they are doing.

There are three groups of symptoms for codependency: (1) delusion, preceded by denial and followed by dissociation from reality; (2) repression, preceded by suppression and followed by dissociation from feelings; and (3) compulsion preceded by obsession and followed by behavioral dissociation. Presenting problems of codependent people often include: (1) low self-worth preceded by guilt and followed by shame; (2) problematic relationships, preceded by assumptions that the relationship is necessary for survival and followed by social, occupational, legal, and financial problems; (3) organ dysfunction preceded by organ stress and followed by organ damage (Wegscheider-Cruse & Cruse, 1989).

Addictive systems could not continue without the aid of codependency. Codependency is as difficult to treat, if not more so, than addiction. The presence of addiction and codependency in families is always accompanied by shame-prone identities in one or more family members. Unhealthy shame and guilt interlace both systems and must be treated for people to become healthy. People trapped within the system may experience depression, isolation, mental and physical breakdowns, and suicide.

Adult Children of Dysfunctional Families

As adults, children of dysfunctional families carry the emotional scars and abscesses of pain acquired from their families of origin into other relationships (Whitfield, 1987). If parents did not meet their children's dependency, intimacy and accountability needs, or failed to meet them in some critical situation, children developed beliefs that shaped their lives as adults. Many of them are shame-prone. Living out their expectations to eventually have those needs met in ongoing relationships leads to constant disappointment for these children as adults. Woititz (1985) lists 13 symptoms that adult children of alcoholics exhibit. They also apply to other troubled families. People may not have all of these symptoms but the ones they have affect them in many ways. These symptoms may also be masked by talents, intelligence, and competent, appropriate behavior in certain situations. The common theme for all of these children is that they have been robbed of their childhood. Adults from these systems:

- guess what normal behavior is;
- have difficulty following a project from beginning to end;

- lie when it would be just as easy to tell the truth;
- judge themselves without mercy;
- have difficulty having fun;
- take themselves very seriously;
- have difficulty with intimate relationships;
- overreact to changes over which they have no control;
- constantly seek approval and affirmation;
- feel that they are different from other people;
- are super-responsible or super-irresponsible;
- are extremely loyal, even in the face of evidence that the loyalty is undeserved;
- tend to lock themselves into a course of action without giving consideration to consequences (Woititz, 1985, pp. 84–98).

Affairs

Not all of those who have affairs are shame-prone, but people who are shame-prone have affairs in an attempt to prove that they are worthwhile and lovable. However, because of a core belief that they are bad and unlovable, they go from one person to another looking for verification. If they get it, they doubt and deny it. In a relationship the partner having affairs may be very dependent on the partner, feel love and loyalty for him, and be very confused and shamed by her own behavior. Because the need for nurturing may be insatiable, a person may have several affairs going at the same time.

In order to be loyal to their partners or to their own or their parents' standards and values and yet have needs met, some people have emotional affairs. They spend excessive time with another person, share intimate thoughts and feelings, and may even snuggle and fondle each other to climax, but they draw the line and do not have sexual intercourse. Feelings of guilt and shame often accompany these activities. Those feelings confirm the "bad me" core belief. Often these people show remorse and experience confusion, with little understanding as to why they do what they do.

People who are not married or committed to a significant relationship may go from one lover to another, never understanding why they do not last. Regardless of the situation, some common themes exists:

- There is a never ending quest to make up for what they did not get as children.
- The more guilty they feel about the affair, the more they will project the guilt onto their partners.
- The affairs may be used to punish and humiliate their partners and/or themselves.

CHAPTER 6

Family Systems Shaming on Issues of Intimacy or Dependency

THE FAMILY ENVIRONMENTS described in this chapter are moderately dysfunctional and may include individuals who are shamed on specific issues, e.g., intimacy or dependency, but not both. In families with intimacy issues, members tend to have unmet intimacy needs accompanied by the interpersonal perception of not being enough. The lack of intimacy affects how individuals get their other needs met—productivity, sense and order, uniqueness, and choices. However, since dependency needs are met, they can count on positive affirmation with accountability. When intimacy needs are met but dependency needs are not, family members may feel worthless. Individual family members from these two types usually fall somewhere in the middle of the identity continuum presented in Table 1.1. Their identities are not as negatively affirmed as people in totally shame-prone families discussed in Chapter 5.

FAMILY IDENTITIES IN SYSTEMS WITH INTIMACY ISSUES AND IN SYSTEMS WITH DEPENDENCY ISSUES

Families described in this chapter have moderate to occasionally extreme shame-prone identities. In terms of family identity, these families either look good and feel bad or look bad and feel good.

Looking Good, Feeling Bad

Both of types of families—those with intimacy issues and those with dependency issues—often appear functional, happy, and productive to outsiders. However, most family members feel bad, consciously and/or unconsciously, about the family, even when its public image is good. While the family identity is poor, family members hold their heads up high in pretense. There is enough strength in individual family members and enough healthy guilt to develop a family image that is deceptive to outsiders. The family and its members pay quite a price to look good. Society's emphasis on looking good at any cost increases both shame and guilt processes when members experience the incongruity between how they feel and what they present to the outside world (Elkin, 1984).

These families look good.

- Families with dependency issues appear to progress with common goals and purposes, but if one looks closely the goals and purposes that are public are rarely completed. Families with intimacy issues tend to be more congruent with goals, but there is plenty of slippage. Justifications and excuses are rational and readily available.
- These families seem to deal well with crises, stress, and outside demands. In actuality, because so much attention and energy are focused on looking good, some of the crises are handled well, but the internal stress is shrouded in secrecy and takes its toll on the family members.
- These families appear to be unique entities with family members bonded, happy, and supportive of one another, but in truth there are many unresolved problems.
- Family members appear to have talents and capabilities to share with others outside the family, but they talk a better game than they perform.
- Family members appear to freely interact with others, but the communication is often superficial and social, rather than interpersonally meaningful.

Nevertheless, they feel bad.

- They experience little sense of pride in the family and in family members with little genuine trust, loyalty, and respect.
- Because of family closeness on values and work ethics, members in families with intimacy issues may perceive themselves as a loving, close family and project that to outsiders, but closeness is elusive, confusing, and sometimes inappropriate.
- Members from families with dependency issues may experience combinations of emotional, physical, and intellectual intimacy, e.g., the parents may be sexual with each other, appropriately physically loving with the children, and yet not feel valued and useful to the family.
- Members may experience the family as unique and separate from

other families based on how bad they are. In spite of the public image, they harbor a belief that "others are good, we are bad."

- Members may experience feelings of unworthiness, not deserving and not receiving abundance. They operate from survival beliefs and what looks good; therefore, they accumulate as much as they can in money, favors, etc.
- Family members experience being rigidly in control yet being acted upon in their environment (victims). They feel that they never get their rightful share of anything.
- Family members experience stress and deception as they pretend to be able to adapt to changes and losses.
- Members are too dependent on family information, while at the same time distrusting information from outside the family. Communication is stressful, with implied expectations for performance outside the family, and negotiation rarely occurs.
- There is a lack of feelings of security and safety. Undefined fear is common in the family. The family and some family members are perceived as not being accountable and dependable.
- Members of families with dependency issues experience confusion and anger about family values and standards. There is much questioning and experimentation regarding rules. The family is governed by vague and incongruent values and standards carried out in manipulative and secretive ways.

Looking Bad, Feeling Good

Families that look bad may feel good for one of two reasons. They place less emphasis on how things should look according to outsiders, or they are blocked from the pain in the family system and within themselves. These families tend to be enmeshed. The family identity and public image are unclear, erratic, and not universally shared by family members; this image seems unimportant to family members.

These families look bad.

- They appear to outsiders to have very few common goals and purposes. These families seem to be chaotic or disengaged and indifferent to either goals or purposes.
- These families seem to be continually dealing with crises, stress, and outside demands in a haphazard, ineffective way (Boss, 1988).
- Family members appear to be bonded, happy and supportive of one another in crazy, unpredictable ways.
- These families appear to need all their talents and capabilities to cope with what goes on inside the family. Members volunteer to do things for others but rarely follow through.
- Family members guardedly interact with others.

Family members feel good because they feel safe, even though they also feel crazy at times.

- They experience irrational pride in the family and in family members through processes of codependency.
- Members perceive themselves as a loving, close family because they need each other.
- They experience unity as a family, unique and separate from others. They are unaware, for the most part, that enmeshment and need keeps them separate.
- Feelings of worthiness are based on serving others in the family.
- They feel in control as a family because they are unified in codependency.
- Denial rather than adaptation is used to cope with changes and losses.
- There is a sameness to family information, while the family remains closed to outside information. Communication and negotiation happen sometimes, depending upon the context.
- Members experience feelings of safety but not security. The family and most family members are perceived as in need of help.
- Families with dependency issues experience family values and standards as vague and useless, without much thought. Questioning and experimentation regarding rules governed by these values and standards are vague, almost as if the values and standards are totally unrelated to the behavior.

The conditions in these families influence the direction of affirmation, negative or positive, for identity formation.

DYSFUNCTIONAL FAMILY FUNCTIONING

Families that foster shame on intimacy or dependency issues have many of the same general characteristics as those listed in Chapter 5 for shame-prone families, with some modifications.

- There is moderate to high dysfunction.
- Coping strategies and conflict resolution skills are inadequate, especially in contexts where intimacy or dependency issues prevail (Lavee, McCubbin, & Olson, 1987).
- Some family members have unhealthy personalities.
- Intimacy, dependency, accountability needs are seldom all met, with many negative affirmations dominant. Intimacy needs may be met and not dependency needs, or dependency needs met and not intimacy needs.

- The quality of the marital/parental relationship, parent-child relationships, sibling relationships, and extended family relationships influence negative affirmation of identities as members experience shame and guilt.
- Such family systems are any of the following: rigidly disengaged, separated, connected, or enmeshed; structurally disengaged or enmeshed; flexibly disengaged or separated; chaotically disengaged, separated, connected, or enmeshed (Olson, Sprenkle, & Russell, 1979). The use of space, time, and energy is such that family members are always distancing from each other or enmeshed, living in hope that is never fulfilled (Constantine, 1986).

The total family affect is much the same as that for families that feel bad and look bad, who have neither dependency or intimacy needs met, with some moderation. The meanings that family members derive from the family interaction are:

- The world is often hopeless.
- Changes do not matter if one is basically flawed ("bad" people can't initiate "good" change).
- The world and especially people in it can be viewed in terms of black and white, right and wrong, good and bad (Beck, 1988).
- Others are necessary to one's existence but cannot be depended upon (Carnes, 1989).

THE CRIPPLED AFFIRMATION TRIANGLE

When parents are accountable, they provide a strong positive base for the affirmation triangle, with intimacy and dependency as the two strong supportive sides. This powerful triangle influences the development of wholeness in family members, as well as in the system as a whole and its subsystems. When either intimacy or dependency needs are not met, it is logical that accountability is not always consistent. Therefore, the base of the triangle is weak. Pulling out one of the sides, intimacy or dependency, also weakens the triangle.

When parents are accountable and meet the dependency needs of their children but have problems with intimacy, the "wholeness" that develops for individuals operates only in certain contexts. Being accountable and teaching children values and standards are forms of intimacy for parents and children. However, this is "pseudo intimacy," a substitute for the real thing. In this case the affirmation triangle works only in situations involving dependency.

When the deficit is in dependency, the reverse is true. Parents are accountable to and for their children in situations calling for appropriate intimacy. However, they do not allow their children to be dependent in essential ways, i.e., values, standards, physical means.

FAMILY CONDITIONS LEADING TO THE FORMATION OF IDENTITIES SHAMED ON INTIMACY OR DEPENDENCY

Families with intimacy difficulties meet dependency needs of individual family members but are threatened by intimacy needs. For example, all members in the Harris family feel comfortable being depended upon for various tasks and responsibilities. Individual family members expect to pitch in at times to help other family members. The physical demands of the children for food, clothing, and shelter are met, and family members do not resent emotional dependence. The parents clearly own their own values and standards, and they expect the children to follow these standards until they develop a set of internalized personal ethics. It is quite easy for the parents to teach their young children values because the parents accept their children's dependency on them. As children grow older, they are allowed to become increasingly independent. Every family member has a sense of being able to depend on other family members to come through. However, family members seem to be afraid of physical contact. There is no kissing, hugging, or touching. The parents seem quite uncomfortable with any display of public affection. Family members also have difficulty sharing personal information, especially feelings. Talk is topic related rather than personal. Although the family environment meets dependency needs, it lacks a sense of closeness.

Other families meet intimacy needs appropriately but are threatened by dependency needs of individual family members. In the Gilligan family, individual family members are able both to receive and to initiate touching without feeling uncomfortable. Personal information, including feelings, is shared openly. However, the needs to provide physical care, e.g., food, clothing, and shelter, and to establish and monitor rules and values seem like intrusions into the lives of parents and the rest of the family. In these families children may do most of the cooking and shopping for food even when the parents have time to do it. No one is sure who will do things or when. Parents sometimes make rules but no provisions are made for their enforcement.

Family members fear having anyone else too dependent on them. Because parents do not feel comfortable with their children's dependency on them, they are reluctant to provide clear standards and values. They are especially reticent about owning any standards as their own and imposing these on the children, regardless of age. Permissive, haphazard parenting is the rule. Consequently, children in these families are confused about values and standards of behavior and have difficulty establishing any set of internal standards as they grow older. To outsiders they appear irresponsible but close.

> • *Family environments that fail to meet the dependency needs of individual members produce individuals who are shamed by contexts or issues that involve dependency* (Kurtz, 1981).

Individuals shamed on dependency tend to withdraw or to be totally dependent; they may flip back and forth. Sharon was shamed on dependency issues in her family of origin. She did not feel shamed all the time, but any situations that involved dependency seemed to "kick in" her proneness to shame. Her response was to withdraw. She typically believed that she should be totally independent and not have to depend on anyone for anything. Consequently, she preferred to be alone. When she was lonely, she wanted to be with people but was mistrustful of them because she did not trust them to be there when they said they would be. It seemed less risky to be alone. That way people made no demands on her to be dependent on them in some way, nor did they allow her to be dependent on them. She did not have to deal directly with her own fear of being abandoned when others did not come through for her.

In contrast, Jack was also shamed on dependency issues, but he wanted to be totally dependent on someone. He typically wanted to just be as little as possible and have someone—anyone—take total care of him. He wanted others to make all of his decisions and face all emotional struggles with him; if they would, he would never be lonely again. He acted on his feelings of wanting to be cared for only when someone initiated a relationship with him.

A woman at work had recently shown some interest in him. He immediately wanted to be with her all the time, and he made many emotional demands on her to take care of him. Overwhelmed and scared, she quickly distanced herself from him. He was confused and hurt, but failed to understand why no one thought him valuable enough to care for him totally.

Both Sharon and Jack appeared to others to "have their act together" except in situations that "hooked" their dependency issues. The way they exhibited their fear of dependency differed; Sharon was withdrawn and isolated from people, while Jack sought relationships in which he could be totally dependent and little. But both of them felt "bad" whenever situations required them to let others be dependent on them or when they seemed to want so desperately to be dependent on someone else. The paradox of being shamed on dependency is that the dependency one wants so badly is the very thing that is most threatening and shaming (Bradshaw, 1988). This type of shame falls under Kaufman's (1989) categories of inter-personal need-shame scenes and purpose-shame scenes and is related to relationship and competence shame in his profile of stages of psychological magnification of shame.

- *Individuals who are shamed on dependency often have patterns of substance (drug, alcohol, food, nicotine, caffeine) and/or behavioral (relationships, sex, gambling, spending, work) addiction in their lives (Carnes, 1989).*

Substance and behavioral addictions serve as medicators to dull the pain and fear (Elkin, 1984). Workaholics, for example, use work performance to try to make themselves worthwhile in their own and others' eyes. The irony is that the dependency needs individuals attempt to meet through relation-ships with work, food, or drugs are never satisfied. The involvement with these things further amplifies the shame, "the inner flaw," that these indi-viduals try so hard to escape.

- *The primary emotions that people shamed on dependency exhibit with others are fear and rage.*

People with dependency issues are afraid of many things, especially social situations. They constantly fear that people will dislike them, and their overwhelming desire to be "taken care of" or their withdrawal often sets up situations in which their fears are confirmed. Then the rage that is exhibited seems out of context or too much for the situation.

Suzanne, an adult woman, was terrified that others would discover her totally dependent relationship with a Raggedy Ann doll that she had re-ceived from her grandmother years before. To her knowledge, no one knew how dependent she felt upon the doll. When alone, she often cuddled her doll close to her, stroking its red, tangled hair. She was terrified of letting anyone know about her doll; in fact, it took months of therapy before she trusted her therapist enough to even mention her doll. She thought being so compulsively involved with a doll must be crazy; nevertheless, the doll helped soothe her ragged dependency needs.

Suzanne arrived for a therapy session very disturbed because she had turned on her doll late one night. She became enraged that the doll was inanimate, angry at herself for being so dependent on a doll, and rageful that the doll could not truly meet her dependency needs. Yet she was terrified that she needed and wanted that doll so much. If it had been possible, she would have been totally dependent on the doll and let it care for all her needs. As it was she was terrified by her rage and confused by the intensity of the feelings that the dependency relationship with Raggedy Ann generated.

The relationship dysfunction exhibited by people shamed on dependency involves three dimensions:

- They are intensely "in" or intensely "out of" relationships.
- They are attracted to others whose dependency needs are not met or who are compulsively codependent (Scharff & Scharff, 1987).
- They go from one person to the next attempting to get relationship needs met.

They want either to be totally taken care of or totally without need to depend on people. These desires become manifest behaviorally by expectations and demands that others will make all their decisions, fix all their confused emotions, and be available to dump on at all times. In some cases the other extreme may be true. Because they sense that no one can really be counted on to fulfill their needs, they disengage from others and become withdrawn and cynical. They tell others they don't care about relationships and social support. They deny that they need to be dependent on anybody for anything.

In relationships where both partners have dependency needs, the manipulation becomes crazy as both desperately seek to get needs met (Scharff & Scharff, 1987). At the same time they are afraid of potential intimacy because of the seemingly "black holish" nature of their drives.

When a partner backs off because of the overwhelming implicit and sometimes explicit demands to be totally taken care of, the dependency-shamed person is confused. The drive to meet dependency needs escalates, and the next person who demonstrates any interest in forming a relationship will be the recipient of the manipulative maneuvers for total care. Because the need is insatiable, it is likely that the new relationship will fail, and the chase will be on again.

- *Family environments that fail to meet intimacy needs of individual members produce individuals who are shamed by contexts or issues that involve intimacy.*
- *Sexual and relationship addictions are common among people who have been shamed on intimacy* (Carnes, 1989).

Lisa sought therapy because of her erratic pattern of relationships over the last year. She was married, had two young children, and her husband worked eight to five as an electrician. She left the house two nights a week to spend time with friends, while her husband took care of the children. In a therapy session she divulged that during those evenings she usually visited singles bars, picked up anyone who seemed interested in her, and ended the evening with a sexual encounter. This pattern had been going on for almost 11 months. She had not been sexually involved with the same person more than once, and she felt more and more driven to increase the frequency of her nights out. In fact, if she had her way and could hide it from her husband, she wanted to cruise singles bars every night. To Lisa's knowledge, her husband was unaware of her activity. He thought she was spending the time with friends. As we talked about her family of origin, it quickly became apparent that Lisa was shamed on intimacy. Although her family had been able to create an environment that met Lisa's dependency needs, her intimacy needs were not met.

- *People shamed on intimacy lack the ability to establish appropriate physical and emotional boundaries with other people. Either they have no boundaries, or their boundaries are rigidly closed* (Fossom & Mason, 1986).

One indication of a person shamed on intimacy is problems with boundaries. These people either have difficulty establishing boundaries or they close themselves off completely and let no one in. Aron was a client who let no one in. If anyone attempted to touch him, his posture became rigid and he literally froze in position. He was not comfortable receiving any type of physical affection and he never initiated touch with anyone. He kept physical distance between him and other people. In short, his boundaries were completely closed.

- *Individuals shamed on intimacy experience body and relationship shame (Kaufman, 1989) and either overcompensate or fail to care for their physical appearance.*

Everyone thought Patricia was beautiful, but she believed that her body was ugly and bad. She kept immaculate care of her hair, skin, etc., and wore very fashionable clothes, but underneath she still experienced her body as flawed and disgusting. Friends tried to convince her that she was beautiful, and at times she felt that way, but in contexts that required intimacy she failed because she was "hooked" by her body shame. In her twisted perception, her partner in any relationship saw her the same way. Consequently, the relationship was shaming to her.

- *Individuals shamed on intimacy issues are blocked to emotional experience or intensely hysterical in situations that involve intimacy issues.*

These people handle emotional experience quite well unless intimacy issues are involved; then they either become blocked to feeling or become "emotional gushers." The "gushers" seem hysterical to others, who are often overwhelmed by the intensity of the emotion that is expressed. Because others feel overwhelmed, they either withdraw or try to help. Sensing that people are expecting something of them that they cannot give, those who seem blocked to feelings are confused by the experience. They often report numbness and loss of energy.

- *Individuals shamed on intimacy issues often experience physical and psychosomatic symptoms.*

Richard and his wife came to therapy as a result of a referral from their physician. Richard had experienced episodes of intense chest pain at night. He woke up in cold sweats with the pain. As the therapist explored the dynamics of both his family of origin and his relationship with his wife, he realized that Richard and his wife were both threatened by any demands for intimacy. Richard's chest pain and accompanying panic attacks were tied into interpersonal events with his wife and children that required emotional closeness. Psychosomatic complaints of this nature are fairly common when people are shamed on intimacy.

As adults, children who are shamed on intimacy but not dependency are able to be clear about rules, expectations, and standards except when issues of intimacy and closeness are involved. When intimacy issues are part of the context,

- *Individuals shamed on intimacy are usually very confused about how to get close to others.*
- *Their timing and amount of affection may be inappropriate.*
- *They may be sexually promiscuous, but they experience isolation and lack of intimacy with their partners.*
- *They may use physical touching and sexual behavior as a weapon, a way to control and handle anger toward others.*
- *Some individuals shamed on intimacy will not risk being affectionate in any relationship.*

They have difficulty sharing personal information and feelings with others and appear to be insensitive. They prefer to avoid talking about emotion and may deny much of their emotional experience. If others show any affection toward them, they become tense and upset.

- *The relationships of people shamed on intimacy issues are either enmeshed or disengaged* (Olson, Sprenkle, & Russell, 1979).

When the physical and interpersonal boundaries are closed and rigid, relationships are disengaged or nonexistent. If the interpersonal boundaries are loose and overly permeable, enmeshment of emotions, thoughts, self, and even physical interpersonal space is the result.

- *Sexual dysfunctions are common in relationships where one or more of the individuals are shamed on intimacy* (Carnes, 1989).
- *Serial relationships are common.*

People shamed on intimacy are similar to those shamed on dependency in that they both go from one relationship to another trying to get their needs met. They hold onto the hope that a different person might be able to meet their insatiable intimacy or dependency needs. In therapy such individuals may report a string of brief, unsatisfying sexual encounters. They tend to be either affectionate and close too fast or never affectionate or close.

- *Individuals shamed on intimacy often tend to be compulsively task oriented and authority guided* (Carnes, 1989).

Because of the emphasis on dependency needs and inadequate intimacy skills many of these individuals tend to be too serious and task oriented. They may be quite compulsive and appear to others to be blind conformists to authority and the rules of a system regarding the accomplishment of tasks. They are often frightened of their own emotions and prefer to avoid what they might be feeling. They are good at setting up standards and expectations in contexts that are task oriented, but they have trouble in interpersonal work relationships.

SHAMING DYNAMICS IN
FAMILIES WITH
INTIMACY OR DEPENDENCY ISSUES

Marital Relationships

Because they meet either dependency or intimacy needs of their children, the marriages in these two family types provide some stability, but they also develop unhealthy shaming and guilting processes. The marriage is stable in terms of providing children a base to count on, but the rules of the marital relationship do not provide all that is needed for family members to develop healthy identities.

In marital dyads in families that are shaming on intimacy issues:

- One or both spouses are confused about, in conflict with, or incapable of consistently meeting the other's intimacy needs.
- They do not share feelings or disclose much personal information. Communication may be low in quantity and in quality as well.

- Spouses fail to adequately nurture each other and other family members.
- Each spouse exhibits some unhealthy personality characteristics.
- Spouses are frightened by growth, development, and change, especially in their spouses.
- Spouses are confused about boundaries or lack of boundaries and often sabotage individual freedom and privacy as a couple and from the children.
- Spouses mistrust each other in some areas, i.e., intimacy is conditional and contextual.

The marital dyad has a responsibility and task orientation, but spouses remain emotionally distant and afraid of sexual and affectional issues. If both partners are comfortable with the low level of intimacy, they may have fairly good marital adjustment (Harper & Elliott, 1988). In such cases, spouses collude with each other not to threaten the system by increasing the levels of intimacy (Slipp, 1984).

As a couple, the dyad is able to be productive and reach goals. Financial and temporal affairs are well managed and handled and parents feel a responsibility to socialize and teach the children. The couple is usually in agreement about how to discipline and set rules for their children and thus presents a united front.

In marital dyads in families that are shaming on dependency issues:

- One or both spouses are confused about, in conflict with, or incapable of consistently meeting the other's dependency needs.
- Rather than being accountable they tend to be codependent.
- Each spouse is sometimes incapable of independent thinking and acting.
- Spouses badger each other about mistakes.
- Spouses can be close and affectionate in interpersonal relationships, but they are not always responsible.
- Spouses demonstrate love based on their terms and needs; they bargain and manipulate in an attempt to get their needs met; they rarely are honest, accessible, and accountable.
- Spouses rarely negotiate personal projects, disagreements, differences in desires and values, conflict, intimacy needs, and other parameters of the coupleship. (Spouses in both family types sometimes sabotage each other in these areas.)
- Pain, momentary doubts, misunderstandings, and feelings serve to confuse attempts to negotiate, listen, and adjust to the other's needs.

The following illustrates marital dynamics in families with dependency issues. A husband who is loving and affectionate, who shares many personal experiences and feelings, may fail to see the need to work or be financially responsible. The dynamics of such a marriage become one in which "being responsible for" people is emphasized over "being responsible to" people. When individuals raised in such systems become parents, they often repeat the same pattern of behaviors by providing intimacy/affirmation needs but not dependency/accountability needs. The couple is very loving and close, with the sexual component of their relationship very active and important.

The parents model intimacy and also practice it appropriately with their children. The values and standards related to intimacy that they practice and teach to their children provide a contextually strong accountability base. However, children get confused messages about dependency. Meal preparation and times may be erratic and shopping forgotten. Work habits and money supplies provide a basis for arguments and instability. Children rarely know when they will get clothes they need or if money is available for school lunches.

Parent-Child Relationships

In families with intimacy issues, parents communicate at implicit and explicit levels that fulfilling children's needs for intimacy is threatening. The family provides for dependency needs, but the intimacy dimension and the accountability that goes with it are missing in one or both parent. The following conditions are common to these families:

- Parents may love each other and their children, but they demonstrate the love inconsistently, with mixed messages and abuse.
- Boundaries are either so rigid that no closeness, physical touching, or affection is allowed, or so blurred that affection and touching are experienced as smothering and engulfing.
- Parents tend to lavish things (clothes, money, privileges) and experiences (swimming lessons, educational vacations, educational toys) on their children in place of affection.
- Hierarchical boundaries between parents and children are present, but often experienced as punishing for the children and protection for the parents.
- Parents have difficulty teaching children how to set sexual limits and boundaries because they attempt to teach them values and standards with no information regarding the feeling and sensual aspects.
- Parent-child relationships will appear respectful, but children tend to nag and hassle their parents, knowing something is missing and having no permission or role model to explore and identify it.

- Children learn to mistrust their parents because they are unpredictably demanding, lacking in understanding, and confusing in providing so much materially and so little personally.
- Religious practices substitute for spirituality, but religious discussions are seen as a valuable learning tool.
- Parents may have conflicting values and standards, with implicit and explicit expectations that children will appease both parents.
- Parents sometimes negate what they say they value or the standards they set because their fear of intimacy causes their behavior to be unpredictable.
- Parents' values, standards, and expectations are clearly identified and owned.
- Usually the rules are fairly consistently enforced by one or both parents and other adults who are a significant part of the extended family system.
- Emotions are neither clearly identified nor owned; nor are parents clear about their own emotions or boundaries regarding closeness with others.
- Children's right to be separate, unique individuals is not affirmed by the parents. Children learn to be emotional extensions of parents, either scared of initiating or receiving affection or inappropriately affectionate.
- Children do not believe that they are loved and valued; they do not experience their world as a loving place or emotional closeness with others in their family.
- Children learn that there is order in the world and that you can depend on authority to establish order.
- When parentification occurs it does so only within an intimacy/closeness context.
- Parents are able to establish discipline, but they can send confusing messages to children about who is in charge emotionally.
- Some parents want their children to take care of their intimacy needs, including their sexual desires.
- Children learn that they are responsible to one or both parents to be sexual; thus, as adults these children have difficulty being close to people without being sexual as well.

In families with dependency issues, parents communicate to children that their dependency needs are an imposition. Accountability and dependency are missing in one or both parents. The following conditions are common to these families:

- Parents lavish children with affection and disclose feelings and

other personal information. Normal hierarchical boundaries between parents and children are missing.

- Parents have difficulty setting limits for their children and teaching them values and standards. Discipline is mostly inconsistent and often alternates between being overly harsh and physical for what the situation requires and appearing totally apathetic about any behavior of children.
- Parent-child relationships will appear cohesive and affectionate, but the parents will also appear irresponsible to others and to older children in the family.
- Spouses are rarely united in parenting their children and tend to abdicate or contend about disciplinary actions.
- Children learn to mistrust their parents because they are unpredictable, undependable, and needy.
- Power in relationships is confusing, and parent-child exchanges are often rigid one-up/one-down exchanges. Or parents act totally powerless by assuming no responsibility to or for anyone in the family, including each other. The distinction between "being responsible to" and "being responsible for" people becomes important. Being responsible to someone means that the other person holds you accountable for your behavior by clearly letting you know what his or her personal expectations are for you. That same person is responsible for you, in that he or she allows you to be dependent on his/her expectations and values until you develop and internalize a set of your own. Family systems with dependency issues are often enmeshed on the dimension of cohesion but chaotic on the dimension of adaptability (Olson, Sprenkle, & Russell, 1979).
- Parents are unsure of or are in conflict with each other about their own standards and values.
- Parents may feel overwhelmed by their responsibility for a child and may act as if they either have no values or are unwilling to impose their values on their children.
- Parents are often loving and affectionate in attempts to get their own needs met.
- Parents fail to socialize the child into a set of structured values and beliefs about how to behave in a variety of contexts, especially in interpersonal relationships.
- Parents are uncomfortable and inconsistent with their stated values and standards and those of society; therefore, their children learn few acceptable values and standards of behavior from them.
- Modifications of rules occur emotionally, rarely, and haphazardly because children receive little direction for assuming more responsibility for their own behavior.

- Children have no role model for being an accountable adult because parents do not declare values and standards for being an adult as well as a parent.
- Children do not learn that they are responsible for how they behave to someone they value.
- Parents do not accommodate and adjust to their children's development stages and day-to-day problems.
- Children are at high risk for parentification, with expectations by parents to meet parents' and siblings' needs.
- Parents often feel very conflicted about having children and are usually overwhelmed by both their roles as parents and the social demands that society places on them.

Sibling Relationships

Sibling relationships in families with intimacy issues are usually distant. They are characterized by respect and courtesy, but self-disclosure and emotional expressiveness are not characteristic of these families or of their sibling relationships. In families that tend to have no clear boundaries, brother-sister incest is common. Siblings in other families deal with intimacy by avoiding it in every relationship.

Sibling relationships in families with dependency issues may reflect either the dynamics of the marital and parent-child subsystem or an exaggerated sibling dependency in reaction to the lack of dependency in the other subsystems. When siblings seek to have dependency needs met by each other rather than by the parents, it will appear to skilled clinicians that the children are really fulfilling aspects of parenting roles with each other. Beneath all the behavior is the pain of a lost childhood. At times children will even set limits for their own parents, reversing the appropriate hierarchy (Haley, 1987).

The relationships between siblings in such families involve conflict over lack of responsible behavior. Brothers and sisters fight because one has used another's belongings or invaded another's privacy. At other times two siblings may collude to behave inappropriately by an outsider's standards. Yet the parents either do not recognize the inappropriateness of the behavior or, if they do, appear powerless to do anything to correct it. Siblings generally learn that they cannot count on each other to be responsible. As numbers in the family increase, the system becomes more conflictual and chaotic. When children have to deal with another sibling or siblings in such a family, the need for sense and order is heightened and the lack of thereof emphasized. The increased complexity combines with the lack of accountability and dependency to increase the potential for dysfunctional family relationships at all levels.

Extended Family Relationships

Shame-proneness on intimacy is transmitted through generations. When grandparents are emotionally distant or overly enmeshed, their children and grandchildren tend to respond to the same underlying fears about intimacy. Whole generations of family members avoid sharing close personal information or physical affection because the implicit rules of the system do not allow it.

Extended family relationships have the potential to moderate the effects of a nuclear family environment that fails to meet dependency needs. For example, grandparents or other extended family members may step in to provide dependable conditions for the children.

However, in the majority of families with dependency issues, the extended system also fails to provide dependency needs. These extended systems are often very chaotic, with all members being affectionate and feeling close to each other, but each individual going his or her own way. Family members learn not to count on each other but to reach outside the family to get dependency needs met.

Friends, Neighbors, Work, and Community Relationships

To outsiders a family with intimacy issues will appear highly responsible and task oriented. The public family image will be one getting things done, being firm with children, requiring family members to meet fairly high levels of performance in school and work settings, but being fairly stoic and distant. The family will look good to outsiders, but in certain contexts the emotional issues associated with either disengagement or enmeshment will create feelings of being bad for each family member. -

Circumstances, particularly relationships outside the family, often determine the outcome of people raised in dependency-shaming systems. Members of these systems are easily exploited by anyone who appears to have promise of meeting dependency needs. The family often appears irresponsible to neighbors and school personnel because parents fail to assume responsibility for teaching and setting limits for their children.

These families look moderately healthy under public scrutiny, but they feel bad when dependency issues and contexts are involved. Families have difficulty mastering tasks of developmental stages because the system is threatened by family members' requirements for dependency.

FAMILY MODEL FOR SHAME

The assumptions in this chapter and in Chapters 4 and 5 are that families must be accountable in meeting dependency and intimacy needs of individual family members in order for those individuals to develop healthy identities. Based on those assumptions, a model of how family environments negatively and positively affirm individual identities is shown in Figure 6.1. This model illustrates the four kinds of family environments we have described. The right upper quadrant represents healthy families, whose members have healthy identities with healthy guilt but no proneness to shame (they do experience transitory shame). The lower right quadrant represents moderately unhealthy family environments that tend to produce individuals shamed on intimacy issues. The upper left quadrant represents moderately unhealthy family environments that tend to produce individuals with "dependency shame." The lower left quadrant represents severely dysfunctional families, which produce individuals who are shamed on both dependency and intimacy.

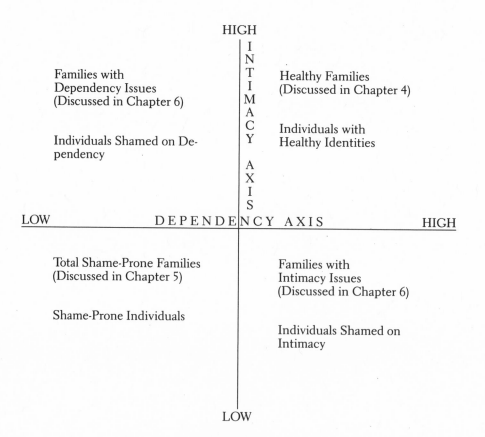

FIGURE 6.1
A Family Developmental Model of Healthy and
Shame-Prone Identities

Accountability is not represented by an axis in the model because it is related primarily to the development of guilt. When accountability is present in the healthy family environment, individuals experience healthy guilt. If, however, accountability dynamics are too harshly enforced or standards too high, individuals will feel excessively guilty and worry too much about mistakes they make. In the other three family environments, families with dependency issues, families with intimacy issues, and shame-prone families, accountability is present in varying degrees. Again, if the accountability dimension is enforced harshly or standards are excessive, guilt will be excessive and will be used to further shame the self. If accountability is not present, individuals will lack conscience development and enter into later relationships doing as they please without regard to how their behavior affects others. For example, a person with an antisocial personality disorder is a shame-prone individual whose early family environment lacked the accountability dimension; consequently, moral conscience is lacking.

SECTION III
Assessment of Shame

CHAPTER 7
Characteristic Response Patterns of Four Systemic Positions

THE SYMPTOMS AND SPECIFIC patterns that shame-based individuals exhibit are related to their systemic position (Bigner, 1971). Knowing this information allows for more effective parenting and therapy interventions.

The assumption underlying the concept of systemic position is that individual family members adopt specific roles in their family systems, roles that have characteristic behavioral, emotional, and cognitive patterns associated with them (Anderson, 1987; Churchill, 1977; Dastrup, 1986; Hanna, 1982; Hardman, Hoopes, & Harper, 1987; Hoopes & Harper, 1987). Specific characteristics of each systemic position are often related to the order in which children are born into the family system (Toman, 1988, 1976); however, in some families systemic position and sibling position may not be the same. For this reason the term "systemic position" is more accurate than the terms "sibling position" or "birth order," even though in most families the descriptions of systemic positions are related to sibling position or order of birth.

This chapter is designed to give the reader enough information to understand how people in different systemic positions respond differently to shaming dynamics. We provide in another book a much more detailed description and understanding of how the interaction between individuals and their family systems results in the creation of each systemic position (Hoopes and Harper, 1987).

Although others have conceptualized the idea of systemic position as a personality theory of birth order (cf. Nelson, 1989), in our model this is definitely not so. The distinctive patterns of interaction between personal and systemic needs are what distinguish the systemic positions, rather than personality traits.

Each child is born into a dynamic family system that is somewhat different from that experienced by the other children in the same family. The family moves through developmental stages, with each parent, as well as siblings, experiencing growth and development. Family and individual needs change; therefore, needs for intimacy and dependency may be somewhat different for each child. Because of children's unique personalities, unique responses to the family based on their systemic position, and separate experiences outside of the home with adults and peers, they will experience affirmation processes differently from other children in their family. Hoopes and Harper (1987) have identified four unique systemic positions: (1) first children join a two-person adult family system; (2) second children join a two parents-one child family system; (3) third children join a two parents-two children family system; and (4) fourth children join a two parents-three children family system. Particular response patterns for each of the four different systemic positions and what factors influence affirmation for each systemic position are addressed in the next section.

THREE PATTERNS OF RESPONSE

Beginning at birth each child responds to the dynamics of his/her particular family. Individual and family system needs interact with other factors to influence the development of a particular style or characteristic response pattern in individuals as they enter the system at birth. Some of the behaviors within the patterns are shared by all family members, but they are consistently more evident in a specific systemic position and for a different reason. The patterns represent healthy development in families. In dysfunctional families patterns may be exaggerated, rigid, or shut down. Although the patterns are holistic, they are divided into three categories so that they can be more easily described; these represent each position's (1) functional family system roles, (2) perceptual orientation, and (3) identity or a sense of well-being.

Functional Family Roles

Specific system roles are consciously and unconsciously assigned by the family and assumed by the individual. These roles describe the ways in which individuals relate to other family members and functionally fit into the entire system. Although functional in that they serve the productivity and maintenance needs and goals of the family system and its members, they should not be confused with an individual's specific abilities, personal capacities, or non-role-related activities. Roles are merely perceptual-behavioral patterns learned and manifested by an individual because of their physical and social survival value within a family.

Family-assigned roles are the earliest learned. Because an infant is totally dependent upon the family for physical and psychological survival, the family easily imposes a role on a new child.

Functional family system roles are organized into three subcategories: (1) job assignments, (2) interpersonal responsibilities, and (3) social interactions. The subcategories together form a coherent role pattern; this, in turn, is coherent with the perceptual orientation and identity and sense of well-being response patterns. (A brief summary of the patterns for family role, perceptual orientation, and sense of well-being for each systemic position is presented in Table 7.1.)

Perceptual Orientation

The perceptual orientation characteristic of each systemic position begins at birth and is heavily influenced by family interaction. Children are motivated to develop a way of perceiving because of their need to make sense and order of their world. The interaction of individual needs, assigned systemic position roles, family needs, complexities resulting from the number of persons and relationships in the system, individuals' perception of how much they are valued by the family, and experiences in and outside of the family shapes the perceptual orientation for each systemic position.

Perceptual orientation as a filtering process leads to a unique psychological awareness and adaptation to environmental situations. Characteristic patterns, discernible for each of the four positions, are organized into three subcategories: (1) focus or awareness, (2) cognitive patterns, and (3) affective patterns.

Identity and Sense of Well-Being

Children's beliefs about themselves are derived from their perceptions of how secure they feel, how they affect others, how well they do things, and whether others value them. Identity, a component of well-being, is developmental and evolutionary and interfaces with all interaction patterns, including confirming and disconfirming experiences, initially in the family and later in society. These experiences form children's *sense of well-being*. Response patterns of well-being are divided into four subcategories: (1) self-esteem, (2) threats to well-being, (3) responses to threats to well-being, and (4) needs from others.

The Affirmation Process

The affirmation process in the family for individuals in each systemic position is somewhat unique to that position. The uniqueness in family role, perceptual orientation, and sense of well-being explains how one child

TABLE 7.1

Characteristic Response Patterns for First, Second, Third, and Fourth Systemic Positions

Systemic Position Patterns		First	Second	Third	Fourth
FAMILY ROLE	Job Assignment	Produce results Central position Explicit rules/values	Monitor process Keep congruence between explicit and implicit	Monitor quality of marriage Balance in other family relationships	Maintain family harmony Monitor accomplishment of family purposes
	Interpersonal Responsibility	To a parent (usually father) for each family member For each family member's productivity	To a parent (usually mother) for affective states of every member	To help parents connect For enforcement of relationship rules	Collect others' feelings and act them out To all members of system for its unity
	Social Interaction	With individuals Performance anxiety	Close or distant Trouble with boundaries	In and out Difficult to make commitment, but loyal once committed	Impulsive, dramatic Feels blamed for disharmony

120

Focus/Awareness	Rule governed aspects of reality Details	Affect, implicit messages Process more than content	Contexts, issues, connections	Whole field, gestalt Power and responsibility in systems
Cognitive Style	Logical/analytical First focuses on parts and then synthesizes to a whole	Images, symbols Creates images to understand Implicit to explicit in parts then to whole	Connections, correlations between parts Choices are important	Conclusions, outcomes before parts May miss details Summarizes prematurely
Affective Style	Often denies feelings Feelings need to be related to outcome to be recognized	Absorbs others' affect Polarizes	May appear unfeeling and detached Share feelings when connected to a context	Impulsive, demonstrative In touch with feelings of self and others Overly dramatic in expression
Validation	External approval of products To be right Being central	Well defined boundaries To have a place Filling emotional gaps	Stable marriage Maintain relationship harmony	Unity and harmony in systems
What is Threatening	No approval Not central Too many details/expectations	Loss of place Incongruency Others' emotional overloads	Choices are restricted Interpersonal conflict Having to decide for others	Disruptive pain Whole becomes overwhelming Sense of being blamed
Response to Threat	Super rational, verbal defenses Looks stony, feels immovable	Overly rational or emotional Looks helpless, aimless	Trapped Uncaring, apathetic Disappear into introspection	Irresponsible Leave out parts of the whole
Need from Others	Approval of products Recognition	Acceptance as a person with boundaries Others own feelings	Offered choices Appreciation for relationship expertise	For others to own responsibility Cooperation in working toward purpose

PERCEPTUAL ORIENTATION   SENSE OF WELL-BEING

in a family can be negatively affirmed and consequently develop a shame-prone identity, while other siblings experience shame and negative affirmation to a lesser degree or not at all.

HEALTHY FAMILY DYNAMICS THAT SPECIFICALLY AFFIRM EACH SYSTEMIC POSITION

Table 7.2 illustrates which family dynamics are particularly positively affirming to each systemic position and how a person in each systemic position typically responds.

In the healthy family all siblings experience intimacy with their parent(s) and know that they count on them and can be dependent on them as they go through various developmental stages and crises. Children understand that they are accountable to parents; likewise, parents understand that they are accountable to children and to each other.

Children in First Systemic Position

Very early in life first children sense the high expectations that their parents and grandparents have of them, some of which are made very explicitly. Consequently, these children set high performance expectations for themselves based on overt and covert ones. To meet these expectations first children believe they need to constantly produce something, finish something, or be planning for the next project. Not meeting such expectations indicates to them that they are off target, not right. This is a shaming experience for them. In their focus on producing results, whether actual products, completion of tasks, or making lists, they may believe that what they do is never enough, but this belief is at the conscious level rather than held deeply about their worth; it is tied to products rather than the self.

Because the job assignment of a person in the first systemic position is to produce results, firsts feel validated when others in the family recognize their unique products. Parents are especially important to first children because the parents were the only other members in the family when they were born. When both parents are explicit with praise for the outcomes that a first child produces, that child will feel positively affirmed. Even when the outcomes are not particularly up to some standard, it is important for others in the family to recognize the efforts and intent of the first. People in the first systemic position are also helped by explicit messages that feelings, mistakes, and spontaneity are valued and acceptable. As shown in Table 7.1, because first children receive validation from being right and from being central, they do not like to admit mistakes or to be seen as wrong. They are relieved when parents and other family members can accept their mistakes and praise the risk they took in trying something

TABLE 7.2
Dynamics in Healthy Families that are Affirming to
Each Systemic Position

Systemic Position	Family Dynamics	Individual Behavior
First	Products overtly valued by at least one, preferably both parents Explicit messages that emotion, mistakes, and spontaneity are acceptable	Emotional expressiveness Healthy guilt Still has issues about being good enough, but these are tied to product rather than to self
Second	Intimacy (emotional and physical affection) is present both implicitly and explicitly A sense of "place" is explicit and implicit The theme of the system is "Behavior is not always acceptable but can be changed; family members as people are accepted unconditionally."	Congruence Spontaneity Healthy guilt
Third	Both parents are accountable to child for providing intimacy and dependency Both parents are clear that they have chosen and committed to a set of values Choices with regard to standards and values are made explicit (values of child can be different from those of parents as long as they are made explicit)	Can clearly identify issues in relationships Enjoys choices and can be warmly attached to others
Fourth	Family system provides intimacy and dependency needs of all family members All family members own responsibility for own standards and behavior Family is productive Family is harmonious, affectionate, and unified Parents have a sense of their own worth and set limits	Spontaneous, sensitive, and caring Can help unify people and systems Sees blame related to behavior rather than self

with the possibility of being wrong. Family members need to let firsts know that they are valuable for who they are as well as what they produce.

In healthy families, one identity issue for first children is: Am I good enough? To get the desired affirmation they think it is necessary to do more and more. When other family members can help them establish what is enough, they will link not being good enough with the product rather than themselves. When parents encourage and allow first children to be dependent and intimate, they affirm being "good enough." The children will then allow themselves the privilege of not doing everything that seems to need to be done or trying to do everything rather than sharing the load. They will recognize that pushing all the time is not healthy and that they are not bad if they are not always producing.

First children in healthy families experience guilt along with transitory shame when they are criticized or if they realize they have done something that is not in line with family rules and expectations. A positive structure as far as rules are concerned, affirmation from their parent(s), and knowledge that they can count on their parents (dependency) provide a climate for healthy guilt.

Part of the family job assignment for siblings is to assume major responsibility for some part of the system. Each child does this according to implicit messages from the family. Because the family system is a three-person system for first children, they choose to be primarily responsible for and to either mother or father. In many families, especially traditional ones, first children choose father because he is perceived by the family system as most responsible for production. When this is the case, the child will learn intimacy behaviors and unresolved intimacy issues from him. If first children choose to be responsible for and to mother they learn intimacy and intimacy issues primarily from mother. Second children choose the parent that the first child did not choose. This balances job assignments. In order for a child to experience intimacy, the assumption is that both parents are affectionate and close to the child. Behavioral expressions of feelings about the child and each other are usually explicit and clear, with boundaries that apply to intimacy making sense to the child.

First children are not afraid to be intimate when their parents praise them for their expression of feelings, for sharing personal information in the family, and for their affectionate behavior. Nevertheless, for first children intimacy issues are often tied to productivity, their primary source of affirmation.

Children in Second Systemic Position

Second children, who enter a three-person family system, need to be accepted and have a sense of place, both within the family system and with each person in the family. This affirmation occurs through the process of accountable intimacy and dependency. In healthy families parents continually reaffirm that children have a place no matter how bad they are or what they've done. They send a message that inappropriate behavior is not acceptable, but the child is. When this message is clear and repeated, the child can accept it. Intimacy with parents, both explicit and implicit, helps affirm second children's place in the family. Parents who are appropriately physically affectionate with the child, as well as self-disclosing, are very affirming.

Second children can easily become overloaded with other people's feelings because they are sensitive to all of the implicit messages in the system. Without being aware of it they can carry the emotional burdens of several family members, but specifically their mother's. Given the systemic family job assignment of being responsible for mother, they become very susceptible to mother's pain and issues. It is particularly affirming to a second child when other family members are willing to be open about their feelings and take responsibility for them. This allows the second child to separate his feelings from others and helps to provide well-defined boundaries and establish his unique place.

Second children with healthy identities are spontaneous and congruent. Because the implicit and explicit levels of their family system are congruent, their individual behaviors are congruent. There is no need to act out the discrepancies in the system.

Children in Third Systemic Position

Third children join a very complex system, two parents and two children. With family members going in many directions and both the family system and individual members having needs, the major identity issue for this systemic position is: Do I have choices? Third children have to experience choices about day-to-day behaviors and what values to follow. For the choices to be explicit parents need to be explicit and somewhat congruent about their values and standards.

Because third children receive the systemic job assignment of being responsible for the marriage, they need positive affirmation from both parents. They thrive when both parents are accountable. The parents' values can be different as long as they are explicit.

Healthy third children are adept at identifying issues in relationships. They are experts at seeing how people connect with each other. While protecting their right to have choices, they see this as something to enjoy rather than a burden to protect. When dependency and intimacy needs are met, third children will be warmly attached to others rather than constantly retreating from interaction.

Children in Fourth Systemic Position

Fourth children complete a very complex system of six people—two adults and four siblings. The family assignment given to fourth children is to be responsible for the peace and harmony in the family. Consequently, if fourth children are not surrounded by harmony their identity is threatened. Accountable parents are those who assist the fourth child by explicating standards and values out of which flow the goals and purposes of the family. Parents' willingness to take stands and enforce family rules add to the harmony of the system. If they do not do this, fourth children, hindered by their lack of power, will try to bring the system into alignment through manipulation and "cuteness."

In order for fourth children to experience guilt, the family system needs to be harmonious and cooperative most of the time. Because fourth children are system experts, a unified, harmonious family affirms their value to the family. Healthy fourth children can be sensitive and caring, and they can help unify people's systems. A recognition within the system that what they do is of value is affirming. The parents convey that sense of worth while setting limits.

SHAMING DYNAMICS IN
SHAME-PRONE FAMILIES

In shame-prone families there are specific dynamics that are shaming to each systemic sibling position, as identified in Table 7.3.

Children in First Systemic Position

In traditional families children in the first systemic position are tuned into unresolved emotional and psychological issues of their fathers. When fathers feel incapable of having children dependent on them and have trouble showing affection and being close, first children are especially shamed. Even though fathers may never talk about these intimacy, dependency, and accountability issues, first children will have some level of awareness of them and carry them in some way.

Jerry was the oldest child in a family of three children. His father left home for eight months when Jerry was born. The burden of caring for both wife and child seemed too much for him; he couldn't cope with his feelings. Eight months later, when Jerry's father returned, he could not bring himself to play or interact in any way with Jerry. There was much distance between them.

Most likely Jerry's father's family had been shaming and failed to provide for intimacy or dependency needs. His father had never been able to hold down a steady job. Sometimes he drank, sometimes he just decided

TABLE 7.3
Dynamics in Shame-Prone Families that are
Particularly Shaming to Each Systemic Position

Systemic Position	Family Dynamics	Individual Behavior
First	Father is neither close nor affectionate and is irresponsible Explicit messages are constantly given that products are not valued	Obsessive-compulsive Depression and anxiety Rigid thought processes Continually searches for explicit structure in rules and relationships
Second	Mother is neither close nor affectionate and is irresponsible Mother has unresolved emotional issues, e.g., anger toward husband, shamed by own parents "Place" is not secure for any member of family	Codependent (tries to serve and take care of everyone) No emotional identity (blurred boundaries between self and others) Hysterical, disruptive
Third	Parents are abusive to each other Marital, parent-child, and sibling relationships create pain	Disappears emotionally and sometimes physically Appears apathetic and uncaring
Fourth	Verbal, emotional, or sexual abuse anywhere in family system Family violence Individual or systemic dysfunction	Hysterical Absorbs everyone's pain Suicidal Runs away Paranoid

he didn't want to work anymore. As a consequence, the family never had enough money, and Jerry's mother eventually went to work as a waitress to try to make ends meet. Although the father never talked openly about shame, he felt deeply shamed by his wife's working, because to him it implied that he was a failure at providing for his family.

When Jerry reached adolescence, he began acting out not only his own shame but the unresolved shame of his father as well. He tried to be perfect at everything; however, no matter how good his behavior was, he still felt bad inside. Because he felt bad, he tried even harder to produce. As an adult he became a workaholic, totally consumed by his job. His total obsession with work led to conflict in his marriage. When his wife tried to talk to him about his work, he became verbally abusive, yelled obscenities, and accused her of always being out to get him. Confused by his obsession with work and his apparent rage toward her, she finally divorced him. The divorce added more fire to Jerry's shame-prone self. He knew inside that the failure of the marriage was his fault, but he seemed helpless to change the endless criticism and abuse he directed at his wife.

Most noticeable in the initial therapy session with Jerry was his rigid thought processes and his obsession with work. He reported that he saw everything he did as a moral issue. It was all black and white; there were no gray areas. What he ate for lunch was a moral decision, and whatever the choice, he felt he always chose the wrong thing. When I tried to confront his false beliefs about this, he either argued or retreated further inside, but the confrontation did not change his beliefs. In the therapeutic relationship he constantly questioned what was happening and wanted me to explain the meaning of everything we did. This compulsive search for explicit structure made it difficult to get much worked through during the therapy sessions.

Jerry's behavior is typical of shame-prone first children. They are usually obsessive-compulsive and have very rigid ideas about themselves and others. They constantly search for structure in rules and relationships but the answers they get never seem to satisfy them. They are usually depressed and anxious. They worry about many little things and are often uptight for no particular reason. It's very difficult to convince them that some of their beliefs are irrational.

Children in Second Systemic Position

Second children are most threatened when the family system of which they are a part does not provide a secure sense of "place" for family members. The idea of place has both physical and psychological components. For instance, having a room of their own helps second children have a sense of place. However, providing a physical sense of place is not enough. The psychological sense of always having a place in the family, as well as a place in the thoughts and lives of each family member, is important to seconds. When families fail to provide a secure sense of place for individual members, second children are likely to be shame-prone.

Because second children are especially aware of mother's unresolved emotional issues, these issues can be shaming to them. When the mother is shame-prone or suppresses emotional issues and avoids dealing with them, the second child absorbs the pain and acts out. The feelings seem crazy because their source is not clearly identified.

Mothers who fail to be affectionate, close, or responsible are more shaming to second children than to children in other systemic positions. Because they are more tied into mother's underlying emotional issues, second children also pick up mother's fear of intimacy and dependency and feel invalidated and of little worth. Second children who are shame-based do not think that they have a place, do not have separate identities, and are mired in other people's emotions, all the time believing that they are their own. Second children who are shame-prone have no emotional identity of their own. Because they absorb others' emotions, they suffer from emotional overload and can be hysterical, stuck in an emotional quagmire. At the same time they can be very codependent, serving others to the point of martyrdom.

Diane, a second child, came to me very depressed, suicidal, and hysterical. I said to her, "You know that those emotions probably aren't all yours." She stopped and thought about that a moment. To deal with this possibility we did several things. First we identified a special place in her house that was peaceful and comfortable, where she could go whenever things got to her. Then we used imagery to relax her and move her out of the "awfulizing" position. For example, I told her to imagine a roomful of beautiful balloons in which she could put feelings as she blew them up. Then she was asked to identify feelings one by one, taking each out of her body, holding it in her hand, and saying what color it was. Her imagery was vivid. She then decided if it was her own feeling or if she was carrying it for someone else. As she did this she sorted out her feelings from those of others and lightened her emotional load. She was instructed that anything that wasn't hers was to be placed in an imagined balloon for later examination. She gradually accepted that she didn't have to feel feelings now out of her body. She was asked to notice that blowing the balloon full of the feeling actually left her body feeling lighter and freer. By focusing on the context in which feelings occurred she learned to sort her feelings from others'. It was amazing what this exercise did for her in a week.

Children in Third Systemic Position

Third children are tuned into relationship issues in the dyads in the family. They are especially vulnerable to the dynamics of the marital relationship. When the marital relationship creates pain for other family members, third children are most shamed; however, they can also be shamed by other relationships in the family because they are relationship experts.

When parents are abusive to each other, the intimacy and dependency dynamics of the marriage become very confusing to third children. Since they feel it is their job to harmonize the relationship, their sense of personal failure is great when they see their parents being so destructive.

Shame-based third children have difficulty in identifying issues. Why would that be? The context of family life is rarely clear when parents are not accountable. The pattern of going away emotionally and even physically in the face of conflict and pain will be highly exaggerated in shame-prone third children. They will disappear and appear to others to be totally apathetic and uncaring. Situations that require commitments will terrify them because committing to something means giving up choices and shame-prone thirds guard their choices intensely but inappropriately. If

someone pushes them to commit, they will look like cornered animals
fighting for their very survival.

When Scott, the eldest child in his family, and Louise, third and last in
her family, came to therapy, they were planning to be married in three
months. This date represented the fourth time that Louise had changed
the wedding date. The last time she asked to change it, Scott told her that
the only way he would accept the change and stay in the relationship was if
they went to therapy to determine what was going on. According to Scott,
the first two requests for changing the date seemed reasonable to him, and
he had made the accommodation for her. The last two evolved into long
tearful discussions, with both of them feeling hurt and confused. Presently
their time together was mixed with fear, pleasure, and stress.

Louise reported that she loved Scott very much and that she wanted to
marry him, but each time they approached the date for the marriage she
thought of many reasons to postpone the wedding. She didn't understand
her feelings and behavior and felt shamed, discouraged, and confused.
Because Louise would talk openly with him one moment and be closed to
discussion the next, Scott thought he must have done something to hurt or
frighten her, even though she denied this. Neither one understood what
was going on and both felt shame and guilt because they couldn't resolve it.

As we examined the dynamics of their relationship in therapy many
things seemed to be in their favor. They were in love, they came from
similar economic and religious backgrounds, and each had stable families
with parents who loved each other. They met in college when they were
freshmen, but hadn't started dating until they were juniors. Since graduating the previous spring each had worked full-time.

After examining a number of avenues I asked them about their families
and how they interacted with their siblings and parents. Scott was embarrassed and angry when his family teased him one moment and the next
freely gave him advice or admonished him to be the "man" in this situation. Louise's parents were confused by her behavior and had tried everything they could think of to solve the situation.

Thinking that Louise's behavior might be connected to the issues of the
third sibling position, I reframed Louise's behavior in a logical way. I explained to them that third children often have difficulty making decisions
and commitments because they have to give up choices in order to do so.
Louise nodded her head and visibly relaxed. I also explained that when
third children feel backed into a corner they often check out of the conversation, either physically or emotionally. So when Scott was confused by her
being there with him one moment and not the next it meant that she
needed time out to be with herself.

Louise told Scott that he seemed to assume so much of the decision-
making that she often felt that she had no choice. When he protested that
he didn't feel that way, that he wanted her to be part of decisions, she

described to him the way he had presented their honeymoon plans, with all reservations made. He agreed that he had gone ahead with the plans, thinking that was what she would want.

All of this information seemed to make sense to them and they were able to quit punishing themselves for the confusion. By creating alternatives with choices for both of them, we helped them to examine all parts of the wedding plans. We were then able to work through the impasse, plan for an orderly completion of their wedding plans, and rehearse ways of meeting this kind of impasse should it happen again.

Children in Fourth Systemic Position

Anything that disrupts harmony and progression toward the family's goals is potentially shaming for fourth children. Since they feel it is their job to harmonize and unify the family, they will feel responsible for either individual or family dysfunction. Violence, addiction, and verbal, emotional, or sexual abuse will be especially shaming to fourth children, even if they are not the recipients of the aggressive acts. To them the system is out of control and nonharmonious, and that means they have failed in their job.

When fourth children are shame-based, they tend to be hysterical and totally irresponsible, to run away, and to absorb everybody's pain. Everything is their fault, nothing they do is right, they are stuck with all of those feelings wherever they are. They become totally irresponsible because no one is helping them keep the system together—it is, as they see it, hopeless. The parents aren't giving enough structure to make the system work; they're not giving the fourth child enough support so that he or she can do something. Shame-based fourth children are often suicidal and paranoid.

Alex came to Dr. Whitman for therapy after crashing his car while drunk and putting himself and his companion in the hospital. Alex realized he needed help. Hysterically he told his father and mother that he was in trouble, he was scared, the family was never there for him, no one listened to him, and he wanted to go to therapy. If he didn't get help soon he was sure that he would kill himself or some other terrible thing. As he went on and on his father denied that things were that serious, but his mother thought back over the past few months and began to feel very guilty. Alex was in trouble and they had missed it. She immediately supported his request for help. This was painful for her because she realized that she, her husband, and her sons would have to be involved. She was aware of some of the denial in the family.

Alex was the fourth son of a family very successful in the business world. As a 17-year-old his future seems to be cut and dried. He had already been accepted to Harvard, the alma mater of both his parents and his three older siblings. His father and older brothers had great plans for him in the business. Although he had consistently told them that he did not want to be in business, it was as though no one heard him. When he talked with his mother she told him he was being ridiculous. Where else could he be as successful and as secure financially? He was intelligent, personable, and would be an asset to the business.

Most of his life Alex had tried to pull the family together into more "fun" activities. His parents' and siblings' serious talk, obsession with making money, and focus on appearance had gradually driven him further from them. He felt alienated and disengaged from them. Whenever he pointed out that someone needed support in the family the situation was denied and swept aside. He had heard his mother cry at night, yet she always denied it when he asked her about it. It was his imagination! She had the television on and someone was crying.

As a senior in high school he began to ignore his classes, spent more time listening to music, and traveled with a group who continually harpooned the "establishment" and experimented with drugs. Alcohol and girls became his obsessions. His weight dropped, he looked distraught, and he had to lie more and more to family, friends, and teachers. Family members noticed that he had changed, but they tossed it off as a demonstration of Alex's growing up and sowing a few "wild oats." Because no one in this family failed or got in serious trouble, it was not an option as far as they were concerned.

After meeting with Alex several sessions, Dr. Whitman consulted with the medical doctor and the psychiatrist. They were in agreement that Alex needed treatment; however, no one was convinced that he was an alcoholic. But they agreed that a drug counselor should assess the situation and determine this. Dr. Allen indicated that Alex was shame-prone, that his parents were accountable in certain areas and had always allowed Alex to depend on them for the physical aspects of life. Intimacy was lacking in all parts of the family. The rules for behavior and success were rigid and demanding. All other family rules, roles, and interactions were dominated by these rules for success.

The following description focuses on what the therapist did because he knew Alex was a fourth child. In the initial sessions Dr. Whitman helped Alex look at his despair and hopelessness by separating his life into parts: school, his relationships with each person in his family, the family as a whole, what he wanted to do with his life. This helped alleviate the feelings of being overwhelmed. In family sessions, working to help family members to acknowledge their own emotions and behaviors, as well as to be explicitly responsible for their part in the things that were wrong in their family took much time, expertise, and patience. They did not know how sensitive Alex was to their pain and how responsible he felt. He thought their pain, their failure to be close and to have fun together was his fault. As family therapy progressed the parents and siblings began to talk about their frustrations and reactions to the distance they felt. Through individual and family therapy Dr. Whitman helped Alex to disconnect from the pain in the family and deal with his own.

DYNAMICS IN FAMILIES WITH DEPENDENCY ISSUES THAT ARE PARTICULARLY SHAMING TO EACH SYSTEMIC POSITION

Table 7.4 identifies dynamics in families with dependency issues that are particularly shaming to each of the four systemic sibling positions.

Children in First Systemic Position

Because first children are particularly tuned into father's unresolved emotional issues, when he has dependency issues the first child will also have dependency issues. These fathers do not allow their children to depend on them. It is difficult to accept the children's littleness and need to be protected and instructed. This dynamic affects first children because they need to be productive. When the focus is on intimacy alone rather than on a mixture of tasks and intimacy, first children have no way of knowing that their parents are accountable enough to make sure that they produce. They end up thinking that they will never be good enough because they can't make sense and order out of their job assignment. What this produces in terms of response from a first child is an unending, obsessive demand for explicit structure in all relationships.

In these families first children believe they can be close to parents; they know parents will be affectionate, hug, hold, and kiss them. But they do not believe that they can count on parents when it comes to completing tasks and pursuing goals. Because of this belief they feel more responsibility to be productive and seek more approval from parents who can't give approval. This repetitive cycle punishes and confuses first children.

Children in Second Systemic Position

When the mother is affectionate but irresponsible the second child is most likely to be affected. That's because it is consistent with a second child's role to attend to mother's unresolved issues. When there are problems with dependency, a sense of order is not provided consistently. The structure remains mostly implicit and inconsistent. Unlike first children, who are bothered by implicit structure because they cannot tell which outcomes they should seek, second children are bothered by the incon-

TABLE 7.4
Dynamics in Families with Dependency Issues that are
Particularly Shaming to Each Systemic Position

Systemic Position	Family Dynamics	Individual Behavior
First	Father is irresponsible but affectionate Expectations are never made explicit so message is "You can never be good enough"	Obsessive search for explicit structure
Second	Mother is irresponsible but affectionate Sense of order is not provided consistently so that structure in family system remains mostly implicit	Irresponsible in work Use charm to manipulate Use intimacy as a maneuver—confused when it doesn't work Theme of "Whatever I do is okay"
Third	Marital partners irresponsible to each other but still close Child tries to save marriage but it doesn't work No rules for dependency in dyadic relationships	Distant from family members but often enmeshed with people outside the family Difficulty in cognitive ability to see connections and issues Doesn't feel an obligation that others count on them
Fourth	No sense of order in family system Most family members are irresponsible but blame each other Family members feel close but cannot count on each other	Out of control Looks irresponsible to others World view that everything is chaotic Feels blamed and dumped on Feels responsible for family's nonproductivity

gruities between explicit and implicit. As seen in Table 7.1, one of the job assignments of second children is to search out discrepancies between implicit and explicit structure. When there is chronic incongruity between the two, second children become shame-prone on dependency issues.

Second children who are shamed on dependency issues will be irresponsible in work but charming socially. They will use intimacy to manipulate others; when it does not work, they will be confused. Since intimacy, but not dependency, was provided in their own families of origin, they assume that anything they do is okay. They really believe that if they do the "right" thing they can make whatever is not working work and get whatever they want.

Second children shamed on dependency issues need to have rules and limits set for them. For example, some families don't have any rules about space. Anyone can walk into the bathroom or the parents' bedroom anytime. This lack of rules about space has different effects on different people in the family. For second children it is problematic, since they need their own secure space.

Children in the Third Systemic Position

When husband and wife are irresponsible to each other, the third child is shamed on dependency issues. The parents can be very affectionate and close, but they do not meet each other's task needs. They provide little structure as a marital system, hindering their productivity. When there are no explicit or implicit rules for handling dependency in the marriage, third children are affected. Sometimes there is an implicit rule, almost a collusion, between marital partners about dependency. Either they are supposed to be totally independent and not exhibit any dependency needs in the marriage or they are supposed to be totally dependent, expecting the spouse to take care of them as though they were little. Because the job assignment of third children is to harmonize the marriage, they are greatly affected when the marriage experiences chronic conflict. Initially they will do their best to save the marriage, to try to get their parents to make it work. But if their attempts fail, they will feel shamed. They will assume in some distorted way that it is because they are bad that the marriage didn't work.

Dependency shamed third children feel no obligation to allow others to count on them. They are afraid of letting others rely on them, and they resent anyone who has dependency needs. Often they will be distant from family members but enmeshed with others outside the family. The message is: You cannot count on family members to come through, so maybe you can be totally dependent on people outside the family; perhaps if you find the right person, he or she can be your substitute parent. Third children raised in these family environments have trouble identifying issues and seeing connections between people because the context is rarely clear.

Children in Fourth Systemic Position

When there is no sense of order in the family system, fourth children are more shamed on dependency than other siblings. Fourth children keep their "sensors" to the ground to monitor whether the family is productive as a whole. In families with dependency issues, most family members are irresponsible in terms of tasks and so the family as a whole usually fails to reach its goals. This shames the fourth. Because family members are loving and close but do not feel they can count on each other, the fourth child may take the blame on himself for the lack of dependency in the entire system.

Fourth children shamed on dependency look irresponsible even though they are trying very hard. They are unable to stay at any one task for long periods of time. They switch jobs and start a lot of things they never finish. To outsiders it appears as though they are out of control and completely irresponsible. Their view of the world is that everything is chaotic. They focus on events that demonstrate a lack of sense and order, and they assume it is somehow their fault that the world is not a more dependable place. If they were just *good*, somehow the world would be better too. Sometimes fourths from systems with dependency issues think that if they just stay close, it will take care of the lack of dependency. When the closeness doesn't solve the dependency issues, they appear confused and disoriented.

DYNAMICS IN FAMILIES WITH INTIMACY ISSUES THAT ARE PARTICULARLY SHAMING TO EACH SIBLING POSITION

Table 7.5 illustrates characteristics of families with intimacy issues particularly shaming to the four systemic positions.

Children in First Systemic Position

When fathers are distant, first children are shamed on the intimacy dimension. The family with intimacy issues is usually concerned about explicit products. This emphasis exaggerates the first child's characteristic response. At times the expectations to produce will be overwhelming.

The kinds of messages first children hear from this type of system are: "Get your work done!" "Learn to take care of yourself!" "Don't expect us to always support you." First children respond with work, work, and more work. In the compulsiveness of work, they'll never feel fulfilled because none of their intimacy needs get met. These first children will be filled with fear and anxiety about producing. Because their intimacy needs have not been met, they feel lonely. Yet their public image will be one of stoicism; they will appear to be content to be by themselves working on some task. They often have difficulties with authority figures because to them authority figures fail to value people but continue to push them to reach

TABLE 7.5

Dynamics in Families with Intimacy Issues that are
Particularly Shaming to Each Systemic Position

Systemic Position	Family Dynamics	Individual Behavior
First	Father is neither affectionate nor close but responsible and owns values System emphasizes explicit products	Fear and anxiety Authority issues Lonely Stoic
Second	Mother is neither affectionate nor close but owns values Explicit family focus on sense and order with an implicit message that intimacy issues are threatening	Fear Flipflops between emotional confusion (overloaded with emotion with no explicit explanation of why they are so emotional) and excessive rationality
Third	Marital partners are not close or affectionate, nor do they disclose personal information Parents have difficulty showing affection and sharing with children (third child as a relationship expert observes the implicit and explicit rules of relationships)	Handles all feelings on own by introspection Disruptive (an attempt to get parents united) Difficulty making interpersonal commitments Difficulty with affection in own relationships
Fourth	No one in family is affectionate Lack of unity and closeness affects family's ability to be productive	Can be responsible in achieving but irresponsible in relationships Either disappears or clings Hassles siblings inappropriately and intensely Accepts blame for no lack of closeness in family

expectations and standards. The expectations feel like a burden, especially in the absence of intimacy.

Children in Second Systemic Position

Families with intimacy issues explicitly focus on sense of order and dependency issues; their fear of intimacy remains implicit. Because it is the second child's job to identify incongruities between the explicit and implicit, this system feels crazy to a second child. He or she will be affected if there is no intimacy with mom and especially if mom is a needy person and isn't being taken care of by dad.

These second children are full of fear. They don't understand where it come from. Without knowing it they have absorbed each family member's concerns and fears about being valued. It will feel to them as if this fear is all theirs. Sometimes they'll go just a little crazy. They act out; they don't like to be home; they don't want to be around mom because of the pain they feel when they are with her. Sometimes they'll hassle mom and try to get her to take care of herself. This is all at a subconscious level; they don't know why they're doing what they're doing. They will be totally emotional at times and flip into excessive rationality at other times.

In one family the second child, 13 years old, was seen as the problem in the family. The therapist observed that when anyone in the family but mom talked this son vigorously rocked back and forth in his chair. And as soon as mom began to talk, he'd stop rocking. When the therapist commented on this, mother broke down and explained that she had some emotional issues that needed to be expressed in the family. The second child was sort of the energy vent for all of her stuff. When she'd begin to talk about that, he didn't need to rock.

Children in Third Systemic Position

It is the lack of intimacy in the marriage that is most shaming to third children in families with intimacy issues. Because third children observe relationship rules and enforce them in other relationships, they become particularly afraid of intimacy in their own personal relationships.

Initially third children will disrupt and act out in an attempt to get mom and dad more united. When they discover that these attempts do not bring their parents closer together , they withdraw and appear apathetic. Their individual response is to handle all feelings on their own by introspection. The process of working conflict through in a relationship is a scary thing for them. They see the self-disclosure of feelings as a violation of relationship rules. They have an underlying belief that relationships will not survive the expression of conflict and emotion.

Third children raised in this type of family have difficulty committing to a relationship. Third children have difficulty with commitments anyway because of their desire to guard their choices, but intimacy problems compound this hesitance. They shy away from showing affection because the rule of their parents' marriage on which they built their identity was to show no affection.

Children in Fourth Systemic Position

Because it is the job of fourth children to unify and harmonize the family, fourth children feel like failures when their families are disengaged.

These fourth children may be responsible in accomplishing tasks but irresponsible in relationships. While feigning harmony and unity, they feel underneath that the relationship is bad because thy are bad. Somehow they cannot separate their own identity from the identity of the relationship or whole system in which they are embedded. They accept personal blame for the lack of closeness in the family—it is somehow caused by their badness. As children they may hassle other siblings excessively and inappropriately as they are attempting to get someone in the system to do something about the lack of intimacy. When fourth children feel overwhelmed by the intimacy and emotional issues in systems, they'll either leave or cling.

Sometimes the characteristic response patterns of one systemic position are shaming to another family member in a different systemic position. Because neither person is explicitly aware of his or her own response patterns, both fail to understand why they become so defensive. The answer lies in the fact that both take defensive action to hide their shame from the other.

DAD TOOK MY RIGHTS AWAY: A CASE OF A FIRST-CHILD FATHER AND THIRD-CHILD SON

Ted, the first child in his own family of origin, was always confused by the arguments he got into with his 15-year-old son Jay. He didn't understand why Jay always flared so readily whenever he tried to offer fatherly help and advice. During the middle of every argument, when Jay screamed at his father to leave him alone, Ted felt enraged. He couldn't understand how Jay could be so ungrateful for all that Ted did for him. In his mind, if Jay would just be responsible and get things done, he wouldn't have to hassle him so much.

Jay complained that his father never left him alone. He tried to control everything Jay did. From Jay's perspective, his outbursts were attempts to protect himself. He thought his dad always took his choices away. He *had* to fight to keep his choices; however, when he fought his dad just got worse and worse. When he couldn't stand it any longer, he just wanted to be left alone to work things out for himself. When his father continued to hassle him, he felt unloved and attacked.

After several years of this pattern, both Ted and Jay felt shamed. Ted assumed he was a failure as a father, but he couldn't admit it to anyone, especially to his wife and Jay. Jay assumed he was a failure because, as he watched himself fight so hard to protect choices and then totally withdraw, he felt ashamed by what he observed and felt. He was a bad son—or so he thought. Ted worried that the way Jay was turning out was all his fault, but thought the only thing to do to change things was to assume more control. That solution seemed to make everything worse between him and Jay. Consequently, he felt that the family was even more out of control.

What Jay and Ted failed to realize was that their interactional exchanges were largely consistent with their systemic positions. Ted, a first child, needed to be right in order to feel good about himself. He was concerned with products and outcome because that was his job assignment in his own family of origin. On the other hand, Jay was a third child, whose job it was to balance relationships in the family. Third children are threatened most when it appears their choices will be taken away. In this context they will fight or flee. Because they have learned from the structure in their family that they can disrupt relationships, they tend to work through conflictual feelings by an introspective process rather than a relationship process. Jay just wanted his father to leave him alone so he could work out his feelings, but the distancing made Ted feel that he was not right, that he was off target. As Ted became more intense in an effort to be right, Jay became more withdrawn in an effort to work through his feelings and protect his choices. Neither could keep from feeling shamed by the patterns of the other. To them they were a bad combination; not only was the combination bad, but each of them was bad also. They could not admit this to each other, even though they both felt it so deeply inside. So they defended themselves by attacking, hoping that the other would not uncover their shame but feeling as though they were uncovered anyway.

A MARRIAGE MIRED IN THE EMOTIONAL BOG: A CASE OF A SECOND-CHILD WIFE AND A FOURTH-CHILD HUSBAND

Mike and Liz, who had been married for six years, couldn't understand why they both felt so bad. Liz was the second child in her family of origin and Mike was a fourth in his own family. Liz's mother committed suicide when Liz was 19 years old. Liz described her mother as an unpredictable person who would fly into a rage one moment and break down sobbing the next. No one in the family ever knew what might set mother off. Liz described her father as a quiet, wimpy man. Overwhelmed by his wife's outbursts, he spent a lot of time at work.

Liz reported how much she appreciated Mike's total focus on her when they were dating. He did everything for her. She thought theirs would be the happiest of marriages. But within a few months after they were married it seemed to Liz that Mike hassled her all the time, that he put tremendous pressure on her.

From Mike's perspective, Liz was always tense. He always felt her tension was his fault. He thought maybe his "hassling" was an attempt to find out if Liz blamed him for how she felt. According to him, it wasn't anything that Liz said or even did that led him to think she was tense—it was something deeper, something he just felt. He had difficulty describing what behaviors or events were related to it. Yet he felt somehow he was to blame. He was a bad husband; he was a bad person. He didn't know *how* exactly, but he knew that if he were good the whole relationship would feel different to him. Nevertheless, rather than focusing on himself, he hassled Liz in the hopes that something would change.

As he hassled, Liz usually became more and more emotional. She threw dishes and sobbed her eyes out. She couldn't explain why she felt so emotional. Sometimes she just decided she wasn't going to be emotional anymore. She would flip into her very logical mode, which Mike hardly understood.

Liz and Mike failed to realize that Liz had been shamed by her mother's crazy behavior. Mike could feel that underlying shame as part of the whole relationship, but neither could put a finger on it because Liz didn't want Mike to know how crazy she felt. On the other hand, Mike didn't want Liz to know how bad he felt either. When he got into the blame he felt, he wanted to get as far away from her as he possibly could. When this happened, Liz felt she lost her place with him, which panicked her even more. When this happened, she became more confused and hysterical, and Mike felt more blamed and paralyzed.

Liz didn't know consciously that she was carrying her mother's unresolved shame. All she knew was how bad she felt. Mike didn't know consciously that the job of someone in his systemic position was to harmonize their system. He didn't know that he could collect Liz's "garbage" so easily and feel blamed personally. Had they better understood the characteristic response patterns of their systemic positions, they might have been able to guard against the shame their relationship engendered and concentrate on resolving the issues of their individual shame.

CHAPTER 8

Assessing Shame-Prone Individuals, Couples, and Families

THE USE OF BOTH standardized and observational or interview methods of assessing clients is common to most therapists (Grotevant & Carlson, 1989). One standardized measure of internalized shame for clinical and research use is described and discussed in this chapter. Other measures that have been used in research are referenced. A checklist for observing individual symptoms of shame that are exhibited in therapy sessions or are derived from interview information is also presented. Shame in couples and families is integrated with Olson's Circumplex Model of family system, and a checklist of family symptoms is presented.

STANDARDIZED MEASURES OF INTERNALIZED SHAME

A number of measures of shame have been used in empirical studies. These include Korpi's Shame and Guilt Test (Korpi, 1977), Susceptibility to Embarrassment Scale (Cattell & Scheier, 1960), the Adapted Shame/Guilt Scale (Hoblitzelle, 1982), Smith-Beall Shame and Guilt Test (Beall, 1972; Smith, 1972), the Perlman Scales (Perlman, 1958), and a system of content analysis that identifies references to shame or guilt in verbal dialogue (Gottschalk & Gleser, 1969). However, since the Internalized Shame Scale (ISS) (Cook, 1989, 1987a, 1987b) represents the best developed measure for clinical use, these other measures will not be described here. They are listed here for the benefit of researchers looking for measures of shame.

The Internalized Shame Scale

The Internalized Shame Scale (ISS) (Cook, 1989) is the result of a sustained and extensive effort to develop a measure of shame. The items were developed specifically to measure enduring, chronic shame that has become an internalized part of one's identity. The Internalized Shame Scale (ISS) consists of 30 Likert-scaled items that yield two basic scale scores. The two scales include a 24-item shame scale and a 6-item self-esteem scale. The 24-item shame scale includes two subscales, an inferiority scale (15 items) and an alienation scale (9 items). The ISS is reprinted in its entirety as Table 8.1.*

The development of the ISS began in 1984. The first set of items was structured so that respondents could rate the frequency (never to almost always) with which they experienced the affect described by each item. The original pool of 90 items was reduced to 48 after a group of alcoholics assumed to have high levels of internalized shame sorted the items into those they experienced frequently and those not experienced at all. Since 1984, the scale has been administered to over 3,000 subjects, both clinical and nonclinical (Cook, 1990). Extensive reliability and validity studies have resulted in four revisions of the scale, the latest of which appears as Table 8.1.

Alpha reliability coefficients for the current version range from .94 for the shame scale and .88 for the self-esteem scale, and test-retest reliability coefficients range from .71 to .84, indicating that the ISS has good reliability. Exploratory factor analysis shows that the items yield two major factors related to shame and self-esteem. The inferiority and alienation subscales within the overall shame scale correlate .74, so it appears that they are not independent of each other.

A series of studies has compared the results of the ISS with three different self-concept/self-esteem measures and concluded that the Internalized Shame Scale was measuring "a trait that contributed more to the development of emotional problems than did low self-esteem alone" (Cook, 1988, p. 18). Self-esteem and shame are conceptually different in that shame is an affect, and shame-prone identity describes the affective experience of a person with such an identity. Self-esteem is not an affect but more of a cognitive evaluation of the self. In factor analysis studies, Cook (1988) observed that the items on the shame subscale and the 6 self-esteem items on the Internalized Shame Scale do not load on the same factor, but load respectively on two different factors.

Ursu (1984), in a study of measures of self-esteem and shame, argued that internalized shame and negative self-esteem are different. Scores on

---

*Directions for scoring and interpretation and clinical and nonclinical norms are available by contacting Dr. David R. Cook at the University of Wisconsin-Stout.

TABLE 8.1
Internalized Shame Scale (ISS)

DIRECTIONS: Below is a list of statements describing feelings or experiences that you may have from time to time or that are familiar to you because you have had these feelings and experiences for a long time. Most of these statements describe feelings and experiences that are generally painful or negative in some way. Some people will seldom or never have had many of these feelings. Everyone has had some of these feelings at some time, but if you find that these statements describe the way you feel a good deal of the time, it can be painful just reading them. Try to be as honest as you can in responding.

Read each statement carefully and circle the number to the left of the item that indicates the frequency with which you find yourself feeling or experiencing what is described in the statement. Use the scale below. DO NOT OMIT ANY ITEM.

SCALE

| *1-Never* | *2-Seldom* | *3-Sometimes* | *4-Frequently* | *5-Almost Always* |

Scale

1 2 3 4 5   1. I feel like I am never quite good enough.
1 2 3 4 5   2. I feel somehow left out.
1 2 3 4 5   3. I think that people look down on me.
1 2 3 4 5   4. All in all, I am inclined to feel that I am a success.
1 2 3 4 5   5. I scold myself and put myself down.
1 2 3 4 5   6. I feel insecure about others' opinions of me.
1 2 3 4 5   7. Compared to other people I feel like I somehow never measure up.
1 2 3 4 5   8. I see myself as being very small and insignificant.
1 2 3 4 5   9. I feel I have much to be proud of.
1 2 3 4 5   10. I feel intensely inadequate and full of self doubt.
1 2 3 4 5   11. I feel as if I am somehow defective as a person, like there is something basically wrong with me.
1 2 3 4 5   12. When I compare myself to others, I am just not as important.
1 2 3 4 5   13. I have an overpowering dread that my faults will be revealed in front of others.
1 2 3 4 5   14. I feel I have a number of good qualities.
1 2 3 4 5   15. I see myself striving for perfection only to continually fall short.
1 2 3 4 5   16. I think others are able to see my defects.
1 2 3 4 5   17. I could beat myself over the head with a club when I make a mistake.
1 2 3 4 5   18. On the whole, I am satisfied with myself.
1 2 3 4 5   19. I would like to shrink away when I make a mistake.
1 2 3 4 5   20. I replay painful events over and over in my mind until I am overwhelmed.
1 2 3 4 5   21. I feel I am a person of worth at least on an equal plane with others.
1 2 3 4 5   22. At times I feel like I will break into a thousand pieces.
1 2 3 4 5   23. I feel as if I have lost control over my body functions and my feelings.
1 2 3 4 5   24. Sometimes I feel no bigger than a pea.

1 2 3 4 5	25. At times I feel so exposed that I wish the earth would open up and swallow me.
1 2 3 4 5	26. I have this painful gap within me that I have not been able to fill.
1 2 3 4 5	27. I feel empty and unfulfilled.
1 2 3 4 5	28. I take a positive attitude toward myself.
1 2 3 4 5	29. My loneliness is more like emptiness.
1 2 3 4 5	30. I always feel like there is something missing.

©1989 by David R. Cook, University of Wisconsin-Stout, 237 Harvey Hall, Menomonie, Wisconsin 54751. Reprinted by permission.

the ISS were also correlated with a measure of depression, suggesting that shame is an important consideration in understanding depression. Studies comparing the ISS with the MMPI subscales yielded validity coefficients ranging from .58 to .76. Highest correlations were with the psychasthenia, paranoia, and depression subscales.

INFORMAL MEASURES OF INTERNALIZED SHAME

The initial task of therapy is finding entrance to a client's shame (Kaufman, 1989). Direct observations of client in-session behavior, as well as information gleaned from therapy interviews, provide important clues to assessing shame. The checklist, Table 8.2, discussed in this chapter provides guidelines for sifting through observational and interview information to determine whether or not a given client or family system is shame-prone.

The indicators of shame-proneness are multidimensional, which means that therapists must assess different aspects of their clients, primarily dimensions of emotional, cognitive, and interpersonal behavior. Observing these three areas in the clinical interview helps the clinician to accurately recognize shame-proneness and to identify points of entrance into the shamed world of the client.

Emotional Patterns

As children, shame-based people did not receive validation for their emotional experiences. The messages they received from their family system convinced them that to feel was bad (Edwards, 1976). As the shame-prone identity solidifies, the part of the person that experiences emotion is split off as a bad part (Slipp, 1988). When this happens, specific emotions or all emotions can be blocked.

Four characteristics of emotional experience contrast shame-prone and healthy individuals.

1. Healthy individuals experience a wide range of emotion, including anger, hurt, humiliation, fear, sadness, surprise, joy, contentment, etc. Shame-prone individuals experience a constricted range of feelings. For example, they may be stuck in anger and not be able to experience sadness.

2. In healthy people, the intensity of each of these emotions varies over time. Sometimes they can be quite angry or quite sad, but they do not stay at that intensity for very long. In contrast, shame-prone individuals exhibit an inappropriate matching of intensity of emotion with events. Their affect is either flat or hysterical in response to events that merit neither flatness nor hysteria.

3. Healthy individuals can usually relate their emotional experiences to the context. As they think about how their feelings are related to events and other people, they can understand how their own internal emotional experience and the environment are connected. On the other hand, shame-prone individuals experience a feeling of badness irrespective of the context.

4. Healthy individuals have an appreciation of feelings as part of their overall makeup. They do not try to deny what they are feeling; rather, they use emotional experiences as cues to understanding themselves, others, and their interpersonal interactions. Shame-prone individuals often deny and defend against feelings.

Table 8.2 provides additional checklist items for informally assessing emotional, cognitive, and behavioral patterns related to proneness to shame.

Thought Patterns

Because shame-prone individuals guard against others' discovering their shame, many of the patterns associated with being shame-prone are cognitive processes (Lazarus, 1984 Shane, 1980). Only through thought processes can people make sense and order of their worlds. Individual belief systems and self-talk, as well as family belief systems, are important in assessing individuals for proneness to shame. However, because thought processes themselves are not directly observable, therapists must infer them from the patterns that emerge from what patients say and do.

The cognitive processes of the shame-prone individual generally include the five basic patterns below:

1. A belief that "something is wrong with me"
2. A perceptual focus on the negative
3. Polarized style of thinking
4. Subjective reasoning
5. Obsessive thinking

TABLE 8.2
Assessment Checklist for Identifying a
Shame-Prone Individual

EMOTIONAL PATTERNS:
- A constricted range of feelings
- An inappropriate matching of intensity of emotion with events. Affect is either flat or hysterical in response to events that merit neither flatness nor hysteria.
- A feeling of badness regardless of the context
- Denial of and defending against feelings
- Systematic increase in frequency, intensity, and duration of any one particular emotion on the horizontal axis of the map for treatment in Chapter 8, but especially in feelings of humiliation.
- Excessive guilt without forgiveness or no guilt at all
- Fears of being abandoned and embarrassed in front of other people
- Emptiness
- Reacting to real or imagined criticism with rage (expressed or nonexpressed) and humiliation (nonexpressed)

THOUGHT PATTERNS:
- Belief that "something is wrong with me"
  - "imposter syndrome"
  - expect to be exploited or harmed by others
  - all information has symbolic meaning about their own personal identities
  - distort incoming information in the perceptual process so that it fits with their world
- Perceptual focus on the negative
  - label themselves and others negatively and respond to the labels as if they were the real thing
  - often believe that working in therapy may make things worse
  - intentions of others as well as of themselves become very distorted
  - make attributions to the character traits and intentions of others rather than to the situational factors
  - disconfirm the context and distort responsibility for the causes of events
  - use mind reading to the detriment of themselves and others
  - overgeneralize and magnify
  - catastrophize by inflating the severity of a particular event's consequences
- Polarized style of thinking
  - all-or-nothing, black-and-white thinking
- Subjective reasoning
  - poor reality-testing
- Obsessive thinking
  - frantic efforts to avoid real or imagined abandonment

BEHAVIOR PATTERNS:

Nonverbal Behavior (occurs within session):
- avoidance of mutual facial gazing and direct eye-to-eye contact
- put head down
- blushing
- staring posture
- frozen face
- mask-like face

(continued)

TABLE 8.2
(Continued)

• head-back look
• using hair to hide one's face
• hands over parts of the face, especially eyes
• looks of contempt

Interpersonal (may occur within or outside of session):
• pattern of unstable and intense interpersonal relationships
• exploitive of others, often make preemptive strikes
• respond with power, contempt, or rage when shame is close to being discovered
• choose to be involved with people and situations that lead to disappointment, failure, or mistreatment even when better options are clearly available
• often reject or render ineffective the attempts of others to help them
• respond to events that should be experienced as positive with depression, guilt, or behavior that produces pain often demand that others always treat them with kindness
• even when treated well, react with rejection and suspicion
• melding/lack of well defined personal thoughts, feelings, desires
• sexualized anger

Individual Behavior (may occur within or outside of session):
• perfectionism and other compensatory behavior
• internal withdrawal
• denial
• sarcastic humor, self-deprecatory humor
• excessive involvement in pleasurable activities that have a high potential for painful consequences
• series of shaming events in person's life

"*Something is Wrong with Me.*"   Often shame-prone individuals suffer from the "imposter syndrome" (Beck, 1988), assuming that "if others only knew [any supposed secret], they would discover that I am flawed." They expect to be exploited or harmed by others. If such exploitation does not occur, it is only because other people, including therapists, have not had enough association with them to discover their "flaw." If they are not immediately exposed they wait, believing that the other person knows and is conning them in some way.

For shame-prone individuals all information has symbolic meaning about their own personal identities (Thrane, 1979). They personalize almost any source of information. For example, most shame-prone individuals distortedly believe that even the most benign acts of others are directed toward them to highlight their badness. These people have very closed perspectives of themselves; outside information does not easily penetrate the rigid belief systems of shame-prone individuals. Rather than modifying their beliefs in response to external input, these people distort incoming information in the perceptual process so that it fits with their world and confirms their badness. If they cannot distort the information, they disqualify it as a fluke or chance happening.

An example relates to changing behavior. Even when it is obvious to all others that they have changed their behavior, shame-prone individuals find ways to disqualify the information. Since their mental template includes the notion that they are incapable of change, actual experiences with changing behavior do not register. Rather, the change is downplayed. The basic core remains "bad" and unchanged even though the behavior may have changed quite dramatically.

Perceptual Focus on the Negative. Individuals prone to shame label themselves and other negatively. Then they respond to the labels as if they were the real thing (Bagarozzi & Anderson, 1989; Beck, 1988). For instance, one client assumed that he was really evil because a woman teasingly called him "a real devil." He took the label literally and assumed she somehow knew about his "badness." From his perception, although his behavior matched the label, he was frightened of being "a real devil."

Shame-prone individuals have excessively negative expectations (Lewis, 1986). From the time these persons get up in the morning, they are braced for things to go wrong. They assume that things will only get worse. In fact, they often believe that working in therapy may make things worse. Consequently, they appear to be ambivalent about the process. They really want help, but they fight it a lot.

Their own and others' intentions become very distorted in shame-prone individuals' minds (Horowitz, 1981). Shame-prone spouses are likely to quickly jump to negative conclusions about their partners' state of mind and what it means for their marriage. In one case, when a wife failed to meet her husband's unexpressed expectations, he concluded, "She really doesn't care about me. She's only interested in herself." It is common for these people to make attributions to the character traits and intentions of others rather than to situational factors.

This distortion process is one in which people depend on ambiguous signals to inform them about the attitudes and wishes of other people (Beck, 1988). By selectively abstracting information from their world (external and internal) that is consistent with their shame, they create a tunnel vision that biases explanations about why things happen and why others behave as they do. The unique coding system they use for interpreting interpersonal signals almost always negatively biases the signal. For example, when his wife wasn't saying anything, Gary assumed that she must be angry with him. When he saw friends at work talking and laughing, he assumed that they must be talking about him and making fun of the things he did.

Attributing such ill will to others is a common symptom of the shame-prone identity. The consequences of such thinking include questioning without justification the loyalty or trustworthiness of friends, reading hidden disparaging or threatening meaning into remarks or events, and being reluctant to confide in others because of unwarranted fear of rejection.

In maintaining their negative focus, shame-prone individuals often disconfirm the context and distort responsibility for and causes of events. They often attribute the cause of others' feelings, behavior, etc., to something they have done (Horowitz, 1981). Outwardly, such people deny any responsibility and often blame others for events. However, on the inside they are terrified that their own badness may be the cause. Internally, they frequently assume blame for others' problems or relationship difficulties. For instance, a wife confessed in therapy that their marriage was not working because she was "bad."

Shame-prone individuals use mind-reading to the detriment of themselves and others. Beck (1988) discussed how spouses develop distorted pictures of each other, leading in turn to misinterpretations of what the other says or does. Undesirable motives are then ascribed. As Beck points out, people are not in the habit of "checking out their interpretations of each other's behavior" (p. 11). Shame-prone persons believe that they can tell what others are thinking and feeling, so they do not bother to gather information or check on reality.

One last aspect of the focus on the negative is the amount of overgeneralizing and magnifying that shame-prone people do. Words such as *always, all, every, never,* and *none* are signals that this process is occurring. Phrases such as the following are frequently used:

- "He never gives me credit for having a brain."
- "She always puts me down."
- "You've never loved me."
- "You never care about how I feel."
- "You're always going to treat me miserably."

There is a tendency to exaggerate the qualities of others, whether good or bad, and to create catastrophes by inflating the severity of a particular event's consequences. Emotions are also "awfulized," as illustrated by the following statements:

- "I can't tolerate all this anger."
- "I can't stand being frustrated all the time."
- "I can't bear being humiliated all the time."

In tracing the thinking patterns of one husband, we discovered the following self-talk:

Why is she so content to be quiet? She must be angry at me. I must have done something wrong that offended her. Now she will be angry with me for a long time. I always make people angry with me. People hate me. Even my wife hates me. I will always be alone because I am bad.

Without checking out his attributions, the husband jumped to highly exaggerated conclusions about the cause of the trouble and the implications for their marriage. It is not unusual for shame-prone individuals to get trapped in such a web of invisible causes. By responding to these faulty conclusions about the meaning of other people's behavior, shame-prone persons set up what they most fear—rejection from others.

Polarized Style of Thinking. Associated with the belief that "something is wrong with me" is a polarized, all-or-nothing cognitive style (Beck, 1988). There is no continuum; there are but two discrete and often opposite categories of thinking. For example, a client once said, "I am either bad or good. There is no in between." This same client felt that she had to either give in or get out of the relationship with her boyfriend, fight or flee in the face of any interpersonal conflict, and shout or shut up. Tasks were either possible or impossible; she was either happy or unhappy, flawed or perfect. For her, if a performance was not perfect, then it was totally flawed.

Subjective Style of Reasoning. When shame-prone people use a subjective style of reasoning, the process is based on conclusions from emotions that are felt very strongly or not at all and a need to justify their reactions. They may arrive at conclusions such as, "I am mad; therefore, someone else has made me angry." There is an acceptance of one's own meaning of an event without reality-testing or awareness of distortions.

Obsessive Thinking. Shame-prone individuals often get caught up in their own impressions of how others might be viewing them. Much of this stems from frantic efforts to avoid real or imagined abandonment (Lansky, 1985). Because they do not check out these assumptions, their thinking gets more and more negative and distorted. These thoughts become so repetitive that they interfere with other cognitive and emotional processes. The individual becomes blocked from seeing alternatives. He or she can only see one thing—if people discover my flaw, they will surely abandon me. Protection against being discovered controls his/her behavior as well as thoughts.

Behavioral Patterns

Shame-prone behavioral patterns include nonverbal indications, interpersonal behaviors, and individual behavior (see Table 8.2). Some nonverbal behaviors have been identified earlier, particularly in the case of Marilyn described in Chapter 1. These clues to shame-proneness are invaluable. The individual and interpersonal behaviors of shame-prone individuals can be observed as they occur between the therapist and client in individual therapy, in therapy sessions with other family members, and as reported to occur outside of sessions in other relationships.

Nonverbal Signs.   Nonverbal indications of shame include avoidance of mutual facial gazing and direct eye-to-eye contact. Some clients become uncomfortable when therapists or others look directly at them. They may avert their eyes, put their head down, or blush. Others may deal with direct eye contact by adopting a staring posture (Kaufman, 1989). They will stare directly into others' eyes in a counter attempt to embarrass them. This type of stare usually involves a quality of emptiness, as if the person is dissociating in an effort to avoid the shame. Somewhat related to the staring posture is the adoption of the frozen face. These individuals fail to demonstrate variation in facial expression. They look the same most of the time, even in contexts requiring smiling, surprise, or sadness. Other shame-prone individuals may adopt a mask-like face. For example, a client might always smile whenever shaming events occur or are discussed; this smile masks the shame. Other nonverbal behaviors indicative of shame include the head-back look; using hair to hide one's face; hands over parts of the face, especially eyes; and looks of contempt (Kaufman, 1989).

Interpersonal Behavioral Patterns.   In individual therapy, clients will describe many of the following characteristics as they talk about relating to others; in some instances the therapist may be able to directly observe the behaviors as they occur in the therapy session. In sessions with couples or families, the therapist can observe the behaviors as spouses and family members interact.

Most shame-prone people display a pattern of unstable and intense interpersonal relationships (Bradshaw, 1988). They are often attracted to people who are as needy as they are, always with the hope that when they meet their partners needs, their partners will take care of them too (Slipp, 1988). This often leads to serial relationships, in which partners' needs to be dependent and taken care of wear them down and prove their shame. The enticement of these kinds of relationships moves them rather quickly from one to another. In some relationships partners feel overwhelmed by the demands for dependency. When shame-prone individuals sense they may be abandoned, they reject first.

Shame-prone individuals are often codependent and form relationships with others who are codependent (Wegscheider-Cruse & Cruse, 1989). The inappropriate mutual caretaking that results leads to great instability in the relationship; yet neither partner will leave the relationship because of the mutual codependency.

Shame-prone individuals are almost always exploitive of others (Lewis, 1987). They often make preemptive strikes against others. Anticipating others' negative feelings and thoughts in relation to them, they strike first so that others cannot abandon them or really discover their shame. In actual therapy sessions, such clients may attempt to control what happens as a way of maintaining power. As long as they stay powerful, they can keep others from discovering their hidden shame. Other may become openly scornful of the therapist or other family members. By turning on others in contemptuous ways, shame-prone individuals distract others away from the shame. When others must defend themselves against personal attack, it will feel to shame-prone persons that their own shame will not be easily discovered. Rageful behavior in the form of yelling, name calling, sarcasm, and even physical threat and violence is often manifested when there is a threat that a person's shame will be discovered. Power, contempt, and rage in interpersonal interactions are strong indicators that shame is involved (Kaufman, 1989).

Shame-prone persons often choose to be involved with people and situations that lead to disappointment, failure, or mistreatment even when better options are clearly available (Gelles & Cornell, 1985). They often incite angry or rejecting responses from others and then feel hurt, defeated, or humiliated. Such chronic victimization is a sign that both dependency and intimacy needs have gone unfulfilled in the family of origin.

In the therapy context, shame-prone clients often reject or render ineffective the attempts of their therapists to help them. When clients report that they have seen a number of therapists, the current therapist should suspect that shame is an underlying dynamic of the problem. In family and other relationships outside of therapy, these clients will sabotage attempts to help them or refuse to be helped altogether. Many times attitudes of "being strong" and "handling things alone" are manifestations of underlying shame.

It is not uncommon for shame-prone individuals to respond to events that should be experienced as positive with depression, guilt, or behavior that produces pain, such as an accident (Lewis, 1986). They behave consistently with their mental template. When some event is positive, they assume that it must be a fluke; it will only be a matter of time before something bad happens.

Shame-prone individuals often demand that others always treat them with kindness. This attitude inevitably leads to a letdown, since even the most loving friend has difficulty being consistently kind. Any single lapse can be transformed into the attitude "people always ignore my wishes" (Beck, 1988). Even when others treat shame-prone persons with respect and love, they often react with rejection and suspicion.

Melding with the desires, wishes, feelings, and thoughts of others should also be an indication that a shame-prone identity is in operation (Lewis, 1958; Severine, McNut, & Feder, 1987). Melding describes the lack of clear differentiation that exists in shame-prone individuals. They have to be either totally isolated from others or just like them in thought, feeling, and desires. There is no comfortable middle ground.

In some cases of proneness to shame, anger becomes sexualized. Consequently, these shame-prone people act out in various sexual activities, which are usually demeaning to themselves as well as the other people involved (Russell, 1984). Men or women who attempt to demean or humiliate themselves or their partners through some sexual act have shame-prone identities. They feel they are flawed. They experience the rage at not having intimacy or dependency needs met, and they lash out in sexual ways (Carnes, 1989). Shame is always at the base of such sexualized anger.

Individual Behavioral Patterns.   Perfectionism or other compensatory behaviors are symptoms exhibited by people who have shame-prone identities (Morrison, 1987). One very successful business executive who supervised the activities of thousands of employees in over 15 different subsidiary companies confessed in therapy that nothing he could ever do would be good enough. Inside he would still be flawed and no good. Overachievement can be a symptom of hidden shame. Observers seldom guess that an overachiever feels so "bad" inside because the achievements cover the shame. However, in these individuals the achievement orientation is an unfulfilling, never-ending, false atonement. It is an obsessive and compulsive attempt to transform one's inner core by doing, but the doing is never sufficient to change one's core.

Shame-prone individuals may withdraw into themselves. When this happens, their personality shuts down and turns inward, keeping the real flawed individual hidden from view. The interpersonal game is one of "keep away, see if you can find me." But this internal withdrawal can also be a type of dissociation, in which the individual splits off parts of himself/herself to avoid dealing with pain.

Denial, a defense that denies access to the self (Lauer, 1961), is common to all shame-prone identities. As behavior it disconfirms other people and the situation while protecting one from having to examine any personal motivations or accept responsibility for behavior. As an attitude it maintains the perceptual distortions and cognitive styles discussed earlier.

Using humor that is sarcastic or self-deprecatory may also be an indication that shame is present. When humor is used in rigid ways to put others off, it most likely is a protection against having to face shame directly. Self-belittling humor is often used by shame-prone individuals to indirectly check out others' evaluations of them. When others respond with reassurance or even praise, shame-prone individuals distort the information and assume they are just being kind and not telling the truth.

Shame-prone individuals often engage in activities that are shaming (Wicker, Payne, & Morgan, 1983). For example, they are often excessively involved in pleasurable activities that have a high potential for painful consequences, such as unrestrained buying sprees, sexual indiscretions, or foolish business investments. A series of such events in a client's life should be seen as one indicator of a shame-prone identity.

Psychopathology and Shame

Kaufman (1989) asserts that current systems for diagnosing psychopathology should be reexamined from the perspective of shame. Shame alone does not produce all forms of psychopathology, nor do all emotional and mental disorders have shame as a contributing dynamic. However, internalized shame should be considered in a large majority of *DSM-III-R* disorders (Kaufman, 1989). Whenever clinicians see cases that involve addictions and codependency, physical or sexual abuse, problems with sexuality and sexual dysfunctions, eating disorders, phobias and anxiety disorders, affective disorders, personality disorders, borderlines (Lansky, 1986), narcissism (Miller, 1988), or paranoia, they should assess these clients for internalized shame.

ASSESSING SHAME-PRONE COUPLES AND FAMILIES

Experience and knowledge in assessing families and couples are essential before one attempts to assess shame-prone systems. It is also essential that one assess all family members for proneness to shame. The order of individual and couple or family assessment should be matched to the uniqueness of each case and to the style of the therapist.

As indicated in Chapter 4, couples and families have identities that influence the attitudes, beliefs, feelings and behaviors of these units. For example, three identities are involved in a two-person relationship—one for each of the individuals and the one for the couple. The makeup of a family's identity is much more complex, with numerous two-person and three-person relationship systems, plus the spouse system, the sibling system, and parent-child systems. Shame-proneness may be embedded in some or all of these units of the family system. To be effective, therapists must deal with all shame-prone identities. It is just as important to include the identity of the system in assessment strategies as it is to include identities of individuals.

While the focus in this section is on families and couples, the methodology can be applied to other systems, e.g., parent-child, sibling, dating, and friendship relationships. It is important to consider the system identity, interpretations of formal, standardized measures, and informal observational measures.

Couple and Family Identity

Family identity has been written about in Chapters 4, 5, and 6 in terms of how families feel inside and how they look to others. Couple identity is similar in that couples can exhibit various combinations of feeling good or bad and appearing good or bad to outsiders. If couples or families have shame-prone identities, treatment goals should include changing the system's identity toward a more healthy one.

Couple Identity.   The basic assumption in working with couples is that like attracts like. Consequently, shame-prone individuals rarely marry healthy individuals. They attract various combinations of shame-proneness; e.g., someone shamed on intimacy may marry a totally shame-prone individual. Table 8.3 identifies possible variations of shame in couples. Using this table, the following hypotheses about couple identity can be formulated:

1. *If the identities of both partners are shame-prone, the couple identity is also shame-prone.* This couple looks bad and feels bad.
2. *If the identity of one spouse is shame-prone and his/her partner is shamed on intimacy or dependency, the couple identity is also shame-prone.* Although couples in this category look bad most of the time, in some contexts they may look good; however, they always feel bad. This couple looks good when they are both being accountable and at the same time balancing out the neediness of the partner.
3. *If both partners are shamed on intimacy or if both are shamed on dependency, the couple identity is shame-prone.* Couples who are shamed on dependency look bad and feel bad when their dependency needs are not being met. Couples who are shamed on intim-

TABLE 8.3
Combinations of Shame-Prone Identities in Couples

Identities	Shame-Prone	Shamed on Intimacy	Shamed on Dependency	Not Shame-Prone
Wife				
Husband				
Couple				

acy look bad and feel bad when the intimacy needs are not being met.

4. *If one of the partners is shamed on intimacy and the other one is shamed on dependency, the couple identity is shame-prone.* Couples in this category may look bad and feel bad, or they can look good, but feel bad.

Family Identity.   What does it take for a family to have a shame-prone identity? Must all members have a shame-prone identity for the family to be shame-prone? What about the family of origin and the extended family? Because of the organizational complexity of families, the answers to these questions vary with families and their situations. Table 8.4 heightens therapists' awareness of various combinations as it examines possible combinations.

Across the top are listed four types of identities, totally shame-prone, shamed on intimacy, shamed on dependency, and healthy. The identity of each subsystem on the right (e.g., wife, husband, couple, sibship, each child) can be charted. For specific families other systems may also be added, e.g., parent-grandparent, child-parent, and numerous extended family relationships.

The following hypotheses about family identities can be developed from Table 8.4:

TABLE 8.4
Combinations of Shame-Prone Identities in Families

Identities	*Shame-Prone*	*Shamed on Intimacy*	*Shamed on Dependency*	*Healthy*
Wife				
Husband				
Couple				
Sibship				
Child xl				
Child xn				
Family				

1. *Families may have a shame-prone individual or a shame-prone relationship within the system and not have a shame-prone identity as a system.*
2. *If parents have shame-prone identities, they will likely create a shame-prone family identity.*

Standardized Assessment of Couples and Families

There are no existing paper and pencil measures that directly assess shame in couple or family systems. However, it is possible to integrate concepts from the Circumplex Model of Family Systems (Olson, Sprenkle, & Russell, 1979) with various characteristics of shame. Either the couple or family version of the Family Adaptability and Cohesion Evaluation Scales (FACES III) (Olson, Portner, & Lavee, 1985) can then be used to formally assess the cohesion and adaptability dimensions of the Circumplex Model.

FACES III identifies four different levels of adaptability, which represent a variety of behavioral patterns in areas of power, control, discipline, negotiation, roles, rules, and type of system feedback. The test also identifies four levels of cohesion, representing varying levels of closeness, affection, time spent together, and expressiveness. When levels of cohesion (engaged, separated, connected, enmeshed) and adaptability (rigid, structured, flexible, chaotic) are combined, 16 different couple or family types emerge.

FACES III consists of 40 Likert-scaled items that can be given to each member to assess the level of cohesion and adaptability in a couple or family. The first part of FACES asks respondents to evaluate each dimension currently in the couple or family. The second section asks people to respond to the same questions in terms of how they desire the system to be. In this way the discrepancy between actual and desired levels of cohesion and adaptability can be determined.

Some of the couple or family types identified by the scale are much more shaming than others and consequently have higher potential for producing shame-prone individuals. Table 8.5 identifies possible shaming characteristics for each of the 16 family types.

Assessing two dimensions of accountability (amount and what kind of enforcement by parents), the level of dependency available to young children and whether the kind and amount of dependency vary appropriately with age, and the amount of intimacy available in each of these family types provides information based on the affirmation triangle. The type of affirmation, negative or positive, that dominates in the family and the potential for producing shame and guilt are also included in the table.

For each FACES III type, the *amount of accountability* varies from low to high and is related to both the development of guilt and whether dependency needs get met or not. When accountability is excessively high, indi-

TABLE 8.5
Shame Dynamics in the Circumplex Model

Characteristics related to Shame	Adaptability	Disengaged	Separated	Connected	Enmeshed
Amount of Accountability		Low	Low	Low	Low
Enforcement of Accountability		Little	Little	Little	Little
Dependency for young children		Low	Moderately Low	Moderately low	Moderately low
Dependency changes with children's age	Chaotic	Remains low	Remains low	Remains low	Remains low
Intimacy		Low	Moderately Low	High	High
Family Structure/Boundaries		Loose	Loose	Loose	Loose rules, very blurred personal boundaries
Type of Affirmation		Negative	Mostly Negative	Mostly Negative	Negative
Potential for Shame-prone Identity		High	Moderately High	Moderately High, on dependency	High, shamed dependency
Guilt		Unhealthy, lacking	Unhealthy, lacking	Unhealthy, lacking	Unhealthy, lacking
Amount of Accountability		Moderate	Moderate	Moderate	Moderate
Enforcement of Accountability		Some	Some	Some	Some
Dependency for young children		Low	Moderately Low	High	High
Dependency changes with children's age	Flexible	Remains low	Remains low	Yes	No
Intimacy		Low	Moderately Low	High	High, Smothering
Family Structure/Boundaries		Moderate	Moderate	Moderate	Moderate, blurred personal boundaries
Type of Affirmation		Negative	Mostly Negative	Positive	Mostly Positive
Potential for Shame-prone Identity		High, shamed on intimacy	Moderately High, on Intimacy	Low	Moderately Low
Guilt		Some Unhealthy	Some Unhealthy	Healthy guilt	Mostly healthy

(continued)

TABLE 8.5
(Continued)

Characteristics related to Shame	Adaptability	Disengaged	Separated	Connected	Enmeshed
Amount of Accountability		Moderately High	Moderately High	Moderately High	Moderately High
Enforcement of Accountability		Firm, May be harsh	Firm, May be harsh	Firm	Firm
Dependency for young children		Low	Moderately Low	High	High
Dependency changes with children's age		Remains low	Remains moderately low	Yes	No
Intimacy		Low	Moderately Low	High	High, Smothering
Family Structure/Boundaries	Structured	Firm, rigid	Firm, rigid	Firm	Firm, blurred personal boundaries
Type of Affirmation		Mostly negative	Some Negative	Positive	Moderately positive
Potential for Shame-prone Identity		High	Moderate	Low	Moderately low
Guilt		Moderately Excessive, Unhealthy	Moderately Excessive, Unhealthy	Moderately Excessive, Unhealthy	Moderately Excessive, Unhealthy
Amount of Accountability		High	High	High	High
Enforcement of Accountability		Harsh	Moderately Harsh	Firm, not harsh	Firm, not harsh
Dependency for young children		Low	Low	Moderate	High
Dependency changes with children's age		Remains low	Remains low	Yes	No
Intimacy		Low	Fairly low	Moderate	High, Smothering
Family Structure/Boundaries	Rigid	Firm, rigid	Firm, rigid	Firm, rigid	Rigid rules, blurred personal boundaries
Type of Affirmation		Negative	Mostly negative	Mostly positive	Mostly positive
Potential for Shame-prone Identity		High	Moderately High	Little	Some, Shamed on intimacy
Guilt		Excessive, Unhealthy	Excessive, Unhealthy	Excessive, Unhealthy	Excessive, Unhealthy

viduals in these families will experience much guilt. Whether or not the guilt is part of a shame-bound identity depends on other dynamics in that particular family type. The *enforcement of accountability* is related to the type of discipline that occurs in the family; that can vary from harsh to permissive.

The third item, *dependency for young children* varies from low, meaning that the family type provides little dependency, to high, meaning that dependency needs are met. Of course, this particular dynamic is related to whether or not individual family members will be shamed on dependency. The fourth item, *dependency changes with children's age,* is meant to identify whether or not children are allowed by their parents and the larger system to become increasingly independent as they grow older.

Intimacy, which can vary from low to high, identifies whether or not a particular family type meets the intimacy of its family members. The *family structure/boundaries* item describes whether boundaries are clear and how permeable or impermeable they might be. This dimension is measured by FACES III. The last three items, *type of affirmation, potential for shame-prone identity,* and *guilt* identify whether or not that particular family type is likely to produce shame-prone individuals.

For example, in the rigidly disengaged family the type of affirmation is primarily negative, and the potential for producing shame-prone individuals is high. The level of intimacy and dependency is low, and dependency stays low as children grow older. Consistent with the model presented in Section II, a family type with low intimacy and dependency would be expected to produce shame-prone individuals. In the rigidly disengaged family accountability is very high and harshly enforced, meaning that individuals raised in this family will experience excessive guilt that will likely be used to shame rather than to influence behavior. And, of course, the firm and rigid family structure and boundaries are related to the way accountability is enforced. Each of these dimensions can be identified for every family type in the Circumplex Model.

These hypothesized relationships between Circumplex Model family environments and the potential for producing shame-prone individuals need to be empirically investigated. These classifications are useful only as descriptions and can be verified in therapy as couples and families are observed and assessed.

Table 8.5 postulates that six couple or family types are totally shaming:

- rigidly disengaged
- rigidly separated
- structurally disengaged
- chaotically disengaged
- chaotically separated
- chaotically enmeshed

Couple or family types with issues of intimacy are likely to be:

- flexibly disengaged
- flexibly separated (mildly shaming on intimacy)
- rigidly enmeshed (moderately shaming on intimacy)
- flexibly enmeshed (mildly shaming on intimacy)
- structurally enmeshed (mildly shaming on intimacy)

The couple or family type with issues of dependency is likely to be:

- chaotically connected
- rigidly connected

Because they feel positively affirmed and experience healthy guilt, the following types will be most likely to produce healthy individuals and healthy family identities.

- structurally separated
- structurally connected
- flexibly connected

Informal, Observational Assessment of Couples and Families

In order to assess whether or not a couple or family system is shaming, clinicians need to observe three areas of process: emotional undercurrents, shared belief systems, and interactional patterns. Table 8.6 provides a checklist of couple and family patterns related to shame.

Emotional Undercurrents.   All couples and families exhibit underlying emotional currents or moods. These moods are created by a multitude of cumulative interactions, beliefs, and events. Although healthy families experience negative moods, they do not get stuck in them. In contrast, shaming families seem to exhibit a prominent set of one or possibly two moods. Like shamed individuals, shaming systems do not exhibit a wide range of affect.

A sense of failure is almost always present in shaming systems (Stierlin, 1974a). Individual family members probably will not talk openly about their sense of failure, but it is often exhibited through defensive postures as family members interact with each other. In working with shaming systems, therapists will often become overwhelmed by a sense of failure. They may feel defeated by the multiple problems the family presents or by the family's complicated interactions. It is important that therapists be able to attribute meaning to the sense of failure they feel. After ruling out

TABLE 8.6
Assessment Checklist for Identifying Shaming Systems

Emotional Undercurrents:
• Sense of failure
• Primary mood of family is anger, sadness/depression, or fear

Shared Belief Systems:
• Negative shared social identity ("we're bad")
• Fear of exposure
• Collusions
• High frequency of negative attributions between family members
• Scapegoating
• Dysfunctional family myths

Interactional Patterns:
• Trauma
• Abusive cycles
• Dysfunctional Communication Patterns
  – No talk/non-expressive
  – Secrets
  – Excessive control attempts to protect system
  – Incomplete transactions
  – Blame
  – Disqualifications
• Perfectionism is a common family theme
• Dysfunctional rituals
• Intimacy/dependency is lacking because of unreliability and unpredictability
• Denial
• Intergenerational transmission of shame and denial

---

that the sense of failure is related to therapist family-of-origin or personal issues, therapists should assume that family members also experience this sense of failure. As participant observers, therapists experience the underlying emotional currents of the couple and family just as other family members do.

How the couple or family appears to the outside world, even to the therapist, is not as important as the underlying sense of failure in the system. Because as a system they do not want others to discover their sense of failure or "badness," some couples and families present an image of being "extra good" or even "perfect." They look very good. They push achievement and doing in an effort to transform or even atone for a pervasive sense of failure. Other shame-prone couples and families may have given up trying to protect their image and so appear "bad" to external observers. Regardless of the outward appearance of the system, when a sense of failure seems to be part of the underlying emotional current in the system, therapists may conclude that the system is shaming.

Different couples and families exhibit different primary emotional moods. These moods should be assessed in four ways. First, clinicians should pay particular attention to the emotional currents in early sessions of therapy. Second, therapists should use circular questions to determine what family members think other family members are experiencing emotionally as they interact in the family (Tomm, 1987). For example, a therapist may ask a child what emotions she thinks her father and brother are experiencing in interaction with each other. Follow-up questions such as, "Who else in the family experiences similar feelings to dad? To your brother?" will help elicit the emotional connections in the family. Third, therapists should ask about the typical mood of the couple or family at home. Again, circular questioning may produce the information quickly. Lastly, therapists should pay particular attention to their own emotional process as participant observers in the couple- or family-therapist system (Alonso & Rutan, 1988a).

The emotional mood in shaming systems will be one of anger, sadness/depression, or fear. Although the couple or family will exhibit one of these emotions outwardly, it is safe to assume that individual family members experience the other two as well. For example, if the couple or family appears to be angry most of the time, the clinician may assume that some family members are also feeling sad and scared. The patterns of unmet needs/issues/affect in the treatment map presented in Chapter 10 are experienced by couples and families as well as individuals.

When therapists encounter couples or families that exhibit the above patterns, e.g., a sense of failure and an outward appearance of anger, sadness, or fear, they should be aware that the system will have many unresolved emotional issues. These may stem from family of origin issues that the parents carried into the nuclear family or they may be related to issues of unresolved loss and grief.

For example, in one family the father was always quite openly angry with everyone. The children usually tried to avoid him when he came home from work because he would lay into them for something. The mother responded with similar exchanges of hostility. In exploring their families of origin, I discovered that father's father was very angry with his mother, but never outwardly expressed it. It seemed to me that my client was the child conduit for his father's unresolved anger, which through intergenerational transmission became part of the prominent mood of this nuclear family.

On the other hand, mother's mother had been very passive in response to angry tirades from her father. She had determined that she would never sit and take it as her mother had done. She would defend herself—and so she did. Although the outward expressions of all family members were of anger, they all shared a sense of failure, sadness, and fear. There were issues of loss over what might have been in their family and not over the family's inability to meet needs for dependency and closeness.

Shared Belief Systems. One of the characteristics of a shaming system is the shared negative social meaning (Reiss, 1981). A systemic identity is created in which the couple or all family members believe that the system is bad. They probably have not talked about their beliefs in an explicit way; perhaps this implicitness makes the belief all the more powerful.

Because the couple or family members share a belief that the system is somehow bad, they learn to fear exposure (Nathanson, 1987c). They believe that, if people and systems external to the system were to discover too much information about the internal processes of the couple or family, the family would be censured, possibly even abandoned. To cope with this fear, couple and family members collude with each other to never let the outside world learn their secret.

One of the most difficult tasks facing a therapist or treatment team is recognizing and breaking through collusions in shaming systems. The contracts formed implicitly and explicitly in every relationship set the stage for major collusions between spouses or family members (Zinner, 1974).

Because members of the couple or family are shame-prone to some degree, hidden in the relationship contracts are several shame issues. Individuals believe, "If you will keep my shame hidden, I will keep yours hidden." Another collusion in marriages is that each partner entered into the contract *knowing* that the other one would *not* meet his or her shame-based needs. Each person adopts the following beliefs (in families the beliefs are similar but more complicated because of the numbers of relationships involved):

1. "I see you, my partner. My badness is so bad that it affects you. Therefore, we have a bad relationship because of me."
2. "I see you seeing me. You'll undoubtedly discover my badness. I know that you see my shame because I see you either uncovering or denying my shame."
3. "I see you seeing me, seeing you see me. I believe that you think the same way as I do about me, but I may argue about it. Now we both know that I am bad, and I know that you know."
4. "I see us as a couple. We are bad."
5. "I see you seeing us as a couple. You too see us as bad. It is my fault."
6. "I see you seeing me seeing you see us as a bad couple. I know that you know, that we both agree."

These colluding beliefs tend to maintain and create more shame-prone issues. For example, partners collude to regulate intimacy because they fear that too much intimacy will uncover shame. They collude to regulate dependency because they know, based on their past experiences, that they cannot count on others. They want to avoid the pain of being disappointed one more time. Out of their own pain they also collude to be codependent, to enable their addictions, illnesses, and affairs. They collude to never reveal not only the other's personal shame but also their shame as a couple.

The games and pretenses flourish in practice and subtleties within the couple interaction, hooking the therapist into focusing on individual and couple issues instead of on the system's shame-prone identity. The games and defenses they represent are key issues for assessment and for the therapist and treatment team. The defenses exhibit the collusion.

Family members will also share negative attributions toward family members who exhibit proneness to shame. Labeling statements, such as, "He's the black sheep of the family," "she's just dumb," "don't expect him to do anything kind for anyone," "she's lazy," are shared by several members of the family. Shaming systems exhibit a much higher frequency of negative attributions between individual members than healthy family systems.

These negative attributions often lead to scapegoating the individual or individuals most shame-prone in the couple or family. The couple or family adopts a mindset that is maintained by members' beliefs that they cannot expect the shame-prone individual to operate in positive ways. Their focus on lack of performance, mistakes, negative personal characteristics, and blaming sets up a chronic vicious circle of beliefs that escalates with rigid thinking. Positive behaviors are then seen as a fluke that happen by chance rather than through any real intent or control of the shame-prone individual.

Dysfunctional couple and family myths are developed out of these shared cognitive processes (Bagarozzi & Anderson, 1989). For example, all family members may believe that a particular family member is fragile and that they must be careful how they interact with her. In shaming systems a common myth is "talking about important things is dangerous" (Kramer, 1985).

Interactional Patterns.   Trauma is a common experience in shaming systems (Wegscheider-Cruse & Cruse, 1989). The trauma may be created by the couple's or family's response to extraordinary events, to the demands placed on the system by normal life cycle development, or by everyday patterns of abusive interaction. In any case, the trauma creates an intensely emotional atmosphere in a family system that already has difficulty expressing and dealing openly with emotion.

All systems that are physically, sexually, emotionally, or verbally abusing are shaming (Elkin, 1984; Lansky, 1987, 1984). Abuse or violence in any form is one indication that shame is an underlying dynamic of both the individual and couple/family identity. Name-calling, threats, and intimidation are abusive maneuvers that always shame family members.

The type of communication patterns that occur in shaming couple and family systems include difficulty in talking, excessive attempts to control, failure to complete transactions, blame, denial, disqualification, and secrets (Fossom & Mason, 1986). Difficulty in talking actually helps protect the system because both feelings of shame and shaming behavior never get addressed directly. This "no talk" rule perpetuates secrets. In some cases one generation of the family withholds information about affairs, unwanted pregnancies, abuse, illnesses, or suicides from the next generation (Pillari, 1986). Likewise, family members in the same generation may hide secrets from each other.

Communication and interaction that are controlling are the vanguard of the shaming system (Fossom & Mason, 1986). Members of the system are so frightened by the thought that outsiders will discover the flaw in their family that they *have* to be controlling. When family members feel they are able to control each other and circumstances, they gain a sense of predictability and safety, false as it may be. These control maneuvers may not take the form of domination. Illness, being overly helpful, cute, seductive, or more competent than others, and analyzing/intellectualizing are all ways that keep outsiders from discovering shame in the system.

In shaming systems it is common for communication to be disrupted in a myriad of ways. Conflict and fighting in these families never end with a resolution of the issue or any commitments to changing behavior. Rather, couples or family members just stop in the middle of the conflict, withdraw from each other, and avoid bringing the subject up. After a few days they seem to pretend that the conflict never occurred; they may even deny that the issue is conflictual. In such a system disagreements may be perpetuated for years and yet not openly talked about. This pseudo harmony protects the system from outsiders' discovering its shame. Transactions also remain incomplete in another way. Frequent interruptions, changing of topics, and inability to focus on the content of messages keep communication from being clear. Decisions are never easily reached in these families because so many communication distractions occur that the family gives up before reaching any type of decision.

Blame and frequent disqualifications are additional patterns that occur in shaming systems (Lansky, 1980). When family members sense that anyone is close to discovering their shame, they lash out with rage and blame. The blame keeps others off guard and helps the shame-prone individual deny the shame.

One theme in shaming couple and family systems is perfectionism (Fossom & Mason, 1986). The messages that family members receive from and give to each other are, "We must appear right to outsiders," "It is important to do the right thing." "Right" is not defined in terms of what would be best for the family or for individual members, but rather in terms of what external systems or people would expect. The image of perfection becomes extremely important, even though family members know internally that it is all hypocrisy.

In many cases the shaming couple/family system sets up rituals that maintain and increase its sense of failure and weakness (Wolin & Bennett, & Jacobs, 1988; Wolin & Bennett, 1984). For example, shaming families may set up council meetings that all family members must attend. The purpose of such meetings might be to plan some family event or talk about some problem. The exchanges during the meeting are often heated and personal. Blaming, disqualification, name-calling and incomplete transactions are usually a part of this particular ritual. At some point family members will withdraw, deny that the conflict is intense, and even eat refreshments together. These ritualistic, patterned interactions maintain the shame.

All of the above patterns of interaction combine to create unfulfilled intimacy and dependency needs in system members. They learn not to expect reliability or constancy in relationships. The shame-prone individual adopts the belief that "my needs can never be met if I have to depend on someone else." Couple and family members eventually readjust their expectations and deny their needs by adopting the belief that all relationships are unreliable.

In most shaming systems, transmission of shame and denial can be traced back for several generations (Hoopes, 1987). Frequently issues of loss and unresolved grieving become prevalent as therapists explore three-generational genograms with families (Scharff & Scharff, 1987). The difficulty with talking and expressing emotion keeps grief bottled up. The consequent inability of those individuals to be intimate and allow dependency sets up the dynamics for shame to be not only perpetuated but multiplied in its intensity and rigidity.

When clinicians first interview couples and families, they should use the checklist in Table 8.6 to determine what kind of emotional undercurrents, shared belief systems, and interactional patterns a particular couple or family exhibits. The more shaming a system is, the more symptoms it will exhibit on the checklist. When a couple or family appears to be shaming as exhibited by the symptoms in the checklist, the clinician should then use the individual assessment checklist to see which, if not all, of the family members are shame-prone. Likewise, when a therapist discovers a client who is shame-prone according to the individual checklist, the client's families of origin and procreation should be assessed using the family checklist.

SECTION IV
Clinical Applications

CHAPTER 9

Confronting Your Own Shame as a Therapist

ONE OF THE REASONS that it has taken so long for mental health professionals to pay attention to clients' shame is that to do so therapists would have to face their own shame. There is no way around it—in order to deal with their clients' shame, therapists need to work through their own shame issues (Fossom & Mason, 1986; Kaufman, 1989). Therapists, like clients, defend against having their shame uncovered, which, consequently, has made it easier to collude in ignoring shame. According to Fossom and Mason (1986), facing personal shame reminds people that they are "never completely finished as human beings" (p. 162).

For therapists to work through their own shame, consultation with other trusted professionals is vital (Fossom and Mason, 1986). Trying to resolve issues of shame on one's own is usually counterproductive, since these issues are best resolved in the context of relationships that can be positively affirming and deal with issues of intimacy, dependency, and accountability. Yet it is difficult for most professionals to really open up and share with each other, especially in their own communities. Most people, therapists included, go to great lengths to protect their shame from being discovered by others.

The assumption that therapists must face their own shame does not mean that all clinicians have shame-prone identities, but that all clinicians have experienced and do experience transient shame from time to time (Chapter 3). When experiencing shame as emotion, therapists may act very different from their normal or usual style. Therapists' attitudes about clients and self, emotions, and behavior both in and out of session all change as they get in touch with shame. It is assumed that most therapists have healthy identities and experience transient shame rather than internalized shame. However, many therapists have unresolved intimacy or dependency issues or both that surface in certain contexts.

Using a modification of Figure 6.1, a model of healthy and shame-prone identities, Figure 9.1 illustrates the range within which therapists' shame responses may fall. The shaded area encompasses most of the top right quadrant, with some overlap in the other three. The shaded area is divided into three parts, A, B, and C. Dividing therapists into these three groups allows a description of each group's responses to shame. The responders in group A experience transient shame in some therapy contexts and respond in healthy ways, acknowledging their feelings and moving through them. Therapists whose responses fall most often in the B area likely have either dependency or intimacy issues that surface as shame in certain therapy situations. Therapists in groups A and B are apt to seek consultation from colleagues to check their shame-reactions and assumptions. The responders in group C have issues in both dependency and intimacy and are more shame-prone. They may have difficulty recognizing these issues for what they are. Unless they already have a consultation process in place, they will have great difficulty working them through.

The first step in acknowledging transient shame is for clinicians to

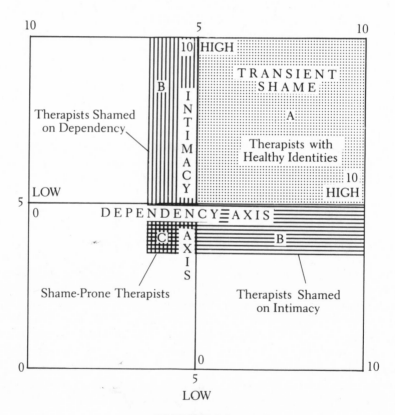

FIGURE 9.1.
Therapist's Shame Responses

become aware of their feelings of shame, regardless of the context but especially in therapy. With some training, clinicians can recognize cues that will help them be more aware when dynamics of shame are operating in their work with clients.

THERAPISTS' SIGNALS FOR RECOGNIZING FEELINGS OF SHAME

There are at least seven signals that indicate therapists are dealing with personal issues of shame with particular clients. These may not apply to every therapist, and therapists, as they become more sensitive to their own signals, can create their own personal list. Shame is likely involved when:

1. Therapists become uncomfortable with their own feelings toward client(s) but deny it.
2. Therapists withdraw emotionally during a session.
3. There is a lack of therapeutic progress, and the case seems stuck.
4. Therapists exhibit codependency and inappropriate caretaking.
5. Therapists experience increased self-doubt and blame themselves for clients' lack of progress.
6. Therapists become outwardly shaming to clients.
7. Therapists dread appointments with specific clients and hope they will fail to appear.

Uncomfortable with Own Feelings

In many training models, therapists are taught that they should not disclose their feelings toward clients, particularly when those feelings involve anger, fear, sadness, or attraction. This supposed position of neutrality helps therapists avoid placing their own moral values, opinions, and feelings on clients (Epstein & Loos, 1989). However, in reality therapists have values and feelings, and it may be impossible for them to remain so neutral (Seymour, 1982).

When therapists become aware of some feeling toward a client and attempt to hide it, they will undoubtedly experience shame. During a supervision session, an intern related that he was quite confused by a therapy session he had just completed with one of his female clients. She had been describing her conflict with a teenage daughter, and the therapist felt he had asked all the appropriate questions. But he was also aware of how beautiful her blue eyes seemed as he listened to her struggle. He sensed a sexual attraction to her that he had not felt in previous sessions. It scared him, and he immediately tried to put it out of his mind. Of course, the more he tried to put it out of his mind, the more his feelings of attraction pushed to the forefront. He said nothing to his client, but at the end of the session he was terribly ashamed of experiencing such feelings.

As we explored the issues in supervision, it became apparent that he was also spending most of the time in therapy sessions listening attentively while his female client "dumped" her problems into his lap. He was a very empathic listener, reflected well, and offered support, but he could see very little change or progress in her. As we explored how he took care of clients—in this case inappropriately—it became clear that the thought of doing anything else was very frightening to him. If he were to insist that therapy be something more than listening and offering support, he would also have to face his own pain, which he was reluctant to do. Through more exploration it became evident that this therapist was shame-prone on issues of dependency.

During a consultation session, a professional colleague reported that he was stuck with a case. When I asked him if he liked the couple he was seeing, he reported that he was extremely angry with the wife. When I asked why he was angry, all he could say was that he did not like her. I tried to explore whether she was similar to anyone in his family of origin or immediate family. As I did so, he withdrew; after a lengthy silence, he blurted out, "Therapists are not supposed to feel this way toward clients! I am supposed to be helpful and caring, not angry and destructive!" When I asked what he had done with his feelings during sessions with this particular couple, he said, "I did everything possible to keep them from knowing how I felt." His own lack of comfort with his feelings and his desire to hide or cover up were indications that he felt shame during his interactions with this couple (Alonso & Rutan, 1988a).

Emotional Withdrawal

A second cue that a therapist needs to recognize in order to face shame is emotional withdrawal during a session. Kaufman (1989) has indicated that the establishment of an interpersonal bridge between therapists and clients is essential to working through shame. When either the therapist or the client moves into experiencing shame, the interpersonal bridge is destroyed unless both can disclose what is really happening to them on the inside. Withdrawing emotionally is just a maneuver to cover some sense of shame. The reasons for the withdrawal may be related to the here-and-now interaction of the session or to the therapist's own personal issues.

The early stages of therapy may go quite well, with therapists emotionally in tune with their clients. If in those sessions the clients begin to work through their denial about their own shame, their needs to be dependent and/or intimate may be sudden, demanding, and unexpected to therapists. These client behaviors may signal within therapists their own shame issues. As a defense, therapists may become distant observers of the process, intellectualizing and giving explanations that take themselves and their clients away from their feelings. As they move into safe territory, therapists may then become once more emotionally attentive. From one session to another, therapists and clients may experience a yo-yo effect as they ride in and out on emotional spurts.

If therapists are aware of their change in behavior and affect, they rationalize it as due to a bad day, the client's craziness, stress, or a phase of therapy. More often than not, therapists avoid having to deal with their own erratic behavior by focusing everything on client behavior.

Lack of Case Progress, Codependency, and Self-Doubt

The three cues of shame, lack of progress, codependency, and self-doubt are related and often occur together. People sometimes choose to enter mental health professions because of their desire to take care of other people. Professional training further convinces these people that they should be caring and helpful. Although it is extremely important for clinicians to exhibit empathy, good listening, and caring behavior, such patterns can turn into inappropriate caretaking. For example, one wife told her marital therapist about a fairly traumatic experience involving her alcoholic father. The therapist was empathic, supportive, and reflected how awful it must have been for her. The more he empathically reflected, the more she "poured" out her heart. Session after session she brought her crises to him and he was empathic and caring. The problem was that nothing was changing.

Although the case seemed to be "stuck," the therapist was reluctant to consult with anyone because he was shamed. He couldn't figure out why she wasn't making progress because he had been so caring. Yet his doubts about his professional competence became more frequent and more intense with each session. Consulting with another therapist meant that he would have to openly explore his doubts about his own abilities. Staying stuck in the rut of increasing self-doubt and codependency with his client seemed preferable. One time when a colleague asked directly about the case, he said that there were no problems and everything was fine, although inside he knew it was a lie.

Patrick Carnes (1989) explained that coaddicts mistake "intensity for intimacy, obsession for love, and control for security" (p. 137). Therapists who exhibit codependency through inappropriate caretaking are similar in that they mistake clients' chronic emotional dumping as helpful and therapeutic, their own empathic abilities as true caring, and the control/countercontrol interactions as security. Through such patterns both clients and therapists collude to keep each other's shame covered.

Experiencing self-doubt, therapists often wonder, "Could I be the reason my client isn't moving faster?" The question is very seldom asked to anyone but the self. Clinicians with shame-prone issues often operate from the same beliefs that Carnes (1989) identified for the addict. In certain contexts, with particular clients, they worry that they might be a "bad, unworthy therapist." They worry that their clients will not love or respect them as they really are. And they worry that their needs to be productive, to help, to facilitate, will not get met if they have to depend on their clients or other colleagues. For many therapists, such beliefs and the feelings associated with them are transient and limited to specific contexts. Others are haunted by these beliefs and behaviors until they actively seek treatment for the shame. All therapists can benefit by actively facing such thoughts and feelings as signals that they are into their own shame, transitory or internalized.

Projecting Shame on Clients

What are some of the signals that therapists might be shaming their clients by projection? Shame-prone clients are easily shamed by the therapist and/or others in the session. Consequently, for therapists to know if they are shaming clients, they must be aware of their own shame issues and changes of their behavior toward clients. When therapists sense their own tendencies to want to do things "to" their clients, this may be a signal that they are projecting their own shame (Pichert & Elam, 1986). Therapists can be not only openly shaming by belittling, using one-up maneuvers, being arrogant, etc., but also subtly shaming by failing to provide appropriate intimacy, dependency, and accountability. For example, if a client is expressing painful emotional experience and the therapist is uncomfortable with the intensity of the emotion, the therapist may be experienced as shaming by the client. The issue may never be dealt with directly, but the client may not be willing to risk sharing emotion again.

Dreading Appointments

Some clients are much more difficult for therapists to like than others. Whenever therapists find themselves wishing that clients would call to cancel their appointment, they should examine the dynamics of shame in the relationship with their clients. While overscheduling and burnout may be the basis of wishing clients would cancel, more often the therapist fears feeling shame in relation to particular clients.

UNIVERSAL ACTIVATORS OF
THERAPIST SHAME

The kinds of contexts that will be shaming to therapists are related to issues of intimacy, accountability, and dependency. According to Kaufman (1989), there are universal activators of shame, meaning that they occur because of the nature of the therapeutic process and are universal across most, if not all, clinicians. There are also shame activators that are specific to every therapist. These particular activators induce shame because they are related to the family of origin, life event history, and personal dynamics of each therapist. Intimacy, dependency, and accountability issues that arise in the process of therapy may include both universal and specific shame activators.

Activators of Therapists' Shame Related to Intimacy

There are basically three kinds of universal activators related to intimacy that have the potential to induce transitory shame in therapists: issues around self and emotional disclosure, touch, and accepting clients' anger and other emotions. The many other specific activators that might exist for particular therapists will be discussed later in this chapter under family-of-origin issues.

Self and Emotional Disclosure. Rules are not clear about how much or how little therapists should disclose about themselves in therapy sessions. Certainly ethical considerations make therapists cautious about talking about any of their own problems. After all, the clients are the ones who are supposed to receive the therapy. Some theoretical approaches assume a more neutral, uninvolved stance in relation to clients than others. Therapists of those orientations follow fairly rigid guidelines about disclosing feelings, thoughts, or experiences. Regardless of theoretical orientation, most therapists experience conflict around issues of disclosing information. There are few therapy guidelines about how, what, or when to self-disclose, so just the uncertainty can become shaming (Kaufman, 1989). Some clients ask for personal information. Therapists' reactions to these requests may be important clues as to whether the request was shaming. At times, therapists find themselves including personal anecdotes about their families or activities and suddenly wonder, "Why an I doing this?" This questioning is often accompanied by embarrassment and a sense of having done something wrong.

If clinicians choose to disclose information about themselves, including their feelings, they become more vulnerable because they become more known. They expose themselves to the "scrutinous" eyes of their clients. However, being aware of personal feelings and thoughts and not disclosing them leads to hiding. And hiding is usually more shaming to most people than taking the risk of disclosing personal information.

Touch in Therapy. To touch or not to touch clients is an issue that most clinicians are forced to resolve. Most clinicians adopt some rule about touching that ranges from not touching clients at all to being willing to offer support in the form of a hand on the arm or shoulder and sometimes even holding a client. Clinicians who adhere to a "no touch" rule may still find themselves wondering how to respond to clients' intense emotional expressions (Kaufman, 1989). While touching must be separated from sexual intentions, not offering some sort of nonverbal support can be a sign that therapists believe they are too inadequate to deal with whatever situations or problems clients present. Some clients will directly ask to be held. In an era where malpractice suits often involve allegations of inappropriate sexual involvement between therapists and clients, most therapists experience conflict about touching clients, and that inner turmoil often turns to transient shame.

Accepting Clients' Anger and Other Emotions. Because the dynamics of shame-prone clients involve restriction in the range and intensity of feelings, the treatment process involves getting clients to share feelings that they have kept covered for long periods of time. The protective emotional layers of shame are anger/hurt and rage. Shame-prone clients will sometimes exhibit intense anger and rage, which gets directed toward their therapists. The task of clinicians is to hear the anger and rage and remain available to the client without getting angry in return (Kaufman, 1989). Of course, these emotionally laden contexts have the potential to shame therapists.

Clients' expressions of other deeper layers of emotion, such as humiliation, fear, and grief, also have the potential to activate shame in therapists. For example, a colleague was doing grief work with a single-parent family because a child in the family had died in an accident. The trauma surrounding the accident accompanied by the intense grief the mother expressed in sessions was overpowering to the therapist. She had lost her own brother in an accident 10 years previously. As her own grief over the loss of her brother welled up inside of her, she did not know whether to follow her impulses to cry or to hide her emotion from the clients sitting in front of her. Having to struggle to make a decision about it was shaming to her. Being able to share a range of feelings, even negative ones, helps create intimacy in relationships. Hiding feelings of which one is aware almost always leads to an experience of shame.

Activators of Therapist Shame Related to Dependency

The nature of the therapeutic relationship is one in which issues of dependency are always involved. Therapists and clients alike worry that clients may become too dependent on therapists for support, consequently eroding self-sufficiency and self-confidence in the client. Therapists are aware that a certain amount of dependency, at least early in the stages of therapy, is needed to create an effective helping relationship. As discussed in Chapter 12, in the early stages of therapy shame-prone clients expect therapists to be total caretakers doing everything "for" them, or they expect to be rejected with therapists doing things "to" them.

When clients are in the mode of wanting to be little and taken care of, they can be demanding and intrusive. Therapists can become very resentful of these demands; at the same time transient shame can be activated because it feels to therapists that they can never be sufficient. For example, a female client told her male therapist that she had become aware that he could never be totally available to her. Hooked by her need to be dependent, her therapist pointed out several ways he really was available to her. The next week he received several calls at home from her, none of which was of an emergency nature. He felt trapped by her neediness, which was now intruding into his own family life. The next session he set limits and told her she could call his house after hours only in times of emergency. She replied, "See, I told you that you could not be available to me." He responded by pointing out that he could be her therapist but he could not assume the role of a close friend whom she could call at any time. He became shamed during the session by her demandingness, which in turn led to his distancing, which in turn confirmed her suspicions that he would eventually abandon her. Thus, client shame begot therapist shame.

Even when therapists do not have unresolved dependency issues in their own families, they may have trouble with the dependency demands of clients. One of the reasons for this is that therapists do not choose to accept the dependency demands of clients in the way they do with children. To be expected to act like a parent to a client can be a frightening and overwhelming demand to a therapist. Such contexts have the potential to activate shame in therapists because of the feelings of insufficiency and intrusiveness that result.

Joan wanted her therapist to be her surrogate husband. Of course, she never expressed this fantasy directly, but she hinted at it a number of times. She wanted to be quite dependent, called just to talk, and suggested that they get together to enjoy social activities outside the therapy session. Her therapist set limits, refused to be involved in any type of dual relationship, and handled her anger and shame around his seeming rejections. Yet, when she informed him openly in a very shameless way that she whispered his name over and over again as she masturbated his shame was activated. Such dependency/counter-dependency scenes are not at all unusual when working with shame-based clients.

Activators of Therapist Shame Related to Accountability

There are several universal activators of shame related to accountability. The therapy relationship involves roles of help-seeking and help-giving, which naturally sets up therapists to potentially experience guilt and perhaps transitory shame. Universal activators of shame related to accountability include limitations of therapist power, recognizing mistakes, being at an impasse with a case, therapist uncertainty, and client discouragement (Kaufman, 1989).

Limitations of Therapist Power.   Inexperienced therapists have difficulty accepting the notion that they cannot heal everyone and every problem. As stated by Kaufman (1989), the challenge for all therapists, experienced and inexperienced alike, is to "accept feeling limited without feeling lesser for the limitation" (p. 230). The power to effect positive change always rests with clients. Therapists need to be caring, but they cannot be entirely responsible for clients' progress. Feeling responsible for change and perhaps even for the ultimate outcome of therapy places therapists in a situation in which they will experience shame. The reason shame is more likely to be experienced than guilt is that therapists usually cannot identify any specific behavior they can change. Rather, the issue turns inward to questioning personal competence.

Recognizing Mistakes.   Most therapists find it hard to recognize and admit mistakes to clients. But mistakes do occur and are a natural result of being human and imperfect. Denying that mistakes happen maintains therapists' shame, whereas "owning up" to their part in the system helps therapists face and even tolerate their own shame. By admitting mistakes, therapists demonstrate that they will share responsibility with their clients (Kaufman, 1989).

Being at an Impasse with a Case.   Seeming failure or feeling "stuck" with a case also hooks therapists' accountability issues and turns them to shame. Refusal to be open with feelings about impasses and inability to admit mistakes prevent therapists from restoring the therapeutic relationship. Both clients and therapists will feel shamed when this happens. In reality, "feeling stuck" can be a part of any relationship at times. In most cases such impasses generate opportunities for evaluation and growth. At such times therapists will minimize their own and their clients' shame by being open about how they feel and by seeking consultation. Clients benefit from watching a therapist who appears to accept mistakes without feeling chronically limited (Kaufman, 1989).

Therapists' Uncertainty.   Because they have not had experience with a wide range of presenting client problems, inexperienced therapists experience uncertainty about a number of things. They have difficulty predicting which cases have good prognoses and can be treated in short periods of time, with observable improvement, and which cases have poor prognoses and may be in therapy for long periods, demonstrating slow improvement.

Characteristics of therapists who usually have positive outcomes in therapy include the ability to openly negotiate and establish specific goals, interventions, and predicted length of therapy with clients, as well as to be persuasive and confident (Jones, Cumming, & Horowitz, 1988). When therapists have difficulty with such skills, it is often because of their uncertainty about being accountable that leads to feeling helpless, limited, and shamed.

Clients' Discouragement. Discouraged clients have the universal capacity to shame therapists. When therapists do not reframe client discouragement as issues of shame, clients are likely to drop out of therapy (Kaufman, 1989). When therapists discover themselves implicitly or explicitly blaming clients for not progressing in therapy, they are using blame to protect their own feelings of shame. Such a scenario is similar to families in which some apparent failure induces feelings of shame, to which family members respond by blaming one particular person or each other. If therapists cannot recognize and experience their own shame, they will not be able to explore clients' discouragement as a form of shame.

THE THERAPIST'S FAMILY-OF-ORIGIN
AND LIFE HISTORY EVENTS

In addition to these universal activators of shame, there are shame activators that are specific to each therapist. These activators induce shame because they hook into family-of-origin issues, life event dynamics that have not been resolved for that particular therapist, or other specific situations.

Unresolved issues in therapists' own families of origin set the stage for the therapy process to activate shame in them. In contrast, ongoing willingness to explore such issues helps therapists face their own ghosts and resolve unfinished business (Fossom & Mason, 1986). These family-of-origin disturbances create opportunities for therapists to grow, provided they will confront their own shame.

In a supervision group Steve presented a case involving a couple and their teenage daughter. Steve felt stuck with the case and found himself extremely angry at the father. As the group observed video segments of therapy sessions, they commented on the difference in Steve's voice tone when he talked to the father. He seemed harsher, more on edge whenever he talked to the father than when he spoke to mother or daughter. Steve admitted that maybe he was taking care of both the mother's and the daughter's issues by fighting with the father. He also noted that both mother and daughter seemed afraid to confront their husband and father directly with how they felt.

When asked whether or not any of these clients reminded him of anyone from his family of origin, Steve turned deep red and his eyes fell to the floor. After several minutes of silence followed by tears, he disclosed that the husband reminded him of his grandfather, who was an alcoholic. During his adolescent years and even into adulthood, Steve had engaged his grandfather in terrible battles because of how his grandfather had treated his mother, who of course had enabled the grandfather and even defended him from Steve's attacks.

As Steve reported the story of how he had tried to get his grandfather into treatment, the group commented on how much his mother had subtly sabotaged the attempt. As he thought about that comment, Steve became aware of how angry he was at his mother for enabling his grandfather. As the supervision group pushed him to make the connection to his current case, Steve acknowledged that he felt some anger toward the wife for allowing her husband to verbally abuse their daughter. Steve had met his unfinished business in the therapy session with his own clients. How therapists face such challenges determines whether they internalize the shame or become positively affirmed by resolving the personal issue.

It is impossible to list every specific activator of shame that comes from therapists' families of origin or life event history. However, when therapists come from family systems that involve addiction, codependency, or chronic trauma of any kind, they need to do some shame work of their own before they can be effective therapists with shame-prone clients. Although they may be helpful in some cases, they will undoubtedly encounter situations in therapy that will key into their family-of-origin issues and interpersonal dynamics.

Discovering Specific Shame Activators

To understand what activators specifically induce either transitory or internalized shame, therapists need to explore the following:

- How shame feels inside.
- What events specifically activate their shame.
- Their own concurrent responses to shame: affects, thoughts, memories, and behavior.
- Who/what in their own lives they explicitly and implicitly shame.
- How they defend against shame.

By being aware of oneself, including emotions that are experienced, therapists can discover exactly how they feel when they experience shame. Feelings of anger, rage, fear, and grief should be seen as opportunities to ask the question, "Am I also experiencing shame?" Being aware of the kinds of words that describe the feeling of shame may also be helpful for some therapists. Words that describe a mild state of shame include *uncertain, lacking confidence, insufficient,* and *unsure of self.* More moderate descriptors include *overwhelmed, inadequate, immobilized, incapable, lacking, deficient,* and *incompetent.* The most severe descriptions of shame might include words like *worthless, good for nothing, inferior, crippled, useless,* and *failure* (Hammond, Hepworth, & Smith, 1980).

Therapists can also use proprioceptive body signals to determine when and how they experience shame. Tension in facial muscles, neck, and back may be specific indicators for some, while for others knots in the stomach, gastric distress, and diarrhea may be indicators.

In identifying what events specifically activate their shame, therapists need to focus on what client needs and feelings seem to be connected to the events and their feelings of shame as a therapist. Many times the expression of some particular feeling by clients, such as anger, hurt, or sadness, will be connected to the therapist's sense of shame. Sometimes certain topics or issues will evoke shame. This is particularly true when clients describe problems that therapists have not resolved in their own lives (Alonso & Rutan, 1988a). During the course of marital therapy a husband disclosed an emotional affair with another woman from which he was having a hard time pulling away. As he discussed the compulsive nature of his attraction to this woman, the therapist became shamefully aware that the client's involvement sounded very much like his relationship with a female colleague who shared office space with him.

As therapists become aware of their feelings of shame, they should pay attention to their associated thoughts, memories, images, other feelings, and behavior. Doing so often facilitates the linking of current experience with past family or life event experiences. In exploring the context of her shameful feelings, one therapist recovered with the help of her supervisor memories about a time when her mother was seriously ill. Her parents' marriage was unstable at the time, and her mother and father retreated to their bedroom each night to fight out their conflict. She reported lying in bed listening to the loud shouts and name-calling emanate from their bedroom. She worried that somehow it was all her fault. When her mother became ill, she remembered thinking that God was punishing the entire family for how bad they were. The identity of the family as being bad was an important clue for the therapist. After sharing the memory, she reported to her supervisor that she hadn't thought about that for years. In fact, she had never been able to recall so vividly what she had thought and how she felt during that time.

In addition to identifying memories and feelings, therapists need to be aware of how they exhibit feelings of shame behaviorally (Pichert & Elam, 1986). Withdrawal, irritation, blaming, criticism, dissociation from events and feelings, and lashing out are various behavioral manifestations that shame is operating.

Because shaming others through blame, name-calling, etc., is evidence that shame may be in operation, therapists need to examine their own lives to see if there are individuals or groups of people whom they consistently shame. Constantly being critical of oneself, family members, and others serves as a way of acting out one's shame. It is also possible to talk disparagingly about situations, objects, or even ideas in a shaming way. For example, one therapist was highly critical of sex addicts. The professional community was quite shocked when they learned that he had been arrested for soliciting a prostitute who was actually an undercover police officer. As the story unfolded, he had been highly involved in pornography and many forms of compulsive sexual behavior. Many times individuals are shaming of people, groups, ideas, events, etc., that are representative of personal characteristics for which they have tremendous dislike or even hatred.

Of course, shaming others is just one way of defending against one's own shame. Therapists need to examine other ways that they characteristically defend against shame. Becoming overly involved in others' problems can be a way of not having to look at one's own shame. Becoming angry or fearful, playing martyr or victim, lying, overworking, overcontrolling, and talking too much are other ways that people defend against their shame.

Understanding their own personal defenses helps therapists better process relationships with their clients. Therapists who work through their own shame can help clients to do likewise. As therapists explore these areas, they become vulnerable along with their clients. Knowing that their therapists can do so gives clients courage (Kaufman, 1989).

EMPOWERING ONESELF AS A THERAPIST

To counteract transient shame, therapists can empower themselves by being accountable "to" and "for" themselves. This can be done in many effective ways. Therapists should experiment until they discover what works for them. They should not hesitate to trade in routines and rituals for newly designed strategies. The following three examples represent possible ways of empowering oneself as a therapist.

Positive Affirmations

Developing and practicing positive affirmations is an important consideration for therapists as well as for clients (Bradshaw, 1988). When therapists feel positively affirmed in their professional role, they enjoy their work more and suffer less burnout. Working with shame-prone clients is not an easy task. Therapists have to guard against having their own shame activated. Even when they do that, it is easy to be overwhelmed by the pain of shame-prone clients.

Paying attention to their internal dialogue can help therapists avoid their own shame traps. The right affirmation will counteract the shameful internal dialogue. Stated very positively, the content of the affirmation describes therapists' strengths at their best. Therapists should create their own positively affirming statements and images; the following examples may serve as a starting point.

These affirmations relate to intimacy.

- "I am warm and loving and others benefit from being around me."
- "Who I am is as important to clients as what I do in therapy."
- "Clients accept me best when I am really who I am."
- "I am real and other people really like who I am."
- "I receive and initiate touch and am clear about the meaning of that touch. I also help clients understand the meaning of it."
- "Expressing my observations and feelings about clients helps them as well as me."
- "I am free to be myself in session—I am free to get out of my chair and move around the room. I am free to structure experiential exercises."

Affirmations related to dependency are:

- "I am free to choose when clients can be dependent on me—I am not bounded by their desires to be totally dependent."
- "I allow my clients to be dependent on me when that is appropriate, but I set limits and work this through in the relationship. I know that my clients will become more independent as therapy progresses."
- "I recognize that clients' desires to be dependent on me indicate that our therapeutic relationship is developing as it should."

The following affirmations are related to accountability/responsibility:

- "My many talents and skills serve clients when they allow me to help them."
- "I love the growth I am experiencing and gratefully explore my own issues as they relate to the therapy process."
- "I let my clients be responsible for their own progress in therapy."
- "I am satisfied with my therapy because I am adept at processing my role in therapy as established by my own criteria."

This last affirmation may have many parts, e.g., "I was myself. I expressed my observations and feelings in a helpful way without feeling restrained by the client system. I pushed clients to look at issues and alternatives even though it was painful for them. I maintained the relationship even when the client felt shamed by me. I enjoyed doing therapy."

Having Fun in Therapy

To have fun in therapy with shame-prone clients, one must be present and alive. Be curious! Be energetic and in tune with clients' energy. Therapists can act each moment as though they have never been in that moment before, because they haven't. Therapists can be alive to their own responses as well as to clients'. It is appropriate to be cautious about the way one creates fun because shame-prone clients distrust having fun. They distrust it because they are unworthy and unpracticed in knowing and experiencing it.

Experienced therapists know the routines of therapy and can execute them in their sleep. Because shame-prone clients often have a history of many kinds of therapy and therapists, they know the typical routines as well. Although it may be frightening to them to have a therapist who meets them with consistent "aliveness," they will learn to trust it and respond positively to it.

Humor can heal many hurts. Appropriate humor can be very effective with shame-prone clients if they trust that it is not at their expense. Telling jokes and funny stories, if not overdone, teaches clients that they can be less serious than they usually are.

Participating in a Vibrant Support Group

A good support group is one that allows therapists to be who they are with all their strengths as well as with weaknesses and fears. People who believe in growth, who welcome feedback and can also dispense it, foster the kind of support and love needed. The group can take many forms, e.g., 12-step, a Patent support group (Patent, 1989), supervision, therapy, group practice, and special interest. The basic criterion for the group is that a therapist's needs are met, including that of being a valued contributing member.

Therapists can be responsible for developing a support group that works for them. In examining reasons for not being currently involved in a support group, therapists may discover that they are worried about being shamed. Facing that shame and owning up to it will be the first step toward getting support.

CHAPTER 10

Treatment Map
for Working Through
Shame-Prone Patterns

THE TREATMENT MAP described in this chapter can be used in three ways: for determining how to enter a client's shame, for guiding in-session work related to unmet needs and associated interpersonal issues and affect, and for evaluating the overall progress of treatment. With modification, it can also be used for assessing and treating shame-prone systems. The map in Table 10.1 illustrates patterns of unmet needs, interpersonal issues, and emotions that together form the basis of shame-prone identities.

The following assumptions underlie the construction of the map:

1. Everyone has a basic need to be whole, to be psychologically healthy in all aspects of their lives; that need for psychological health has a direct bearing on all other aspects of living.
2. If the psychological needs are met with some consistency, children develop healthy identities.
3. Individuals whose needs are not regularly met are likely to be shame-prone.
4. With assistance shame-prone people can work through the layers of patterns of unmet needs and associated interpersonal issues and emotions to eventually attain health or, more specifically healthy identities.

DESCRIPTION OF THE MAP

This map utilizes the concepts presented in Chapter 3, Table 3.1. However, the map adds internal and behavioral responses to needs not met; in

TABLE 10.1
A Map for Treatment of Shame

EMOTIONS

INTERNAL RESPONSES TO NEEDS NOT MET	BEHAVIORAL RESPONSES TO NEEDS NOT MET	PSYCHOLOGICAL NEEDS	(Nonspecific) RAGE	ANGER/HURT	HUMILIATION	FEAR	TERROR	GRIEF	JOY
Cynicism	Reclusiveness	(1) INTIMACY	INSUFFICIENCY						
Passive-Aggressive	Immobility	(2) PRODUCTIVITY		REJECTION					
Powerlessness	Victim Martyr Abuser	(3) DEPENDENCY			WORTHLESSNESS				
Helplessness	Craziness Addiction Co-dependency	(4) SENSE AND ORDER				ABANDONMENT			
Hopelessness	Suicide Disease	(5) UNIQUENESS					EMPTINESS		
Blocked	Unstable	(6) CHOICES						LOSS	
Hope	(NEEDS MET) Adaptation	(7) WHOLENESS							ACCEPTANCE

SHAME-PRONE ISSUES

addition, it is in a form that can be easily referred to during treatment. The column on the left identifies seven psychological needs. The first six needs are often unmet for shame-prone individuals, and so the column also identifies internal and behavioral responses when the needs go unmet. The last need of wholeness is the goal for good emotional and mental health. The internal and behavioral responses associated with that need occur when the need is met. Interpersonal issues associated with each unmet need are represented in the diagonal boxes. Emotions associated with each unmet need and interpersonal issue are represented across the top of the map.

Unmet Psychological Needs

The regular meeting of several needs is important to everyone's emotional and mental health. These needs, identified in the left column of Table 10.1, include: (1) to be *intimate*; (2) to be *productive*; (3) to be *dependent* on one's parents; (4) to make *sense and order* out of one's world; (5) to be recognized and valued as *unique* by parents, other family members, and others outside the family; (6) to experience and welcome *choices* as part of making changes; and (7) to be *whole-healthy*. Accountable adults in healthy families meet the needs of their children, at least enough of the time for their children to develop adequate coping skills and healthy identities.

When these needs are not met on a fairly consistent basis, individuals respond internally as well as behaviorally. The internal responses that correspond to specific unmet needs include: (1) *cynicism*; (2) *passive-aggressive* attitudes; (3) beliefs and attitudes of *powerlessness*; (4) a sense of *helplessness* and *littleness*; (5) a certainty of defeat or *hopelessness*; and (6) uncertainty with an awareness of being *blocked*. When the need to be whole is met, individuals respond internally with *peace* and *excitement* to the possibilities in life.

The behavioral manifestations to unmet needs include: (1) *reclusiveness*; (2) *immobility*; (3) *victim, abusive,* and *martyr* patterns; (4) *crazy behavior* with *addictive* and *codependent* patterns; (5) *suicidal thoughts* and *actions and physical diseases*; and (6) *unstable behavior*. The behavioral response to the met need for wholeness is *competent congruent behavior—adaptation, negotiation,* and *conflict resolution*. The behavioral manifestations serve as clues that lead the therapist to the internal responses.

Interpersonal Issues

The interpersonal issues associated with the unmet needs are presented on the diagonal. These issues occur in pattern with specific emotions and unmet needs. The issues identified within the diagonal boxes are: (1) *insufficiency* ("I'm not good enough"); (2) *fear of rejection* (how soon and by whom); (3) *worthlessness* ("Everyone knows I am bad—no one wants me"); (4) *abandonment* ("Because I am bad I will be left alone"); (5) *emptiness* accompanied by *loneliness* and *isolation*; and (6) *loss* accompanied by *grief*. The interpersonal issue of *acceptance* is related to wholeness and is reflected in mature acceptance of what "never was" (e.g., a loving, kind father) and "never will be" (e.g., no one can be a child again and reclaim what was missing).

Emotions

Across the top of the map are listed seven emotions that represent some of the basic emotional experiences of healthy individuals: (1) *rage (nonspecific)*; (2) *anger/hurt*; (3) *humiliation*; (4) *fear*; (5) *terror*; (6) *grief*; and (7) *joy*. Shame-prone individuals have a limited range of these emotions. Sometimes they appear to be totally shut down, and they have difficulty getting in touch with any emotional experience. Others seem to be stuck in one or two emotional categories. Whatever emotion they seem to be exhibiting can be used as an entrance point to their shame. For example, if clients seem to be expressing predominantly anger and rage, the therapist can focus on interpersonal issues related to insufficiency and rejection and unmet needs of intimacy and productivity.

With the exception of joy the affect represented in this map reflects individuals' responses to a disruption or a conflict in achieving or maintaining psychological needs over time. A person moves from experiencing transient feelings of shame toward being shame-prone when feelings of humiliation increase in frequency, intensity, and duration. When a person has been shame-prone for a long period of time, he cannot remember when he ever felt different. Although an increase in frequency, intensity, and duration of humiliation is a definite indicator of the shame-based syndrome, increases in dimensions of rage, anger/hurt, and fear can also signal shame as an underlying dynamic.

PATTERNS ASSOCIATED WITH SHAME

Each set of unmet needs and accompanying interpersonal issues and emotions is referred to as a pattern. The need, issue, and emotion occur together and often simultaneously. These unmet need/issue/emotion patterns are also referred to as layered because, when one pattern is operating, the other patterns may be present as well.

The following assumptions are made about the unmet need/issue/emotion patterns:

1. Each pattern is complex in and of itself.
2. All of the patterns interact with each other, increasing the com-

plexity. Inside shame-prone individuals the interactions are dynamic, confused, integrated into shame-prone identity, and holistic from a dysfunctional perspective.

3. All but the last pattern of wholeness/acceptance/joy represent manifestations of proneness to shame.

4. People who are shame-prone have affective residues and interpersonal issues related to life experiences within every pattern, some more debilitating than others.

5. Discussing each pattern as if it were a separate dynamic is an arbitrary separation necessitated by language.

6. The goal of treatment is to help clients meet the seventh psychological need—to be whole-healthy. The seventh pattern suggests what the result can be for clients who successfully work through the other six patterns.

Pattern of
Intimacy/Insufficiency/Nonspecific Rage

Individuals. Table 10.2 illustrates the characteristics of this pattern. The internal and behavioral responses of individuals who do not have their intimacy needs met greatly influence the dynamics of this pattern. Individuals shamed on intimacy in their families of origin build walls of protection and skepticism. Anyone who attempts to be intimate with them meets a solid wall of cynicism that seems to say "I don't care." This cynicism is protective. Underneath the protection lies a different message, "I don't dare care—I have been disappointed too many times." Others' attempts to be close elicit other messages full of skepticism: "Who are you trying to run a number on? We all know that I am not worthy of being close to you, so what do you really want?"

Reclusiveness, a set of behaviors that minimizes interaction with others, is a way to guarantee that the individual does not have to deal with intimate overtures or the lack of them. To avoid being disappointed, such people practice the often unconscious "game" of dismissing or discounting others. By ignoring others and devaluing what they say or do, they avoid risking disappointment again. Even positive attempts by a spouse or friend can be brushed aside because the shame-prone individual is too bruised to accept the act at face value. Whether reclusive or cynical, these individuals may be sexually involved with others, e.g., marital partners, or superficially with friends, but they never feel satisfied and many encounters are either painful, superficial, or artificial. Whether they can achieve real intimacy with sexual partners depends on the severity of the internalized shame. The seeming "normalcy" in these relationships may mask severity of the interpersonal issue of *insufficiency*, not being worthy, not being enough.

TABLE 10.2
Pattern of Intimacy/Insufficiency/Nonspecific rage

	Emotion
	NONSPECIFIC RAGE
Unmet Need	Shame-Prone Issue
INTIMACY cynicism reclusiveness	INSUFFICIENCY

1. States to be defended against: insufficiency—not worthy.
2. Primary affect: nonspecific rage
3. Beliefs: "I'm not enough! I'll be found out!"
4. Games: protective maneuvers, coverup, conning, cynical remarks, reclusive behavior that sometimes looks like exclusiveness.

To mask the pain, shame-prone individuals may practice obsessive, addictive behaviors that involve alcohol, drugs, sex, and relationships.

Children are shamed when intimacy is withheld and when the context is abusive physically, emotionally, or sexually. Unconsciously, children harbor all incidents of failure, e.g., the times they were brushed aside, sometimes brutally; when they were discounted, pushed away, hit; when they were cuddled one moment and ignored the next. Such children are shamed and feel and accumulate *nonspecific rage*. It is nonspecific because no one ever acknowledged it consciously, and the child did not know how to label or acknowledge the rage. Experiencing themselves as bad and unworthy, they tend to hold the rage inside and deny its existence. Sometimes the rage becomes unmanageable and they get out of control, e.g., breaking things, hitting a sibling, teasing and abusing a pet. These incidents become another indication of their unworthiness and further shame them.

Shame-prone individuals use games to hide their shame and remain insulated from their rage. Children maneuver and manipulate to get what for them is perceived as necessary for survival. The games or maneuvers are representative of behavior that works to protect them. Sometimes they are self-debasing; other times they are smooth, conning as they go. They may be angry, with a "why are you treating me this way!" attitude, or they may be snarling and sullen. Experiencing the rage and helplessness of being little, children sometimes strike out. Sometimes they kill animals. Not understanding their behavior, they feel out of control. Ignoring, intellectualizing, covering up, hiding, hassling over the meaning of words, making flip comments, hiding behind hair, refusing to answer, and making fun of someone or something to change any perceived focus or possibility of focus are some of the games that are used to cover the shame. These actions may appear as efforts to manipulate and control everyone and everything. The games or strategies are created to meet survival needs, even though deep inside such individuals believe they do not deserve to survive.

Systems. When the couple or family identity is shame-prone, intimacy needs are rarely met within the relationships. Superficial and perfunctory behaviors may substitute for real intimacy. In two-person relationships one of the partners may not have intimacy issues even though the other one does; the partner shamed on intimacy is incapable of meeting the other's intimacy needs. The internal response to not having intimacy needs met is one of *cynicism*—one more empty promise, one more proof of unworthiness. Other people may experience such couples and families as cynical when they interact with them.

Outwardly the couple or family may appear to be reclusive, turning down invitations to extended family events, work-related functions, neighborhood parties, and community functions. Couples who always choose to do things by themselves or with selected couples can avoid being found out as partners who are not intimate, and therefore bad.

The nonspecific rage that such couples feel interacts with that which one or both partners brought into the marriage. The pseudo-intimacy of the marriage, e.g., living constantly in each other's personal space, sex that is often empty, daily verbal conversations that become predictable, with the promise of the intimacy remaining always an illusion, fuels the rage. If the rage is held in check, cynical comments and attitudes by one or both partners about marriage, family, parenting, and society permeate the relationship, masked by pretense for the benefit of outsiders. Although pretending to the best of their ability, couples and families that house many such relationships believe everyone knows about their badness so they socialize little with others. When they do things mostly by themselves, the collusion about their "badness" grows stronger, yet they feel less vulnerable. Some couples circulate socially, carried by the social skills of one of the partners. For example, on the surface it looks like Tom is the life of the party while Marjorie is the quiet one. As a couple they are unable to develop intimacy with other couples.

The rage hidden and smoldering within such couples and families is often exhibited in sudden vicious fighting over what seems a small issue. No one remembers how it got started, and no one can account for why there was so much rage. After the fight is over, the anger seems irrational and inappropriate for the situation. In some couples or families the emotional onslaught is accompanied by physical beatings and physical combat.

Because of the shame, people in these systems rarely talk about what happened. Some people who associate with them in social situations sense this rage, although they may not identify it as such. They are more apt to identify uneasy feelings and a desire to leave their presence. Some members in the family, social, or work circles who are codependent may try to "fix" the couple or the entire family in some way.

These couples and families believe they are not good enough, insufficient. The game they play is one of pretense with a number of variations. They may pretend that they do not think that there is anything wrong with them as a couple or as a family. Instead they direct the feelings of inadequacy toward themselves, their partners, or other families. They know on some level that something is wrong with their couple or family relationships, but they are too afraid to examine what is hidden underneath the rage—the anger, hurt, and fear.

In couples, one or both may participate in both sexual and emotional affairs. The affairs are usually short-lived, because these people cannot get their needs met in outside relationships either. The temporary intimacy is always lacking in some way. Their shame prevents them from fully accepting intimacy as something that they deserve.

The following case illustrates some of the shame dynamics when intimacy needs are not met and the couple and family are shame-prone. Ben and Eva brought their family to therapy because their three young children fought all of the time and nothing they did to stop the fights seemed to make any difference. This couple presented themselves as intelligent, well-dressed, and concerned parents. They were concerned for the children's safety and emotional well-being. They also were tired of the hassle. After the first family session, the therapist sensed the seething rage between the parents. He hypothesized that the children fought to keep the parents from fighting. When the therapist proposed this to the children, they seemed relieved and indicated that they were frightened when their parents fought. The fighting erupted so suddenly, and one or both of their parents seemed so angry and out of control.

After assessing the couple, the therapist determined that the father was shamed on intimacy and the mother was shamed on dependency. The couple's collusion to keep each other's shame hidden intensified the frustration each felt as they failed continually to get their needs met. At times when this frustration peaked, fights usually broke out.

Pattern of Productivity/Rejection/Anger

The characteristics of this pattern are described in Table 10.3.

Individuals.   No matter how dysfunctional their families, children receive messages about how they can serve the family system. Many of these

TABLE 10.3
Pattern of Productivity/Rejection/Anger

	Emotion
	ANGER/HURT
Unmet Need	Shame-Prone Issue
PRODUCTIVITY passive-aggressive immobility	REJECTION

1. States to be defended against: fear of rejection
2. Primary affect: anger
3. Beliefs: "I'm not enough! I'll be found out and rejected! No matter what I do, it is not enough!"
4. Games: "The hell with you. Don't even try to get close to me."

messages have to do with productivity, e.g., "Clean your room. Rub my back. Take care of your little sister. Fix my pain. Be close to your father." When children live in dysfunctional families where they are never able to fully complete these implicit and explicit assignments for the family and rarely receive any recognition and approval, they tend to view themselves as *unproductive*. Recognition and acceptance by parents for products and results are foreign to children in these circumstances. Positive affirmation is often so sporadic and unpredictable that children experience every comment and act by parents and other adults as punishing. Because of criticism and perceived demands for perfection by their parents, early attempts by children to be *productive* in their families are experienced as *rejection*. They become shamed. Consequently, they live in fear that what they do will be criticized, ignored, or receive perfunctory notice. They feel dismissed as contributing members of the family. Any reaction may be seen as confirmation that they are unacceptable as a person, intensifying their fear of rejection. They defend against the entire pattern by projecting *anger* or *hurt*.

As children, and later as adults, these individuals may appear to be very successful, very productive. Even though they are successfully doing a number of things (e.g., working in respectable jobs, having pleasant relationships with peers, completing grades in school, living in lovely homes, and being recognized by many for a specific talent, such as singing), they fail to view themselves as productive. None of these accomplishments nullifies the feeling of shame created by the negative affirmation received in their family of being unproductive.

The psychological games that shame-prone children practice do not save them from being concerned about the need to be productive. From their perspective, their failures are self-evident, and their anger surfaces. Expressing anger is not acceptable in many dysfunctional families. Yet in other dysfunctional families anger is the emotion most often expressed. Shame-prone children react to the accumulation of anger connected to shameful experiences in two major ways. They express it in *passive-aggressive* behavior, or they repress it and stuff it, burying it deep where it can abscess and constantly trigger pain. It is not unusual for children to utilize both methods of expression, very much at the unconscious level.

Passive-aggressive behavior is a natural response to frustration as children vent their anger in indirect ways. Eight-year-old Michael, for example, went into the woods and killed small animals with his hands, and then had nightmares about the blood on his hands. Five-year-old Sally, in suppressed anger, slammed the dishes on the table as she set it, apologizing every time she did it, and feeling shamed by her "clumsiness." Both of these children believed that they caused the constant fighting between their parents. They felt they were failures in their perceived job of keeping peace in the family.

Repeated failures, mixed with real or imagined criticism and insensitivity by parents, other adults, and other children, can push children to the point of *immobility*. They set goals or make plans and seem incapable of making them happen. The immobility protects them from criticism when they make mistakes or perform below perceived expectations. When they are immobile, however, the anger and pain are not expressed outwardly in any way.

The interpersonal issue associated with this pattern is *fear of rejection*. Because they are shamed and "bad," children believe that no one wants to be with them. This fear fosters both the passive-aggressive behavior and the immobility. When parents ask these children to do something, the children whine, complain, do slipshod jobs, or say they will do it but do not. Usually these parents are not meeting their children's intimacy needs, they are not affirming their children as productive contributors to the family, and they do not teach them how to be acceptable contributors. Therefore, their children believe that they are not enough, that they will never measure up, that they can never do enough to please their parents. In reaction to this belief, the message sent from children to their parents and adults through their behavior is: "To hell with you! You never meet my needs and you are never satisfied with my attempts to please you."

Systems. Productivity needs for couples and families are judged by how the couple or family members believe they are seen by the outside world in a number of areas. How they want to be measured for productivity varies from system to system. Are they a loving couple or family? smart?

wealthy? happy? Are they good parents? Good neighbors? Do they make enough money? Is their house good enough? Do they read the right books? Can they talk a good game? Are they fun at a party? Do they give good parties? Do they wear the right clothes? Do they go to the right church? Do they work hard? Do they play hard? Much of this has to do with image-building, and as members of a shame-prone couple or family, they are convinced that they are continually being judged on the short side. For example, although they have never given a party and turn down most invitations, they are sure that they would fail as hosts and as guests.

As they evaluate themselves as viewed by outsiders as being inadequate in productivity, they tend to be angry and act in passive-aggressive ways. Or they will be very quiet, often immobile in interacting with others. Bill and Sarah had been in a shame-prone marriage for 12 years. Sarah did only part-time work and was responsible for the upkeep of the home and the care of the children. As a couple they believed that life was hard and that they never had enough of what they needed. They were critical of each other about almost anything they did. A specific job wasn't done right; the money was not enough; their children misbehaved; they were not trained well enough to make more money. All their criticisms were negatively affirming.

Bill worked in the shipping department of a large company where he had been for 10 years. His present boss and others before this one evaluated him as a reliable employee, quiet with little outward drive and ambition. One time he manifested enough courage to apply for a job as a supervisor and, as he expected, he did not get it. He never tried again, nor did he ask why he did not get the job. His fear of rejection blocked him from asking. When a friend at work tried to talk to him about it, he angrily told him it was none of his business and walked away.

At home his anger spilled over in his relationship with Sarah and their three children. Sarah retaliated with her own anger. Most of their fights started about Bill's work. Sarah told Bill that more money was not the issue for her, but she thought Bill would feel better about himself and would be easier to live with if he made more money. Convinced that Sarah wanted him to make more money and be more successful for her, and convinced that he was not worthy or capable of more success, Bill continually defended himself. Anything set him off—a comment on television, the neighbor's new car, Sarah's silence, looks, behavior, or words. The following dialogue illustrates a typical fight.

Bill came home from work quiet and moody. Sarah knew the signs. She kept all of the children in the kitchen as she finished preparing the meal. When the table was set and the children were ready to eat and at the table, she called to him.

"Bill, we are ready to eat."

No answer, no Bill. The children looked at one another and began to tease and reach for whoever was closest. Sarah ignored them and walked into the living room, where Bill slumped staring at the paper, still in his work clothes.

"I've fixed your favorite, pot roast. Please come to the table. The children are waiting."

"My favorite food. Right! Yours is steak. You are never satisfied. Maybe if we had two men bringing money into this house, we could feed you what you want. Have you thought about that? Why don't you get a wealthy boy friend? I wouldn't care. He could even live here."

"What are you saying? I don't want another man." With tears, "I like what we are having for dinner. Come and eat your supper."

"Do you think I don't know what you want?"

"No, you don't, but you sure think you do."

Sarah returned to the kitchen to calm the children and urge them to eat. Bill pulled out a cold beer from the refrigerator and moodily sat drinking and glaring at his family.

Much of the anger generated in this couple and family stems from the rejection each anticipates and invites out of fear of rejection. The complexity of the feelings are fed by individual, couple, and family issues around fear of rejection—rejection from each other and from the world. To outsiders they say, "To hell with you. You can't hurt us. We won't let you." They do many things to protect the couple and family by angrily or passively rejecting invitations, friendships, casual contacts, etc.

Pattern of Dependency/Worthlessness/Humiliation

The characteristics of the dependency/worthlessness/humiliation pattern are identified in Table 10.4.

Individuals. Dysfunctional parents are inadequate in meeting their children's need to be dependent. These parents resent the fact that others have dependency needs. Implicit messages include: "This is too much to expect of me. Why should I have to feed you from my breast? Why do I have to change your diapers? I can't do it. I can't keep up with the bills. Stop nagging me or I'll leave. I may leave anyway." Or, "I love you. You can do anything. I need you to take care of me. You can do what I can't."

Some of the explicit messages are: "It costs a lot to feed you, clothe you, and have space for you. Life is hard. I never can get ahead financially. I can't do what I want. You are in the way, but I will take care of you."

Parents' messages of victimization and martyrdom permeate the family. The individual's response to these messages is one of *humiliation,* a response that goes much deeper than *rage, anger,* and *hurt.* It strikes at the

TABLE 10.4
Pattern of Dependency/Worthlessness/Humiliation

	Emotion
	HUMILIATION
Unmet Need	Shame-Prone Issue
DEPENDENCY powerlessness victim, martyr, abuser	WORTHLESSNESS

1. States to be defended against: worthlessness
2. Primary affect: humiliation—shame
3. Beliefs: "My needs must in some way be bad; therefore, I am bad."
4. Games: "I'm no good! I'm not worthy!"

very core of one's being. The shamed individual believes, "I am bad. No one can love me or want me near them."

With parents' refusing to be accountable for themselves and to their children, children's beliefs of their own *powerlessness* are magnified, and they become *victims* of their parents, teachers, peers, and society. Victims easily succumb to the role of *martyrs*. In turn they may *abuse* others, much as they have been abused. These roles of *victims, martyrs,* and *abusers* develop in direct response to parents' and other adults' inability and unwillingness to allow children to be *dependent* in healthy ways. The interpersonal issue associated with this pattern is *worthlessness.* Beneath the *anger* at not being allowed to be *dependent* is a sense of shame integrated with the fear of rejection and of worthlessness. Because of their implied "badness," these children feel neglected and unworthy of parental care. They perceive that their unworthiness is the reason for this.

These individuals are powerless, feel powerless, and believe that they are powerless. Their survival games often do not work. Their anger only drives adults farther away. Children strike out in their frustration; often they are *abusive* toward their parents but mostly toward their siblings and other smaller children. Likewise, their parents are abusive—emotionally, physically, and sometimes sexually. They believe that they are unworthy of their parents' love, that they are no good, and that everyone knows it. They believe that they are not worth bothering about, that their parents are justified in their actions.

Systems. As already indicated, all relationships have implicit contracts. Within the implicit contract for shame-prone relationships is the belief that their partners will allow them to be dependent. This belief may be in opposition to another part of the contract, which says, "We each know we are incapable of meeting each other's dependency needs." Interacting with the need for intimacy is implicit begging of one's partner to "baby" them and to allow "leaning" to take place. These pleas permeate the unspoken negotiations. Because neither partner knows how to be dependent or to allow another to be *dependent*, they are constantly humiliated by their own feelings and behaviors and the responses they get. This cycles into more feelings of worthlessness as individuals and as a relationship unit.

Such couples and families look to outsiders, extended family members, friends, and people with whom they work and associate to take care of them. Implicitly they spread messages of "We need help. We don't know how to do this." Sometimes they are attracted to older couples who will allow them to lean on them a little. At the same time, they make it very difficult for others to help them and give to them because they act powerless and easily assume roles of victims and/or martyrs.

In families where both parents came from families where their dependency needs were not met, confusion about moral values and standards dominate. This may surface in very permissive behavior, with few rules or boundaries to guide the couple or their children. Or there may be a constant fight between partners as they try to enforce rigid rules for each other, indicating that it is for the good of the couple or the family. Or one will be very permissive and the other very rigid and punitive. Although some may follow a religious formula (e.g., church attendance, reading scriptures, helping on church sponsored projects), personal feelings of humiliation and a sense of worthlessness as individuals, couple, and family dictate the belief that they are unworthy to have a relationship with a higher power, God. Spirituality lies dormant for most of these couples and families.

Suspicious of authority figures and confused by a lack of explicit rules for their relationship, such couples and families either adopt harsh rules, which are often followed or enforced irrationally, or act out of implicit rules based on their unmet needs. Either model creates disharmony and uneasiness in the system, which is held together by the notion that it is not worthy of anything better.

The couple or the entire family may act as a victim and/or martyr in the world in which they operate. Believing themselves powerless to change things, they function with few rights or privileges. They do not ask for what they want from others and seem incapable of giving even though they see a need for it. These are the couples and families who want others (e.g., spouses, bosses, friends, and agencies) to do everything for them. They are rarely satisfied with what is done for them because it does not "fix" the pain or change the beliefs about their "badness." They are so humiliated and feel so worthless that having others attempting to fix what is wrong adds to the shame.

In couples, if one or both spouses are shamed on dependency, the issue will surface in the relationship. Behind the collusion to not uncover the other person's shame is an unspoken plea for one's spouse to take care of his or her *dependency* needs. When one spouse has been shamed on dependency needs, he or she is suspicious of his/her mate and frightened of the other's needs, implicit and explicit. Although shamed partners may meet the physical needs of the relationship, e.g., work, shopping, gardening, sex, they are terrified of allowing their spouses to be *dependent* on them. On the other hand, they manipulate and maneuver to get their mates to care for them, much as a child would for a parent. They are humiliated by their wishes to be cared for and their inability to care for the other.

Pattern of Sense and Order/Abandonment/Fear

Table 10.5 lists characteristics associated with this pattern.

Individuals. When the need for *sense* and *order* is not met, deep pervasive *fear* of a senseless, crazy world and issues of *abandonment* result. Parents of these children usually can't make sense of their own world, and the order they manage is one of rigidity and unreasonableness, prompted by their own fears. When parents are not accountable, refuse to take re-

TABLE 10.5
Pattern of Sense and Order/Abandonment/Fear

	Emotion
	FEAR
Unmet Need	Shame-Prone Issue
SENSE AND ORDER helplessness craziness, addiction, codependency	ABANDONMENT

1. State to be defended against: abandonment
2. Primary affect: fear
3. Beliefs: "I am bad. No one wants to be with me so I will be abandoned."
4. Games: "I'm afraid. You scare me. Come closer. No, stay away."

sponsibility for their children, and have difficulty being intimate, they have little to offer in terms of *sense* and *order*.

These children experience the opposite of what sense and order provide—senselessness and disorder. The internal response to this is a feeling of helplessness. At this point the pain is very intense and reality is terribly distorted. They seek some kind of release or a buffer for the pain. With the reality that parents cannot, or will not, make sense and order of the world and provide some kind of structure, fear intensifies. Out of the fear develops the following beliefs: "My life is overwhelming. I am worthless. I am found out and I will be cast out. I am abandoned. No one wants to be with me."

Shame-prone people fear exposure because they sense that being vulnerable will lead to abandonment. Shyness, embarrassment, and self-consciousness are forms that this fear takes. The fear exists irrationally, meaning that even in safe environments with safe people shame-prone individuals assume they will be embarrassed and eventually abandoned. However, most shame-prone people will not own up to these feelings easily. To admit to feeling such ways would be risking further exposure and vulnerability.

Sensing their helplessness and feeling intense pain and fear, individuals medicate the pain with *addictions* of all kinds (e.g., substances such as alcohol, tobacco, drugs, and food; behaviors such as relationships, gambling, sex, religion), with the intention of escaping their untrustworthy world. In *codependent* relationships they seek "distorted and disabling connections with substances, persons, institutions, and rigid beliefs" (Wegscheider-Cruse & Cruse, 1989) in an attempt to find security without fear. If the world they lived in made sense, then all the fear and pain would go away. Through medicating the pain, an allusion of safety and order can be maintained for a time.

They become masters at games of manipulations and power, always unsatisfied, always hiding the "truth" about themselves. Knowing the extent of their badness, their shame, they become willing servants to others, trying desperately on one level to "serve" their way out of their shame. The fear and humiliation deepen with each attempt, ending in failure and abandonment, perceived or actual.

The craziness of their world is partially created by other unmet needs in the map—intimacy, productivity, and dependency. The interpersonal issues of insufficiency, rejection, and worthlessness lead children to fear that their parents will leave them, abandon them. Confirmation occurs as children are left, often with inadequate babysitters. When parents return to the family after absences, children face uncertainty. Parents may come home drunk and uncaring or riddled with guilt, making promises to do better to themselves and others. Other parents may appear to have benefited from being away and are more pleasant to be around—for a while. Some come home and reinforce the idea that only the child can meet the parent's needs. Whatever the message, the pressure builds and the cycle starts again. The fear of abandonment is strong, and in some way these parents do abandon their children. This confirms the beliefs of the children that they are bad and worthless.

Individuals from dysfunctional families integrate with this fourth pattern beliefs accumulated from dynamics of other patterns: "I'm not enough! No matter what I do it is not enough! My needs must in some way be bad; therefore, I am bad." The dysfunctional family system that they live in is frightening and crazy to these children. Parents are not accountable *to* or *for* the children. What there is of structure does not protect or nurture the children. Rules are harsh, nonexistent, or liable to change with no explanation and certainly without rationale. At a deep inner level children learn not only that they are "bad," but also that their parents, and adults in general, are not to be trusted. The fear generated from these experiences is pervasive and overwhelming. They believe that at any time they will be cast out, thrown out, left alone, abandoned. These beliefs intensify their feelings of helplessness, littleness, and lostness. Justice, fairness, and dependability are myths—longed for but rarely a part of their familial patterns. Instead, family loyalty and perceived expectations by parents are embedded in secrecy, mystery, unkept promises, and punishment.

Because their world makes little sense to these children, they tend to lose, or never fully develop, a sense of appropriate behavior. They act out the craziness they experience. Other structures, e.g., schools, court systems, church, and community agencies, hold little meaning or respect for them. Rules are to be broken. They often seek out peers who have the same beliefs and needs that they do. They assume, "If we can't trust our parents and definitely not the establishment, we will make our own rules." Being part of a gang or a cult with clear rules and boundaries appeals to their need to count on something or somebody. The violence and abuse in gangs and cults are a version of the same kind of behavior in their families. In some of these groups leaders are addicted to power and followers are codependent.

Presently our world lives with the results of this syndrome. Our society operates as an addictive system with all of the attendant abuses and pain (Schaeff, 1987). Millions of dollars are spent in treatment for addiction and codependency.

Systems. Because shame-prone couples and families cannot make sense of the outside world, they also live in "craziness" within their relationships. The fear, promoted by the lack of order, fosters elaborate and desperate schemes to control whatever in their lives seems to give momentary stability. Very often a spouse or other family members are the object of this manipulative control. Anything can upset this precarious and untrusted stability. Such things as changing the arrangement of the furniture without notification, arriving an hour later or earlier than planned, and forgetting to do something they had promised to do are regular aspects of this pattern.

Patterns of Uniqueness/Emptiness/Terror

The pattern that includes the unmet need to be unique, the emotional response of terror, and the interpersonal issue of emptiness is illustrated in Table 10.6.

Individuals. When individuals experience a chronic failure to meet their need for *uniqueness*, they end up feeling *terror* and experiencing *emptiness* that accompanies the deep-rooted belief that they are bad and worthless and that there is no hope for them. The internal response of hopelessness springs into full bloom and moves the individual toward suicide or disease states.

If the psychological needs for intimacy, productivity, dependency, and sense and order are not met with some consistency by parents and other adults, children cannot experience being valued as *unique* and separate family members. Parents who appear to be unique, separate, and successful, but who do not meet the needs of their children by positively affirming their uniqueness, are into pretense, uncertain themselves as to their own value. On some level children sense the incongruity, accumulate pain from the knowledge, and add it to their burden of worthlessness, failures, and

TABLE 10.6
Pattern of Uniqueness/Emptiness/Terror

	Emotion
	TERROR
Unmet Need	Shame-Prone Issue
UNIQUENESS hopelessness, suicide, disease	EMPTINESS

1. States to be defended against: emptiness, with aloneness and isolation.
2. Primary affect: terror.
3. Beliefs: "Nobody cares!"
4. Games: "I am a zero. No one can change that!"

expectation of abandonment. They deny their feelings, and as a result experience emptiness, nothingness, and severe aloneness, leading to a sense of helplessness. Emptiness is an emotional by-product of the shame-prone identity. As Bradshaw (1988) has stated, to feel any feeling is shame-reducing. This is most likely because any feeling replaces the void, the empty hole created by shame.

When shame-prone people sense they are being criticized, they respond with rage and humiliation, regardless of the reality of the situation. Although the rage is often expressed, the humiliation remains hidden. The person may seethe inside, with the humiliation taking its toll in terms of energy, leaving very little for more functional purposes. These people operate on the belief, "It is safer to be with myself than to be unrecognized and uncared for in the presence of others." Being with someone can be a very lonely experience because of the constant fear of *abandonment*.

The issues and behaviors of aloneness and isolation are different from the behaviors of reclusiveness in response to not getting intimacy needs met. In that pattern reclusiveness is a behavioral response to the interpersonal issue that involves being unworthy to be intimate with others. When the intimacy need is not met, nonspecific rage is the result. Individuals defend against the issue of insufficiency, not being enough, and protect with rage that is buried underneath the fear and terror. In the uniqueness/emptiness/terror pattern, individuals know that they have been found out, that everyone knows that they are "bad." They are dealing with terror— unnamed, pervasive, controlling. Their identity is weakened to the point that they are left with nothing that is strong enough to counteract the strong emotions of fear and terror; they are left with emptiness. Most of these feelings are irrational, with the terror stronger than any other current feeling or behavior. For example, a phrase of music, a glimpse of a color, or the tone of voice may trigger buried memories that in turn trigger terror connected to childhood abuse and neglect.

A common part of the human experience is loneliness. Everyone has a way of being by oneself. Loneliness can be healthy when it leads to the belief, "I'm on my own, oneness. If I choose, I can have people with me." Sometimes feelings of aloneness have negative effects on people. Shame-prone individuals believe that they have no choice, that aloneness is connected to their emptiness, an expression of their unworthiness and shame. The emptiness felt by them is existential, often unnamed, unacknowledged by anyone, but relentless in its presence and in its pressure. Individuals defend against the emptiness by the game of "Nobody cares! You are too stupid to know anything about me!"

Hopelessness pervades their beliefs, attitudes, and behaviors. Knowing that they are "bad" and that no one is going to change that leads many of these individuals to wish for death. The death wish may be met through a slow disease or through suicide. For some individuals suicide seems the only way to effectively deal with the huge abscess of accumulated pain and existential emptiness. Attempts at suicide are often final tests to gain recognition, to get acknowledgment that they exist as separate, unique individuals, worthy of help. On the other hand, if anger and passive-aggressive feelings turned against the shameful self predominate, a disease such as cancer may prevail.

One defense against the emptiness is manifested in intense dissociation from reality, feelings, and behaviors. When the games fail, when *addiction* does not ease the pain, when *suicide* attempts fail, the person may move further into dissociative disorders such as multiple personality.

Systems.   Couples and families in this pattern are very dysfunctional. They believe that they have failed as a couple or family, that they are very bad. Although blaming the other for their failure, spouses both live in terror that they will be found out and labeled for everyone to see. They know that they are not unique or special in any way. The relationship is empty and each couple or family member is empty. Each feels very hopeless, although they may go through the motions. Suicide attempts may be serial and serious. One or all family members may experience disease that is life-threatening and debilitating. Cancer, heart disease, colitis, and severe headaches are but a few examples.

Some of these couples divorce, especially if one is somewhat stronger than the other. Others are too immobilized by the emptiness to initiate and follow through with a divorce.

Often, one partner in couple or a member of the family will be hospitalized for a psychiatric disorder and receive treatment as an individual. Couple and family work is difficult to do unless individuals receive some therapy first.

Pattern of Choices/Loss/Grief

The characteristics of this pattern are described in Table 10.7.

Individuals.   The belief that they do not have choices, or at least that their *choices* make no difference, minimizes shame-prone children's very existence. When parents meet their children's dependency needs, they make choices that are appropriate for their children. When their needs go unmet, shame-prone children experience the results of their parents' poor decisions or their failure to make effective decisions.

In dysfunctional families, children get mixed messages about their right to make their own choices. Dysfunctional parents want their children to make choices that keep them out of trouble and that put fewer demands on them, the parents. The need to make their own choices in the social arena motivates children as they struggle with parents for control of these

TABLE 10.7
Pattern of Choices/Loss/Grief

	Emotion
	GRIEF
Unmet Need	Shame-Prone Issue
CHOICES blocked, unstable	LOSS

1. State to be defended against: losses
2. Primary affect: grief and sadness
3. Beliefs: "I am so bad that I can only make mistakes. I need someone to care for me. I can't do it."
4. Games: "Find me if you can."

choices (e.g., what they wear, whom they associate with, whom they bring home, what they do with their time, how they do in school, and whom they date). Guilt and shame interactions often consistently erode children's perceptions of their right to make choices.

The following are examples of the kinds of comments that may negatively affirm individuals about their ability to make choices. "If you loved us you would not make that choice." "I work my fingers to the bone while you are out gallivanting and doing nothing for us." "This is one more instance of your not being able to do anything right. You can't even tell time." "How many times have I told you that you look terrible in that color. Go put on another dress."

The world these children live in does not make sense, and they do not feel positively affirmed as a unique, contributing members of the family. In their lives there have been too many times when the right to make a significant choice has been denied them or the choices they have made have been derided, resulting in deep feelings of *grief* over losing themselves and losing other relationships. Most shame-prone clients cannot recognize the grief until they have worked through all of the other patterns. Personal wants and plans are *blocked* by the unresolved grief, which remains mostly unconscious (Scharff & Scharff, 1987). The outward reaction in this pattern is *unstable* behavior. The internal manifestation is a sense of being *blocked* and restrained. A deep unconscious fear of losing control and being labeled as bad adds to the block. Depression often accompanies these dynamics.

The interpersonal issue, *losses*, is also buried under other patterns in the map. The losses, real and imagined, focus on all of the unmet psychological needs in all the patterns, on the parents who were not there for them, and on many other lost relationships, broken dreams, and failed attempts at success. This choice/loss/grief pattern encompasses all of the dynamics in the other patterns. In dysfunctional families parents' attitude in situations involving responsibility and accountability for their children is one of angry rejection. Their fear of their children's *dependency* is masked by anger, criticism, and abuse. This punishment leads to *humiliation* and negative affirmation for children. The perceived message is "I am bad!" and "The picture others have of me is bad." The repetition of this and similar messages convinces children that they are worth less than their parents and others. The conviction is followed by beliefs and fears about rejection, worthlessness, and abandonment. Children whose intimacy, dependency, and uniqueness needs have never been met have many unresolved losses.

Children with shame-prone identities learn to manipulate and fantasize to gain some semblance of control in their lives. Usually they hold needed change as a process controlled by others—parents, teachers, police, and society. Feeling their impotence and being left out of the decisions that affect them, children feel the loss along with the shame of not being worthy, of being bad. Hiding out, covering up, lashing out, experiencing abuse and abusing others, using drugs, breaking rules and laws—all confirm their badness, helplessness, and hopelessness. They feel and act unstable. Not only is their world crazy, but it feels unstable, as if it, and they, could fall apart and be destroyed.

Buried deep under the other patterns, they grieve for lost parts of themselves, for lost relationships, for lost childhood. Until the other patterns are resolved, the grief cannot be worked through. Depression, melancholy, lassitude, and loss of contact with reality mask the sadness. Only through conscious grieving and acceptance of the losses can shame-prone individuals heal and make choices that energize, strengthen, and give purpose to their lives.

Systems.   These couples and families are pervaded by a sense of emptiness and lack of choice. Fate is seen as natural, and self-initiation is foreign. Many losses fuel unresolved grief. Such relationships are empty of positive energy, of hopes, dreams, and fulfillment. Daily rituals, habits, and fear keep such couples together.

Patterns of Wholeness/Acceptance/Joy

The characteristics of this last pattern are identified in Table 10.8.

Individuals.   In this last pattern on the map, *wholeness* is the psychological need. Some shame-prone people have areas of apparent adjustment

TABLE 10.8
Pattern of Wholeness/Acceptance/Joy

	Emotion
	JOY
Met Need	
WHOLENESS peace, excitement, adaptation	ACCEPTANCE

1. State to be recognized: mature acceptance
2. Primary affect: joy with a full range of feelings.
3. Beliefs: "I am enough! I am lovable and loving. Mistakes are fixable."
4. Games: habits

and health in their lives, but somewhere inside they believe that they lack something because they are bad; because they are flawed, they are not whole. Only by successfully working through the issues, emotions, and needs in the six patterns can individuals experience this last pattern. Although others can offer support in the quest for wholeness, the pattern must be internalized and related to a positive affirmation of self. *Peace* and *excitement* characterize the internal response to knowing one is whole. The behavioral expression of wholeness is *adaptation* to life events and circumstances. As they exchange faulty beliefs for more accurate perceptions, as their behavior is congruent and ethical for them, and as they feel the natural range of feelings without shame, individuals with healthy identity experience *joy*.

As shame-prone individuals learn that some of their needs can be met, they begin consciously to experience all of the emotions across the top of the map. The rage gets labeled and acknowledged, and it eventually dissipates. The anger and the deep hurt are reconciled. Shame and humiliation are faced with the fear and terror brought to the forefront; then they are experienced and released. Individuals are supported as they face the monsters from their childhood. The size of the sadness they feel is overwhelming as they grieve for what has been lost in their lives and accept those losses. The grieving may occur for the father who never met their needs and abused them, the alcoholic mother who was never there for them, the marriage that was punishing, the unrealized dreams, a lost childhood, and lost opportunities.

Exercising choices helps create stability to bring hope and spiritual peace. Satisfaction, new goals, newly appreciated talents and knowledge, relationships that are fun, accomplishments, and possibilities bring joy into their lives. The full knowledge that they are loving and lovable people, capable of correcting mistakes and adapting to a given situation, enhances their lives. They still experience shame, a transient shame that allows them to fully accept who they are and the moment-to-moment reality of their existence.

Negotiation, conflict resolution, healthy and satisfactory relationships, acceptance of mistakes as opportunities to grow—these are characteristics of this last pattern. Accepting the past with its pain and losses and acknowledging the present as a time for growth and exploration cultivate for them the wholeness of identity they seek.

Systems.   As couples and families achieve therapeutic goals, they move toward a sense of wholeness. Having received individual therapy, spouses are free to work on their marriage toward a wholeness, joy, and acceptance of themselves individually, as a couple, and as a family.

CHAPTER 11

Setting the Stage for Therapy

W HEN SETTING THE stage for the treatment of shame-prone clients, one must consider a number of factors. This chapter discusses a treatment approach and some important aspects of setting the stage for therapy. Pitfalls that often befall therapists are identified, and some guidelines for therapists working with shame-prone clients are suggested.

A TREATMENT APPROACH

Therapy may begin with very little evidence that clients or their systems are shame-prone. Therefore, identification of shame-proneness can occur in individual, conjoint, or group therapy, some time after therapy begins. Initially assessing all clients for shame may help avoid this delayed discovery of shame, but it won't be true for all cases. Denial and coverup may be so ingrained that defenses have to be lowered before the shame surfaces enough to be assessed accurately. With this in mind, therapists can assess for shame in the early stage of therapy and continue to monitor for signs during the middle and late stages.

The Therapy Team

When a case has been diagnosed as shame-prone, therapists may want to shift to a different treatment approach. Working with a therapy team can be very helpful. The team need not be involved in every session, nor does the teamwork have to follow a particular format. It is effective for team members to have different strengths and share common philosophies. For example, one may be more skilled in working with groups, another with couples, another with multigenerational issues, another with individual therapy.

Some therapists are already in a setting where the team approach is utilized. In this case, they need to negotiate with the team members for their cooperation in treating shame-prone clients. Some therapists in solo practice or in various other arrangements may find it difficult to adapt a team approach. Even in such cases some type of team approach can usually be developed in cooperation with other professionals.

Length of Sessions

Because shame-proneness is so difficult to treat, the typical 50-minute, once-a-week therapy format proves to be slow and often ineffective. At times therapists should negotiate with clients to meet for longer sessions. Explicit, structured negotiation for longer meeting times is important. When therapists allow sessions to run overtime without planning to do so, clients learn to manipulate. They may talk about irrelevant topics for the first 45 minutes and then dump a very serious issue on the table in the last five minutes. Therapists are more effective when they openly structure the length of the sessions and then manage them so that they end on time.

Treatment Modalities

In dealing with the various shame-prone issues, a treatment team should consider the following modalities.

Individual Therapy. While individual therapy may be part of treatment, clients who begin in individual therapy should be informed as soon as the diagnosis is completed that group and conjoint therapy is expected. When shame-prone clients are seen only in individual therapy, the therapist may be overwhelmed by their dependency demands and the emotional accumulation of pain and abuse that they can exhibit.

Individual therapy sessions for shame-prone clients are more effective when they last approximately two hours once per week. The structure of the individual session can be negotiated with the treatment team. One therapist in individual therapy is usually not powerful enough to break through the layers of affect and resistance within the individual or the family system.

Conjoint Therapy. To deal with couples' and families' shame-prone issues, conjoint sessions are essential. These should also be planned with the therapy team, integrating goals and strategies with both individual and group therapy. When shame-prone clients begin in conjoint or group therapy, it is helpful to inform them as soon as possible that individual sessions are also expected.

Group Therapy. Group therapy for individuals, multiple couples, and multiple families is a powerful tool when working with shame-prone systems. Group therapists can develop a supportive atmosphere for group members. The group is a powerful force, capable of helping members break through denial and release accumulated pain from shameful incidents.

Support Groups. The therapy team can utilize support groups in conjunction with therapy. For those who are addicted or codependent, 12-step groups are very helpful, but they are insufficient in and of themselves for the full working through of shame issues. Other types of support groups, such as Arnold Patent (1984, 1989) support groups, can provide unconditional love and a stable base. Support groups are often more effective with shame-prone individuals who have been in therapy a little while than with those who have just begun.

Intensive Experiential Workshops. Intensive experiential programs lasting several days are available or can be created by the team. These workshops focus on exposing and eradicating the emotional pain attached to issues of shame; in this way they speed up the process of breaking through denial and releasing the pain. The decision to be involved in such a group should be made with the input of the therapy team.

If treatment team members are not directly involved in the experiential workshop, they should be aware of the effects of the experience and be available when clients return. Support and integration of therapeutic issues and individual progress with the marital and family systems are important.

SETTING THE STAGE

One of the factors that determines success or failure in meeting client goals is the quality of the early stage of therapy. The initial contacts with the therapist or agency, paperwork and some assessment, telephone conversations, and subsequent sessions create the beginning stage of therapy. The quality and direction of relationships between clients and therapists develop during these early contacts and sessions. The type of relationship that the agency or office staff establishes with clients is also crucial during this time.

Who Attends the Early Sessions

Who attends the first few sessions is often dictated by circumstances and/the philosophy held by the therapists and agency. Children, adolescents, or adults may be seen in individual therapy or with a parent or both parents, with parents and siblings, and with extended family members. Insurance companies' policies and referral sources also influence the

choices. Hospitalized clients usually fit into a prescribed program of therapy with a team approach, e.g., with a psychiatrist, an assigned staff therapist or a therapist from the community who referred the client, group
therapy, and some family related sessions. Regardless of practices and policies, a family systems approach is highly recommended in dealing with
shame-prone individuals, couples, and families.

Therapists' Welfare

When working with shame-prone clients, it is essential that therapists
take care of themselves. Traditional diagnostic categories for emotional and
mental disorders do not directly address shame. Consequently, shame is
often ignored in the treatment planning. Yet, shame-prone clients are demanding. It often appears that they will never be ready to terminate. They
need a viable support network and so do their therapists. It is advisable to
therapists to do the following:

(1) Establish external support systems. This can be in the form of a
group practice that is structured to provide support as well as therapy,
formal and regular supervision, or informal but consistent and reliable
networking and sharing. Therapists in agencies, treatment centers, hospital settings, or group practice should not assume that the support will just
happen. This support structure needs to be deliberately organized, with
clearly established goals and commitment by all members to support each
other.

(2) Review therapist/client(s) relationships often, using the therapy team
for feedback and support. The burden of relationships with shame-prone
clients needs attention by the support group. At times therapists may need
to enter therapy themselves to work through issues.

(3) Consistently review and work on personal shame and guilt issues. If
therapists are feeling stuck, blocked, complacent, confused, and/or manipulated, these are signals to examine therapist/client relationships. As described in Chapter 9, these and other signals may mean that therapy has
triggered personal shame and guilt issues.

Therapist and Client Expectations

Therapists' and clients' expectations for what happens in the early
stages of therapy affect therapy processes and outcomes. Some clients
come to therapy with expectations based on previous experiences with
other therapists in other circumstances. A therapist's history with other
clients creates expectations for the therapist as well. Clients who have
never been in therapy develop expectations from their needs and beliefs
about themselves and therapy. Some of the expectations can be verbalized;

some will be implicit. Shame-prone individuals expect the worst, at the same time wanting the impossible. At the very least they want to be rescued. Exploring and verbalizing expectations in the early stages of therapy can be helpful to clients even if they feel shamed by the process. Giving direct information about the mechanics of therapy, e.g., setting of appointments, fee collections, late attendance, nonattendance, insurance claims, and emergency calls, is necessary.

PITFALLS FOR THERAPISTS

Rarely do therapists know before therapy begins that their clients have shame-prone identities. Undoubtedly, the indicators of shame-proneness are masked in the symptoms presented by the clients, e.g., addiction, child abuse, anxiety, depression, and relationship issues, and in the experiences therapists have had with other clients with the same symptoms. In the case described in Chapter 1, Marilyn went to therapy, one more time, to try to do something about her depression. She did not say, "Please help me with my shame."

Shame is likely to be an issue if clients have been consistently abused, emotionally, physically, and sexually; are addicted to substances, relationships, or behaviors; live in families in which other family members are addicted; come from a dysfunctional family; dissociate easily; are depressed; or have long histories of failures. As a general rule, therapists should consider in first interviews the possibility that their clients may be shame-prone. Therapists need to be cautious, however, because the very nature of the therapy process with its exploratory and uncovering aspects is potentially shaming to a client.

Knowledge of common pitfalls for therapists in the early, middle, and late stages of therapy assists therapists to avoid them. If clients are shame-prone or shamed on dependency or intimacy, the issues presented in therapy may be magnified to hide the shame. Clues from clients' behavior readily provide information about the therapist-client relationship if the therapist is not complacent or blocked by a pre-diagnosis. The following pitfalls should be avoided:

- *Assuming that the joining techniques used for nonshamed clients in the first sessions of therapy are appropriate for shame-prone clients.*

Joining techniques resemble the social skills practiced in people's homes when guests arrive. They are designed to comfort clients as they find a chair to sit in and prepare for interaction with the therapist (Haley, 1987; Minuchin & Fishman, 1981). These behaviors include shaking hands, taking someone's coat, talking about the clients' experience in finding their way to the office, asking general questions about what clients do, where they live, etc. Shame-prone clients may be able to exhibit basic social skills in many situations, but rarely is it easy for them. They fear exposure of their ineptness, doing something wrong, being found out. Handshaking, causal comments, and questions may all be greeted with suspicion and reserve.

- *Being careless and miscalculating what the trust issues are.*

Shame-prone clients do not trust very many people. Even those very dependent clients who solicit therapists' care very early do not trust therapists to really come through. They do not trust themselves.

- *Ignoring or misinterpreting shame-prone clients' responses to typical information-seeking interventions.*

In the case in Chapter 1, the therapists's attempt to join with Marilyn through questions and comments was shaming because Marilyn experienced it as an uncovering process in which she was going to be found out. Her fear was that the therapist would find out how bad she was. The therapist's personal reactions to Marilyn's responses triggered feelings of anger and confusion. These feelings were clues for the therapist that eventually led to the hypothesis that Marilyn might be shame-prone.

GUIDELINES FOR THERAPISTS

In the early stages of therapy therapists should be aware that most shame-prone clients have issues about trust and fears about being uncovered or found out. When therapists ignore clients' shame and "badness" or try to talk them out of it by giving evidence of their worthiness, they immediately lose credibility. The following guidelines will help therapists be more aware of clients' issues of trust.

- *Expect that clients have no reason to trust therapists and that very likely they have trust issues with everyone.*

Awareness of the possible lack of trust prepares therapists to search for behavioral cues that indicate trust or lack of it. Where clients sit, how they look at the therapist or other people in the setting, posture and facial expressions, a handshake or lack of one, other touch behavior, tone of voice, eye contact or lack of it—are all indications of how the client is experiencing the session. On some level, clients experience therapists through the same type of signals. A rule of thumb is to assume that clients have no reason to trust you in the early stages of therapy.

Working with a therapy team raises complex issues about trust for clients. It is not unusual for clients to see a therapist for quite some time before they are diagnosed as shame-prone. Building relationships with various members of a therapy team requires a great deal of shame-prone clients. Therapists need to be patient and look for ways to create interpersonal bridges with such clients (Kaufman, 1989).

- *Acknowledge to clients that they have no reason to trust you, but that you are willing to earn their trust.*

In the first stages of therapy no one knows anyone very well. Therapists can openly acknowledge that there is no reason for new clients to trust them. In the same breath, therapists should assure clients that they are trustworthy and that they are willing to demonstrate that. Invitations for questions and comments will help build a foundation for trust.

- *Be patient and give information to clients about your behavior.*

Therapist calmness and attentive energy toward everyone in the session, backed by patience, set a stage for exploration by clients. Therapists can talk about what they are doing, what their expectations are, what the time limitations are, and any other appropriate structure. This can be done patiently in every session, if necessary, but particularly in the early sessions. To effectively offer information about one's own behavior to clients, therapists must be constantly aware of their own reactions, thoughts, feelings, attitudes, prejudices, and conclusions. No matter how clear or direct therapists are, shame-prone clients make up information about the implicit and explicit signals given out. They often misread all behavior to verify their own attitudes and beliefs, so that they can make sense and order of the world congruent with their experiences. Checking with clients to determine how they are interpreting behavior will bring this misreading out into the open.

- *Encourage clients to ask about anything that you do or say.*

Therapy need not be mysterious to clients. Therapists need to assure clients that they do not keep secrets from them. Encouraging clients to ask about anything happening in the therapy setting allows shame-prone clients to have a different experience than they typically have with others. When clients do ask, therapists can acknowledge that asking is not always easy and thank them for doing so. The process can be facilitated by the therapist's asking if clients want to know more about anything that has happened.

Shame-prone individuals believe that they are bad and that people do not respect them because of their badness. Encouraging them to ask questions demonstrates respect for them. Timing is crucial because in the beginning encouraging clients to ask questions may put them too much in view of the therapist's "watchful eye." At times clients judge therapists as stupid, naive, or as "conning" them. If the therapist's interactions do not verify their badness, they may believe that the therapist is pretending or not smart enough to know.

Therapists must be judicious about what they say to clients. Many clients are codependent and constantly looking for information so that they can "help" therapists. Their identity may be tied to being helpful; they know of no other way to relate. Some client questions are aimed at comparing therapists to their parents, to them as parents, to their spouses, or to a previous therapist.

- *Give normalcy and credibility to anything that clients do in the session.*

If clients are untrusting and fearful, give credence to their behavior by commenting on how normal it is for them to experience these feelings. For some shame-prone people, "normal" means being like everyone else and having similar experiences. Therapists will need to clarify that there is no one standard for "normalcy" and that emotional reactions that match the circumstances of an experience are "normal." Therapists can validate clients for noticing their internal reactions.

- *Acknowledge that clients have reasons to believe that they are "bad."*

Acknowledging that clients believe that they are "bad" without verifying that they are bad takes sensitivity and skill. For each client the nuances will be different. In the early stages, therapists cannot afford to argue with clients about whether they are bad or not. Allowing clients to express their feelings and thoughts will be more helpful than confronting them, at least in early stages of therapy. In conjoint or group therapy, therapists need to help others not to get hooked into arguing or acting in disbelief about whether a person is good or bad.

- *Match humorous comments with your client's style of humor.*

The use of humor in therapy sessions can be helpful, but it may also be very detrimental to shame-prone clients. Shame-prone clients do not see the humor in common situations. For example, when everyone in a group laughs, shame-prone clients may assume they are being laughed at. Because of their beliefs about themselves and the energy and caution it takes for them to protect themselves, they may not clearly hear what is said or understand why it is funny. Family members often comment about the shame-prone client's failure to see humor. "Mom, you never get it. What planet do you live on?" "I thought it was funny. How come you don't?" "I was only teasing. Do you always have to be so literal?" These kinds of experiences are shaming, and clients begin to believe that whatever is said, or inferred, about their ability to respond to and with humor is "bad."

Therapists need to be aware of their own style of interaction and beliefs about humor. Ask yourself the following questions: What is funny to me? How do I respond to humor with others? Do I tell jokes with some clients and not others? Do I ever use exaggerations to humorously prod clients to learn to laugh at themselves a little? Do I use books or audio and video-tapes that have elements of humor to teach clients? Do I have humorous sayings and colloquial expressions that are part of my normal delivery? Do I tend to see humor in serious situations? How do I evaluate my style of humor? How do others evaluate my humor? Is it gentle? Sarcastic? Timely? Slow? Quick? At my own or others' expense? When others laugh, do I? Is my laughter controlled, spontaneous, loud, appropriate? Do I share what is funny in my life? Therapists who are aware of their own humor and can sensitively match the style of their clients can teach shame-prone individuals to use humor to lighten their burden.

CHAPTER 12

Treating Shame-Prone Systems: Early Stage

A S A PROCESS, therapy can be conceptualized as having a beginning, a middle, and an end. This conceptualization provides a way of writing about processes of therapy common to all therapists while allowing for variations in therapist style and approach. Such variations would be true for a treatment team as well.

This chapter discusses some general considerations about the relationships between shame-prone clients and therapists and identifies therapist-client issues for the early stage of therapy. Intervention strategies and expected outcomes for the beginning stage of therapy for shame-prone systems are also identified. It is important to remember that we are focusing primarily on the dynamics of shame, which can be part of many different presenting problems. We do not address ways of working with specific presenting problems; rather, we focus on how to treat proneness to shame as a dynamic in any presenting problem. Such an approach can be added to any therapist's style of therapy, and it can be integrated with other knowledge about specific presenting problems.

CLIENT-THERAPIST RELATIONSHIPS

Therapists are simultaneously "in and out" of the therapeutic system because they are both participant and observer (Auerswald, 1987; Becvar & Becvar, 1988; Luthman & Kirschenbaum, 1974). They must be able to operate on several levels at once. In addition to observing self and the unit of therapy (e.g., the individual, couple, or family system), therapists are also forming relationships with each person and with each system (Luthman & Kirschenbaum, 1974; Stahmann & Harper, 1983). The therapist-client relationship has the power to heal as well as to hurt and to block healing.

When therapists utilize accountability, dependency, and intimacy behaviors to affirm clients, they provide a solid base for the therapeutic
relationships and contribute to the process of healing shame. When therapists are accountable for the dependency and intimacy issues within the
client(s)-therapist relationship, they provide appropriate opportunities for
working through the issues. These properties add a healing aspect to other
therapy interventions. What does this accountability look like? The answer
is found by examining each one of the dynamics of the affirmation triangle. The limitations of language force us to write separately about the parts
of the affirmation triangle; nevertheless, it is important to remember that
accountability, intimacy, and dependency always interact.

Recognizing clients' needs for a safe secure environment, therapists
should develop a relationship with clients slowly and patiently and should
provide explicit information. The latter should include a conversation
about the appropriateness of clients' needs for safety and security in therapy. Not having experienced safety and security as children or in adult
relationships, clients find it difficult to know what therapists are talking
about. As a key ingredient of the relationship, positive affirmation by therapists is a constant challenge because of the characteristics of shame and
the doubt carried by clients. Providing validation for the worth of clients in
the therapeutic relationship sets the context for all interventions. Only by
experience, and gradually, as shame issues are resolved, will clients eventually believe that they are capable of providing their own safety and security.

Accountability

Shame-prone clients usually lack the experience of being in a relationship with an adult who can separate and act on the differences between
being responsible "to" someone, "for" someone, and "for" and "to" oneself. These distinctions of "to" and "for" are housed within the rights and
ability of individuals to make their own decisions and in every way to be
their own agents. Each of these distinctions calls for accountability, the
process of accounting to self and others according to a personal set of
values and standards. Dependency and intimacy issues also interact with
these processes. When therapists are accountable in the therapist-client
relationship, it provides experience for clients of working through responsibility issues.

Being responsible "to" one's clients calls for integrity, structure, professional skill, and an accounting for one's beliefs, values, standards, and
actions. For the therapeutic relationship, this means that the therapist
provides a structure for therapy backed by professional standards, values,
and ethics, as reflected by the therapist's expectations. What takes place in
sessions, how long issues are pursued, what types of interventions are used,

demonstrations of respect and acceptance of who the clients are and what they do, and setting the rules for in-session behavior with explicit limits are examples of the structure for which therapists are accountable.

If therapists working with shame-prone clients have neither the professional skill nor the resolve to work on their own shame-prone issues, they are not capable of being accountable to their clients. Although the context may be a bit more sophisticated, the relationship that clients have with their therapists will at times feel much like the one clients had with their parents (Alonso & Rutan, 1988b). Therapists may be reproducing or modeling in the client-therapist relationships their relationships with their own parents and children (Kramer, 1985).

In the early stage of therapy, it is often appropriate for therapists to be responsible "for" their clients. Because of their basic belief that they are "bad" and their consequent lack of skill acquisition, sometimes shame-prone clients need their therapist to be "for" them. For example, clients cannot consistently ask for what they want, set limits for themselves and others interacting with them, manage relationships effectively, or stand up for their rights with authority figures. It is important to remember that all interventions should be aimed at affirming clients—no easy task with the shame-based client.

Being accountable "to" and "for" oneself as a therapist requires congruence in integrating beliefs, values, and standards. To speak or act "for" clients out of impatience or a subconscious belief by therapists that they have the right answer may be incongruent with therapists' stated values of respecting clients and allowing them to explore and learn from their experiences. Cultivating a heightened sense of responsiveness to clients and sharing what is appropriate are part of this congruence.

Emphasis on choices, clients' right to choose, and interventions that actually require them to make choices reduces therapists' tendencies to inappropriately do "to" and "for" clients. With this focus, there is an atmosphere of trust and respect. However, identifying when clients are capable of making choices challenges therapists' sensitivity and diagnostic skill. Having to choose may send clients into fear of making mistakes and blaming themselves because they are "bad." These issues are not usually resolved in the early stages of therapy.

Dependency

Shame-prone clients with dependency issues often have difficulty with authority figures. Since the therapist is in an authority role, the therapeutic relationship provides opportunities to work through authority issues. How do therapists maintain control of therapy, give their clients agency, and not shame them in the process? This is often the issue as therapists set limits, explicate expectations, and model relationship behavior with clients (Pichert & Elam, 1986).

Setting limits is a dependency issue because parents who failed to set limits sent the message "you are not worth much" to their children. When therapists do not claim the limits as their own, they are replicating the experiences of shame-prone clients whose parent(s) issued reasons and often consequences for behavioral guidelines without owning the values themselves. For example, clients may have heard their parents setting limits in the name of the school, God, or the other parent:

- "You will be in trouble with Miss Wilson if you do not finish your homework."
- "If you steal, lie, masturbate, etc., God will punish you."
- "Do that garage cleaning again. You know how your father wants it done."

When one is confident about one's boundaries, setting limits comes from one's values, standards, and expectations for self and others. Shame-prone clients need the limitations of a safe environment and modeling to learn to set limits themselves. Therapists need to be very clear and explicit about what their limits are, in and out of the sessions, and to own the limits as theirs rather than intimating that they belong to someone else.

The following are examples of attempts by a therapist to set limits regarding clients' telephone calls. Because the limits are not personally owned, they will very likely shame clients.

- "My wife gets very upset when clients call me at home; so do not call."
- "The agency I work for does not allow us to give out our home telephone numbers or our addresses. I cannot give you my number."
- "Our own research indicates that clients have greater success reaching therapists through an answering service than if we give out our numbers. Please use the answering service."

All three of these statements may be accurate and rational, but they may also be similar to shaming messages that clients have previously received.

What can therapists who want to own their values say to clients?

- "I do not receive calls from clients at home. The answering service or the office staff always contacts me in case of emergencies. Please use the answering service if you think it is an emergency."
- "I will be available to you, but I must set the limits on how that will occur. You may call me at my office between the hours of 9 a.m. and 5 p.m. on Monday through Friday. If I am in a session with

someone when you call, I will return your call. If you have an emergency at another time, the answering service is available to you. They will contact me."

When working with shame-prone clients, it is very helpful to have a receptionist and an answering service as well as a support therapy team. The personnel who operate these services should be trained in how to communicate with clients. Staff people who accept calls need to make some information available to clients, e.g., "Dr. Brown is out of the office at this time. May I take a message?" Personnel must learn to interrupt shame-prone clients' stories and demands. One of us, in Guam en route to Japan for a professional workshop, had a call from a shame-prone client in the middle of the night. This client very cleverly manipulated a secretary into giving him my whereabouts. Angry about my leaving for two months, this client was acting out his anger and refusal to work with the new therapist. It may be that I had never made it clear to the client what was inappropriate and what the boundaries and limits were. It is not unusual for therapists to report that shame-prone clients call their home day and night for nonlife-threatening reasons.

For some therapists, accepting shame-prone clients' emotions and demands offers a real challenge. When therapists accept clients' full range of emotion in the therapist-client relationship, clients learn that emotions in and of themselves are part of every relationship. Eventually they may learn that feelings do not have to be shameful. Therapists who stay "with" clients through rejection, resistance, acting out, incessant demands, and manipulative behaviors have ample opportunity to model negotiations, boundary awareness, limit-setting, and health in relationships. No matter how many mistakes are made, clients learn that they are acceptable as *people* even though they may be criticized for their *behavior.* Given enough time to work through many relationship issues and emotions, clients turn their internalized shame to transitory shame.

Intimacy

Setting limits pertaining to intimacy issues requires clarity within the therapist and in all messages, implicit and explicit, given to the clients. First, therapists must be aware of clients' boundaries or lack thereof. Therapists need to be respectful as they make observations of where the boundaries seem to be. Therapists should then adjust their boundaries and limits to match clients'. Personal space, shaking hands, touching, and hugging—all involving intimacy—can be shame-inducing to clients and traps to the insensitive and unwary therapist. Although they are not completely worked through until the final stages of therapy, these issues must be addressed in the early stages.

Focusing on personal space in a two-person system is an intimacy issue, and being accountable for personal space is a dependency issue. Clients who in the past have used sex to manipulate or who have been victims of sexual abuse may misinterpret any kind of touch. Therapists need to be very careful to eliminate sexual innuendos from conversation and nonverbal behavior. Direct focus on what is being felt and expressed, as well as explicit conversation if sexual behavior is exhibited, can be therapeutic. Being close without being sexual is a challenge for many therapists and clients, especially if they are shamed on intimacy issues. Sharing thoughts, feelings, beliefs, and positive affirmations creates a different kind of closeness, one that models intimacy for clients and provides practice for them in a safe environment.

Validating the Systemic Positions of Clients

Information about clients' systemic position coupled with information about their family of origin and their shame-prone issues provides another avenue for positive affirmation of clients. For example, first children shamed on intimacy were taught by their parents to get their work done, to take care of themselves, and to not expect intimacy from their parents. In reaction to these messages, they felt compelled to work. No matter how much they did nor how well the work was done, they always felt unfulfilled.

Lori, a 24-year-old shame-prone first child, made the comment in a therapy group that she was very discouraged with her job. Slumped in her chair and with little energy, Lori said that, no matter how many hours of overtime she put in, she could never finish what she had to do. She indicated that she felt so desperate about the work that she was thinking of quitting her job. Graduating first in her college class in humanities, Lori had secured a junior position as an editor for a well-known and successful publishing house. From previous conversations in the group, the therapists and group members knew that after two years on the job Lori had an excellent salary and had completed a number of successful projects for the company.

Dr. Brown, one of the group therapists, hypothesized from Lori's family history and details recounted by her of experiences with her father that Lori was shamed on the intimacy dimension. Her numerous affairs, each of which had ended unhappily, coupled with her feelings of inadequacy and hopelessness, added substance to Dr. Brown's hypothesis.

Acting on this data, Dr. Brown said to Lori, "I have something I would like to explore with you. Are you willing to do that?"

Without looking at him and with apparent suspicion, Lori responded, "What is it?" (Notice that she did not give him permission, but wanted more information.)

"I have a hunch that you have worked all of your life, doing job after job, chores at home, babysitting, getting good grades, president of the student body, going the extra mile for every employer, and always feeling that it was never enough and never good enough. No matter who told you that you had done an excellent job—your dad, your mom, your teachers, the university by graduating you first in your class, or your present supervisors who continue to give your raises—you never believe them, do you?"

(Raising her head and looking directly at him) "How did you know that?" (Dropping her head) "Yes! Yes! That is the way I feel. Why am I never good enough?"

"This all began in your family, with you trying to meet the responsibilities and job assignments given to you. With more exploration you will understand, work through some issues you have, and begin to feel different about your job performance."

This interaction gave Lori hope. Although the issues were not worked out in that session, Lori did some significant work in later sessions. In one of those sessions, when the group discussed trust, Lori indicated that when Dr. Brown seemed to know her feelings and her motivation for working so hard and never feeling good about it, she felt understood and accepted by him. This allowed her to move forward in therapy even though she was very frightened at times.

By knowing the systemic sibling position model for first children, Dr. Brown guessed that work was substituted for the intimacy that Lori never had with her father. Using information from the systemic sibling position model discussed in Chapter 7, the therapist provided support and understanding to Lori. Knowing the model for all four sibling positions and the characteristic shame-prone responses provides the therapist with some shortcuts for building relationships and choosing interventions (Hoopes & Harper, 1987).

ASSESSMENT GOALS

Although assessment is an ongoing process in all stages of therapy, it is particularly important in the early stage of therapy. Only those processes that have to do with shame-proneness are identified here; certainly, other assessments may be appropriate for particular cases.

Assessment for Individuals, Couples and Families

One of the first tasks in therapy is to assess shame-proneness for individuals, couples, and families. The following case illustrates some of the methods available for assessing shame-proneness in clients.

Barry, age 12, had a history of poor school attendance and achievement. The oldest of three children, Barry and his siblings lived with their mother,

Angie, who was an alcoholic. Angie worked when she could, but she was often on welfare. All three children, Barry, Burt, and Dan, were currently in a foster home while their mother received treatment for alcoholism in a nearby center.

No one knew where their father, Don, was. A hard drinking, sometimes construction worker, he moved in and out of their lives, most often with confusing behavior. His clumsy attempts to get love and get attention from them were often followed by violence. He beat Angie when he was drunk, then made remorseful attempts to love her and the boys and to gain their forgiveness. Although he did not beat the boys, he was verbally and emotionally abusive, e.g., calling them names and telling them that they would never amount to anything because they were such stupid sissies. On the one hand, he commanded them to take care of their mother; on the other, he derided their intimacy with her and their attempts to defend her from him. Angie responded to the stress with increasing bouts of drinking.

Barry was sent to therapy by the foster home agency because he seemed depressed, failed to attend to personal hygiene, and would not comply with the rules in the foster home. As the therapist gathered information about his client, he wondered if Barry was shame-prone on both intimacy and dependency or if he was shame-prone on one and not the other. As the therapist interviewed Barry, he used the assessment checklist (Chapter 9, Table 9.1) for identifying shame-prone individuals. In regard to emotional patterns, Barry had a constricted range of feeling, responding with anger to almost everything. He acted as though he were bad. He felt he had failed his mother and his brothers because they were not together as a family and he could not stop "them" from taking his mother away.

Based on Barry's behavior, the therapist hypothesized that his thought patterns had some indications of shame. He seemed to believe that he "had something wrong with him," and he distorted reality, as he rarely described events the same way twice. His nonverbal behavior patterns included avoidance of looking at the therapist. He looked down most of the time; when he did look up, he didn't seem to know what to do with his eyes. The reports from his teacher and his foster parents were that he kept to himself, didn't try to make friends, and acted with suspicion when others, both adults and children, treated him well. When he thought no one was watching him, he watched other children playing and having fun, with a great look of longing. His foster parents heard him crying at night.

Looking at the treatment map in Chapter 10 (Table 10.1), the therapist thought that Barry very likely had intimacy, productivity, and dependency issues. He sensed the anger and the rage and heard Barry make comments about how he could never "do it right." Based on Barry's history, the therapist thought that his client would probably have abandonment issues as well.

Assessing Family of Origin

In the early stage of therapy patterns of shame in clients' families of
origin need to be explored (Boszormenyi-Nagy & Ulrich, 1981; Guerin &
Pendagast, 1976; Kramer, 1985). Children often cannot give all the details
and history of the family. However, they can provide many clues. It should
be remembered that clients may construe and experience gathering historical data as evidence of their "badness." In response, therapists should
provide additional information and alternative ways of construing the facts.
In asking questions about clients' families, therapists need to be sensitive
to their shame. While some will be overwhelmed by emotion, others will be
very cerebral, completely blocked from emotion connected to the incidents
or facts. Therapists must be "with" their clients by maintaining an interpersonal bridge (Kaufman, 1989), acknowledging them for their survival
skills and resilience, for what they know, and for what is possible.

Family history and genograms should be used to identify major family
events (birth and age at present, death and cause of death, adoption, marriage and place of residence, divorce and with whom children live, serious
illnesses—physical and mental, geographic moves and pertinent data, accidents and losses in addition to those already described, miscarriages, abor-
tions, stillborns and children who died in infancy), occupations, special
interests, ethnic backgrounds, religious affiliation or lack thereof, education and training, family roles and relationship issues (McGoldrick & Gerson, 1985). Therapists may want to develop separate genograms to identify
addictions and codependency within the family.

Experienced therapists have their own way of developing genograms
and collecting information about clients' families of origin. Therapists who
have no experience collecting genogram information may want to consult
McGoldrick and Gerson (1985) or Pendagast and Sherman (1979). In collecting family information, therapists should search for events that contributed to shame-proneness and unhealthy guilt in family members. Diagram-
ming recurring patterns can be very helpful. Separating out maternal and
paternal sources helps create awareness for clients.

To assess Barry's family of origin for shame-proneness, his therapist did
a number of things. First he had Barry draw a picture of his family that
included the children and both parents (Scharff & Scharff, 1987). Second
he had Barry complete FACES III (Olson, Portner, & Lavee, 1985). Then
he had Barry's two brothers attend two sessions with Barry. During this
time, he encouraged the boys to recall and describe events in their family.
He also saw the brothers without Barry and had them draw pictures of the
family.

Getting permission from the treatment program personnel, the therapist visited Angie for three hours. During this time, he answered her
questions about the boys. Then he had her complete Faces III and did a
detailed genogram with her that included information about her family of

origin and what she remembered about her husband's family. A few weeks later, he saw Barry's Aunt Debra, his father's older sister, who had remained in touch with the family and seemed quite concerned about the boys. He did a genogram and a special event history (Duhl, 1981) with her, with special emphasis on her brother and FACES III concepts.

Using all available interview information, the therapist completed the assessment checklist for identifying shaming systems (Table 8.6). The emotional undercurrents of a sense of failure and emotions of anger, depression, and fears were evident in all of the interviews. Family members seemed to share the belief that they were losers, that they received very little help and support from society, and that things would never change for them. Some of the interaction patterns noticed from conversation and from the genograms and event histories were general emotional and physical abuse, lack of clarity in communicating, and intimacy and dependency needs that were rarely met. Chemical addiction, divorce, and serial marriages were common in both extended families. Based on this information, it appeared that both of Barry's parents came from families that looked bad and felt bad. The FACES III data indicated that the father came from a family that was rigidly enmeshed and the mother from one that was chaotically enmeshed. Both of these families were shaming systems that had many unresolved issues. The therapist concluded that Barry was shame-prone on both intimacy and dependency and that his parents were likely shame-prone on both dimensions as well.

THERAPEUTIC GOALS FOR THE CLIENT

Therapeutic goals for clients are different from the goals that clients bring to therapy and are able to articulate. Therapeutic goals are determined by therapists and or by the therapy team. The following goals illustrate what needs to be accomplished during the early stage of therapy.

Begin the Uncovering Process

Shame-prone clients live with myths, secrets, and denial of reality. The uncovering process to expose what the client is hiding from self and others extends through all stages of therapy, leading clients to eventual health and acceptance of reality. The goal for the first stage of therapy is for clients to uncover and release some of the family-of-origin secrets and myths.

Establish Supportive Relationships

Shame-prone individuals and systems tend to mistrust all relationships, even those that they participate in most of the time. Knowing that they manipulate and con in an attempt to get want they want, and knowing that they never really get what they want, shame-prone clients have little reason to trust relationships. Paradoxically, shame cannot be transformed into healthy guilt without honest, caring feedback from those who recognize the pain and fear. The therapeutic goal of clients' establishing a trusting, validating relationship with therapists and others involved in their therapy experience (e.g., family members and group members) proves to be a challenging task.

The first relationship to establish is one with the therapist(s). This relationship forms a model from which the client can generalize to relationships with other people. Interpersonal behaviors, thoughts, and emotional patterns all need to be examined as clients work to change their relationships with others. In family and group therapy, those attending the sessions are usually working on similar relationship issues from among those identified in the treatment map in Chapter 10: insufficiency, rejection, worthlessness, abandonment, emptiness, and loss. These issues arise for clients in the very first contact with a therapist. They need to be addressed in a validating way in the early stage of therapy, even though they will not get completely worked through until later stages.

Connect with the Inner Child

Whitfield (1987) defines the inner child as that part of a person that is "ultimately alive, energetic, creative, and fulfilled" (p. 1). People who live in dysfunctional families were not nurtured and allowed to freely express feelings, likes, and dislikes. This stifled the inner child, allowing a false self to front for the individual. It is the false self that covers and hides the pain and despair of shame (Bradshaw, 1988). The façades and barriers erected by the false self work so well that the inner child is wounded and lost.

In order for clients to connect with the pain of the inner child, they must begin to trust their own feelings (Wurmser, 1987). Secrets of sexual, physical, and emotional abuse eventually have to be uncovered and faced as the inner child is allowed to be little, protected, and nurtured by therapists and supportive relationships. The initial goal is to connect with the inner child and begin to risk sharing feelings in a healing process. Such a connection may be unstable and frightening for shame-prone clients in the early stages of therapy.

Whitfield (1987) identified one part of the child within as the feeling child. People who are shame-prone may be connected to some aspects of the inner child, e.g., the creative child may have full rein in an artist's life, the thinking and reasoning child may function very well in tasks that require thinking and reasoning. However, shame-prone clients are almost always cut off from the feeling child. Gaining access to the whole inner child requires freeing all aspects and moving toward high energy and a consistent sense of self. In the early stage of therapy, the goal is to get clients to connect to the feeling aspect of the inner child. Most of the work with the inner child occurs in the middle stage of therapy.

Join a Support Group

If one or more family members are addicted or codependent, it is appropriate that they join or continue membership in a 12-step program (Lawson, Ellis, & Rivers, 1984). The first five steps of the 12-step program focus on stopping destructive behavior and returning to a balanced life. To do this, clients must work through some of their denial and begin to uncover their fears and secrets. This focus fits nicely with the goals of the early stage of therapy. The therapy team should be aware of clients' progress in the 12-step program and integrate therapy with their program. The support given by sponsors and group members needs to match the goals of therapy. Focus on shame in therapy is a plus for any 12-step program.

Other types of support groups may also be very helpful. Team sports, individual sports with a consistent group, and other organized groups may provide the needed support. Support systems work if participation is voluntary and group members are committed to the principles that run the group.

Patent (1989) support groups are a viable alternative. The groups have a suggested procedure for operating each session, with an 11-step problem-solving procedure, the purpose of which is to encourage support. Unconditional love is both the goal and the model for giving support in these groups. However, shame-prone individuals, depending upon the degree of dysfunction, may not be able to tolerate these groups in the early stage of therapy.

Acknowledge and Own Spirituality

Acknowledging and owning one's spirituality may not occur in the early stage of therapy, but it is an important goal to address. Shame-prone individuals, couples, and families may have experienced shame in formal religion. Messages from the pulpit and interactions with religious leaders and fellow churchgoers may have been very shaming to clients. Some clients are church attenders and others are not. Some may have participated in religions that have a focus on consciousness-raising and New Age ideas, thereby having had experiences different from those of their parents and most of society. It is not religiosity that needs acknowledging but spirituality. Whether clients regularly attend any religious service is not a concern. Rather, whether clients are in touch with their own empowerment and a "power higher than themselves" is the spirituality issue that needs to be identified as a goal.

Those clients who have participated in addiction treatments and 12-step programs may have already addressed the issue of a "higher power outside of self," but it is not necessarily true that they have worked through their shame issues enough to have connected with their own spirituality. In this context therapists must be very aware of their own issues. Therapists who have their own biases regarding organized religion or a particular religion may shame their clients even when they think they are supporting them.

PROCESS GOALS FOR THERAPISTS

Process goals for therapists act as stabilizers, as markers of progress, and as indicators of directions in which to move. These goals also help the therapy team determine if they have moved through the early stage of therapy and are moving into the middle stage. Intervention strategies connected to these goals are described later in this chapter.

Establish the Therapeutic Contract

A therapeutic contract with clients does not just happen. It develops from the quality and clarity of the relationship between clients and therapists. Even therapists who are used to having an element of trust as part of the contract will find that trust is rarely a component in the early stage of therapy with shame-prone clients. For these clients, the contract may be based on needs and hopes that are constantly denied and counteracted by their own pessimism and cynicism.

As part of the contract, therapists need to reassure clients that they will be "with" them. This means that in the face of all the games and rejection that clients exhibit, the therapist will not abandon them. Shame-based people think that any punishment that comes to them is well deserved. They often do their best to prove to themselves that therapists will punish them. Even though their sense of identity is negative, it is affirming to them, and they seek consistency with their mental frame in actual experience. When therapists do not recognize their clients' "badness," they lose credibility. If therapists indulge the "child" or the "deceptive adult" and do not set limits, clients recognize the "con" they can run (for example, one client tried to seduce her male therapist so that she could say, "I don't have to listen to you. You sleep with your clients.").

Therapists need to avoid retaliation with both children and adult clients. Being "with" them is crucial. No matter what else is going on, therapists must stay "with" shame-prone clients. Caring in this way is central to therapy and to the therapeutic contract. Therapists have to be clear enough that they notice the shame, patient enough so that they are not punitive, sophisticated enough to match client games, and structured enough to work through shame step by step.

Choose Where to Begin

Therapists should acknowledge clients and their reasons for coming to therapy. After assessment is completed, therapists can turn to the treatment map in Chapter 10. The presenting problem or the predominant emotion of shame-prone clients often indicates where on the map to begin. When a client is exhibiting primarily anger, for example, the therapist should begin with the productivity/rejection/anger-hurt pattern. There is no right place to begin; in keeping with principles of equifinality and equipotentiality (Von Bertalanffy, 1968), it is assumed that any starting place on the map recursively leads to all patterns that needs attention.

The basic thrust in treating shame-based behavior is to get at the basic feelings and needs of clients, affirm them as legitimate, and legitimize clients' feelings, even the bad ones. The identification of where to begin on the map starts with the symptoms and stories offered by clients. "I'm depressed." "I lost my job again." "I don't have any energy." "My son won't mind me. He won't go to school." Therapists should take this information and ask what the client wants at a deeper level beneath the words. The client who said, "I never get anything done, or at least done right," was focused on the many rejections he had experienced. By noticing the anger and commenting on it, the therapist legitimized his feelings: "I notice that you are angry. It makes sense to me that you would be angry given that your dad seems to constantly reject whatever you do."

Work the First Three Patterns of the Treatment Map

The major treatment goal for the early stage of therapy is to intervene to some degree in the first three patterns on the treatment map (Table 10.1). This includes identifying and confronting games of individuals and systems, identifying and connecting beliefs with shame-prone issues for individuals and systems, and creating awareness and a connection with the client's inner child. The major emphasis, beginning in the early stage and continuing on into the middle stage of therapy, is on breaking through clients' denial and uncovering secrets and dysfunctional myths.

INTERVENTION AND THERAPEUTIC STRATEGIES

So far we have described *what* to do and said very little about *how* to do it. Here we identify intervention strategies and specific techniques for intervening in shame-prone systems in early stages of therapy. Table 12.1 summarizes the various elements involved. A therapist, co-therapists, or

TABLE 12.1
Areas for Intervention

| Therapists | Therapy Modalities | TARGET AREAS FOR INTERVENTION | | | |
		Feelings	*Belief-Cognitive*	*Behavioral*	*Affirmation Imagery*
Therapist	Individual				
	Relationships Dyadic				
Co-therapists	Triadic				
	Nuclear				
Therapy Team	Family				
	Extended Family				
	Groups				

the therapy team can enter through different levels of the system, all of which are independent subsystems but at the same time interdependent and interactive. These levels are: the *individuals*; the *dyadic* subsystems—the couple, parent, parent-child, and sibling subsystems; the *triadic* subsystems—parents and a child, a parent and two children, and three siblings; the *interactional framework* as a whole or the *family* system; the *extended family* system—family, dyadic, and triadic subsystems with marital interfaces and transgenerational patterns; or a *therapy or support group.*

The ultimate goal of therapeutic strategies and interventions is to lead clients through the unmet need/interpersonal/emotion patterns identified on the treatment map (Table 10.1) and resolve issues of insufficiency, rejection, worthlessness, abandonment, emptiness, and loss. As those patterns are resolved, the identities for individuals, couples, and families begin to change.

Treatment strategies encompass various interventions in master plans to accomplish client and treatment goals. Numerous considerations enter into planning strategies, including where to enter in which system, what therapist should be involved in the therapy (e.g., one therapist, co-thera-pists, the treatment team, or some special program such as a five-day extensive treatment for codependency or a 28-day treatment for chemical dependency), how to track the progress and plan strategies for the various treatment modalities (e.g., individual, couple, or group), and what interven-tions to use.

The top of Table 12.1 lists four targets of intervention. These targets are feeling patterns, belief-cognitive patterns, behavioral patterns (including verbal, nonverbal and interpersonal, and unmanageability), and affirmation and imagery patterns. Of course, therapists' theoretical models may influ-ence specific interventions for each of the target areas, but experiential interventions should be included in these choices.

It is assumed that almost any intervention will influence more than one of the target areas. Although an intervention may be primarily focused on changing feeling patterns, the other target areas (e.g., beliefs, imagery, and behavior) may also be indirectly influenced. Some interventions contain components that target all of the areas.

Using the Treatment Map in Therapy

The map (Table 10.1) is designed to keep therapists and therapy teams focused on shame-prone issues, regardless of what else they do in therapy. Using the map may seem awkward, but with practice it becomes a useful tool.

Steps for Working the Map.   In the early stage of therapy, the following steps are useful in working the patterns on the map for both individuals and systems. More steps will be added to these in the middle stage of therapy (see Chapter 13).

1. *Based on what a client presents, the therapist identifies an unmet need, an interpersonal issue on the diagonal, or an emotion.*

The therapist infers this information from observation of in-session inter-action, interview data, and other assessment. It is unusual for shame-prone clients to talk about their needs in the early stage of therapy. Usually clients talk about emotions or issues. The affects of rage, anger, and humili-ation are usually much easier to identify than issues or unmet needs. Shame-prone individuals tend to talk about themselves in disparaging ways, which points to the issue of insufficiency. The issues of rejection and worthlessness may be more obscure but will emerge as they are connected to emotions and needs.

2. *Therapists assist clients and systems to express emotion and experi-ence unmet needs and interpersonal issues.*

Later in the chapter interventions are listed that target the areas of feelings; these can be used in accomplishing this step.

3. *Therapists confront games and beliefs.*

The games and beliefs for each of the three first patterns are described in Chapter 10. Interventions from all four targets areas, e.g., feelings, beliefs, behavior, imagery may be used to confront games and beliefs. Each pattern on the treatment map has its games. One of the most effective tools for confronting games is the therapist's ability to comment on the games in a way that maintains the interpersonal bridge, the "being with the client."

Clients' systemic positions influence the ways in which they use games to cover shame-prone issues. These games are related to their job assignments and identity issues in their families of origin. Whether children or adults, clients can explore and uncover these patterns. Clients can then decide whether to continue the games and retain the beliefs or give them up.

People in the first systemic position develop games to cover their feelings and beliefs about their inadequacy. Emphasis on the meanings of words, open hostility, and instant amnesia are typical games. People in the second systemic position develop games to hide that they are lost and feeling totally inundated. They are so overloaded with their own and others' feelings that they have very little knowledge of what is going on for them. Their games carry themes of helplessness, lostness, and stubbornness. People in the third systemic position develop games to cover the sense of being locked in with no choices, imprisoned forever. Their games carry themes of detachment, not caring, and "you can't get to me." People in the fourth systemic position develop games to cover their feeling of incompetency. In dysfunctional families children in fourth systemic positions have the job assignment of keeping peace and harmony in the system. They are never able to achieve this except in piecemeal fashion with little continuity. They are negatively affirmed as incompetent. Themes of "cuteness," helplessness, and barter permeate their games.

The games related to the first pattern of unmet intimacy needs/insufficiency/rage are numerous, but they are all designed to cover shame. The major theme of games for the second pattern—unmet productivity needs/rejection/anger-hurt—is "to hell with you." The anger fuels the energy to maintain the game, as it takes on whatever form is needed by the individual or system to defend against rejection and hide shame. Games connected with the third pattern—unmet dependency needs/worthlessness/humiliation—communicate a theme of "I am no good." Playing the game "I am bad" somehow protects these individuals from fully feeling the pain and feelings of worthlessness.

In the early stage of therapy, therapists usually only touch on these games and clients respond with rage and denial. Recognizing the games and acknowledging them as protecting pain are usually the most that can be done. Most of the work that releases the pain and teaches clients honest ways of dealing with it is done in the middle stage of therapy.

Work Clients' Patterns of Denial.   Some clients are quick to label themselves as "bad." They have little awareness of the denial they use to cover the pain that accompanies the label. Denial is distorted thinking rooted deeply in the identities of shame-prone people, expressed as "I am bad." The denial includes dissociation from real events that were and are too punishing and debasing to tolerate. Wishes, wants, and needs that constantly shielded family members from reality taught individuals to live with denial and delusion.

Working through clients' denial in the early stage of therapy includes examining and reexperiencing shaming events represented in the first three patterns of the treatment map. Issues of insufficiency, rejection, and worthlessness in these three patterns represent the denial of the wholeness or health of self. Clients' presenting problems will probably include problems very different in description from the language of the treatment map. For example, a couple came to therapy because the wife was threatening to divorce her husband. He was physically and emotionally abusive to her and their children, and she had attempted suicide twice. Based on what they were presenting, two unmet need/interpersonal issue/emotion patterns on the map were involved: dependency/worthlessness/humiliation and uniqueness/emptiness/terror. No matter where therapists enter such a system, the objective is to move from the presenting problem to the patterns on the map.

The first level of involvement for therapists is represented in the pattern of intimacy/insufficiency/rage. The protective maneuvers and manipulative games presented by clients serve to deny that intimacy is an unmet need in their life. The therapeutic task is to break through the resistance and get them to stop playing games.

The second level of involvement for therapists is to engage the productivity/rejection/anger pattern. This pattern is also protected by games. When these games are taken away, clients experience anger and anticipate rejection. In fact, they will work at getting the therapist to kick them out of therapy—or at least out of any favorable relationship with the therapist. This is a familiar pattern for shame-prone clients. The therapeutic task is staying "with" the client no matter what. Sometimes the therapist will be angry. The anger is usually not the therapist's anger. Therapists sometimes take the client's anger as if it were their own because such a strategy protects them from the client's anger.

The third level of involvement for therapists is the pattern of dependency/humiliation/worthlessness. This pattern is often buried under the first two and does not emerge until those are experienced. As the denial games of the first two patterns are exposed and rendered useless and the anger is faced and tolerated, the worthlessness is uncovered. At this point some clients will say that they are not worth bothering with. The emotional, cognitive, nonverbal, interpersonal, and individual behavior patterns will be evident in the insession interactions. At this point, the therapeutic task is to stay "with" clients and begin to focus on symptoms identified on the individual and systems checklists (Chapter 8, Tables 8.2 and 8.6).

Clients may then begin to experience fear and terror associated with the other patterns on the treatment map. Clients' fear may lead them to abandon therapy in anticipation that the therapist will eventually abandon them. At this point, clients are feeling a double whammy—they know that they are "bad" and now the therapist knows it too. The shame is intense, and they do not know how to deal with it. Leaving or threatening to leave tests therapists and requires them to prove to clients that they will stay with them. At this point, therapists should not allow clients to put themselves down. The focus must be on facing the shame and talking about where they got the feelings of shame. The therapist can then provide additional insight on possible sources of shame.

Interventions

As identified in Table 12.1, interventions target four areas: feeling patterns, cognitive-belief patterns, behavioral patterns, and affirmation and imagery patterns. Although these separations are artificial, they are helpful in identifying interventions in relationship to the therapy goals. Many interventions are complex enough that they affect all four target areas. Certainly therapists can use interventions not listed here that work for them as well.

Targeting Feeling Patterns.

1. *Identify clients' range of feelings and which ones are predominant.*

Emotions of rage, anger, humiliation, fear, terror, and grief are important, but therapists should look for others as well. Most of this emotion can be identified from interaction with clients. If it seems appropriate, therapists can share their observations with clients. Clients often offer nonverbal recognition that the therapist is on track. Although some may verbally deny or even ignore therapists' observations, clients may internally acknowledge these observations and retrieve them at a later time.

2. *Encourage and provide opportunities for clients to release some of their shameful feelings.*

When therapists verbalize their observations of the patterns on the treatment map, client are able, at times, to release some of the emotion. Many interventions that move the client into memories of shameful experiences bring feelings to the surface. With support, these can be released. Such releases may come in the form of crying, hitting on something, screaming, swearing, or other verbalizations.

3. *Begin a process of supporting and encouraging clients' expression of feelings.*

As therapists work on the patterns from the treatment map, they can model how to express some of the feelings that they expect are there. Other interventions, such as drawings (Burns, 1982), other-handed writing (Capacchione, 1988), storytelling, sculpting, and body work, will help clients to uncover and express what they are feeling.

4. *Assist couple or family systems and subsystems to get in touch with and own their anger, sadness, depression, or fear.*

As individuals in couples and family systems begin to identify their feelings, therapists can focus observations or questions on how they must feel. This is partly an educational process to get clients thinking that feelings can be shared by more than one person. A recently divorced woman was in the first session of therapy with her two children. Her stated reason for coming to therapy was that she felt depressed. Her observable symptoms also indicated depression. Although the children had more energy, when the focus was not on them their behavior and mood matched their mother's. When she commented on this observation, the therapist had the immediate attention of all three family members. They all wanted to know how that could be, but they did not deny it. Focusing on the divorce, the therapist indicated that they shared some but not all of the same feelings prior to, during, and after the divorce. Then she asked them a number of questions. "Which of you feel sad?" "Which of you feel angry and do not know what to do with it?" "Have you felt scared and do you now feel scared?"

After getting responses that indicated that all three shared some of the same feelings, the therapist talked about their being part of each other as a family. They could say that the family is feeling sad, scared, or depressed. This led to a discussion of how they felt about these feelings as a family. The children both indicated that they thought they were "bad" as a family.

The mother was so busy reassuring the children that this was not so that she denied any feelings she had about this issue.

Targeting Cognitive-Belief Patterns.

1. *Begin family-of-origin work.*

Cognitive-belief interventions appropriate to this stage of therapy include participation in early family-of-origin work such as starting a genogram (Guerin & Pendagast, 1972) and outlining nuclear family history and/or couple or relationship history (Stahmann & Hiebert, 1987). Cognitive therapists are generally inventive in developing strategies to examine cognitive constructs. Arnkoff (1981) blends Gestalt techniques with a cognitive viewpoint to disrupt the client's usual pattern. Freeman (1982) demonstrates the use of dream material as a way of restructuring cognitive processes.

2. *Therapists assist clients in becoming aware of family rules and their effects on individuals and all systems* (Ford, 1983).

This is an essential step toward examining fears, secrets, and myths and their relationship to clients' feelings of humiliation and their conviction that they are bad. Family histories, sculpting, metaphoric work, enactments, and other interventions that help them experience the family rules are useful (Minuchin & Fishman, 1981; Papp, 1983; Satir, 1972). When clients appear to be shamed by making the rules of their systems explicit, the therapists can validate their experience of shame by commenting on it and staying with them in the experience. The feeling of shame can then be labeled as a feeling rather than the concept of "I am bad."

3. *Teach clients ways of conceptualizing and owning their needs, e.g., the seven listed on the treatment map and others that are current and conscious.*

Many shame-prone clients do not know how to think and talk about their needs. One way to begin is by talking about basic needs that everyone experiences. Maslow's (1970) hierarchy of needs—physiological, safety, love and belonging, esteem, and self-actualizing—offers a vocabulary for beginning the conversation. Kaufman's (1989) interpersonal needs—need for relationship, need for touching/holding, need for identification, need for differentiation, need to nurture, need for affirmation, and need for power—offer an alternative. The needs on the treatment map (Table 10.1) also serve as a springboard into more personalized experiences. Most people have an intellectual understanding of these needs, but shame prevents them from examining them in the context of their lives.

Targeting Behavioral Patterns. Behavioral patterns rarely change in the early stage of therapy. Almost anything therapists might do to focus on behavioral patterns could be overwhelmingly shaming to clients. Because of this, therapists may be able only to keep behavioral interventions in the back of their mind to be retrieved during the middle stage of therapy.

1. *Use nonverbal, verbal, and interpersonal patterns to teach clients about their shame patterns.*

Following the nonverbal, verbal, and interpersonal patterns in the session provides many clues for the therapist and opportunities to teach clients about their shame patterns. Comments by the therapist on the process assist in the uncovering of shame for clients, although it may be shaming to clients.

Jessie and Vern were in the third session with their therapist. Jessie spent most of her time looking down at the floor, and Vern took great care in examining his fingernails. Intermittently one would look at the other. Rarely did either one of them look directly at the therapist. Dr. Tourley, speaking very gently, commented that she noticed that they were having difficulty looking at her. Teasingly she asked if they could look at her if she were a big purple rabbit. Vern and Jessie looked up and smiled and dropped their eyes again. Then the therapist said that she knew how difficult it was for them to talk about their shameful experiences with her—or anyone. She encouraged them to look at each other and occasionally asked them to look directly at her. Observation and comments on verbal and patterned behavior by the therapist start the uncovering process for shame-prone clients.

2. *Examine dysfunctional communication patterns and model and rehearse alternatives.*

Most therapists have chosen specific models for observing interaction patterns and teaching more effective ways of communicating. For example, Dr. Tourley utilized the interaction patterns of placating, blaming, computing distracting and leveling (Satir, 1972; Satir & Baldwin, 1983). She noticed that Vern and Jessie often interacted with each other in a placater-placater interaction, with Vern occasionally switching to the computer style. When he switched to the computer style Jessie sometimes moved into a distracter style. During the fourth session Dr. Tourley had them exaggerate these interaction styles with body position and words in a role play of a recent conflict between them. Asking them to then get in a body position that would be more comfortable, she coached them into the leveling style. This early in therapy the goal was awareness rather than behavior change. As expected they were shamed by the experience of observing their own behavior, but they also learned from the experience and made frequent comments about their interaction styles.

   3. *Assist clients in becoming aware of dysfunctional self-talk and how it affects interactions with others.*

As clients identify shame and the behavior that accompanies it, therapists can assist them to be aware of the self-talk that goes along with it. In the early stage of therapy clients are often reluctant to disclose their shameful thoughts, e.g., "What I just said, or did, was bad or wrong. I never do anything right. I am bad. I am not lovable." Sometimes therapists can accurately guess what clients are thinking and verbalize it for them. Often clients will deny the "guess," acting under the assumption that they must cover their shame, but later they will acknowledge that the therapist was accurate.

   For example, as Dr. Tourley worked with Jessie and Vern while they acted out their interaction patterns, she sensed that they were shamed by the experience. At one point Vern was standing in the "computer interaction style" with his arms folded over his chest and staring into the distance and talking. Jessie was in the "placater interaction style" on one knee with one hand raised toward Vern, pleading with him to listen to her. After asking them how they were feeling at the moment and not getting a reply, Dr. Tourley said that she would make some guesses about how they might be feeling. If they chose to they could acknowledge what was true for them. These are some of the therapist's statements: "I am bad. I am doing this all wrong. Dr. Tourley knows how bad I am. I don't like this position, but I am helpless and cannot change it." Vern said that he did not like the position and Jessie remained quiet. After commenting that what they thought about themselves affected the way they interacted with each other, Dr. Tourley went on with the activity.

   Near the end of the session the therapist asked them if they had learned anything about their shame and how they interacted with each other. Shyly, with head bowed, Jessie said that she wondered how Dr. Tourley knew what she was thinking. Vern said that he too wondered that. This session marked the beginning of acknowledging their dysfunctional self-talk and led to exploring how they could substitute positive self-talk for negative.

   4. *Examine clients' system pattern—couples, families and subsystems— for patterns of interaction that are shaming.*

Knowing the assessment checklist for identifying shaming systems (Table 8.6) and being conversant with the dynamics of the affirmation triangle (Chapter 2) assist therapists in recognizing shaming patterns in clients' system patterns. Each therapist's knowledge and epistemology about relationships and family systems can be utilized to explore and uncover these patterns with their self-talk and shaming behaviors.

Targeting Visualization, Metaphors, and Affirmation Patterns. Using the imagination to experience something in the past or the future may include all of the senses, but especially the client representational systems (Bandler & Grinder, 1975). Clients' language allows therapist to know their representational systems—kinesthetic, visual, or auditory (Dilts, 1983; Lankton, 1980). By focusing on clients' strongest representational system, therapists can construct visualizations that will be productive and meaningful.

Shame-prone people tend to use their own visualizations to confirm how bad they are and how terrible their world is. Some of them experience visualizations as overpowering and terrible. Others say that they have no ability to visualize. Often clients interpret being able to visualize as literally being able to see picture-perfect anything imagined. Teaching clients how to visualize often increases their awareness of ongoing visualizations, heretofore denied.

Metaphors and affirmations usually involve visualizations in their structure. For example, metaphorical stories require some kind of visualizing to connect to the client's world. Positive affirmations require getting in touch with what is wanted and visualizing it as actually happening.

Numerous sources are available for teaching visualization techniques and for examples of how to use the technique, e.g., guided imagery, rerunning movies of one's life, re-creating interactions, and creating and using an inner guide (cf. Bry, 1978; Combs & Freedman, 1990; Denning & Phillips, 1987; Goodbread, 1987; Sherman & Freedman, 1986).

Visualizations are helpful in completing the steps for working the treatment map that were identified earlier in this chapter. Asking clients to close their eyes and see, hear, or feel something in the past requires visualization. When resistance to visualizations is experienced, both clients and therapists need to make reality checks and see where more work needs to be done.

As with other interventions listed in this chapter, most of the work for the interventions listed below will be completed in the middle stage of therapy, although they may be useful earlier in interpreting shame-prone behavior earlier.

1. *Assist individuals and systems in identifying the differences between negative and positive affirmations.*
2. *Design and practice a few simple positive affirmations.*
3. *Use guided imagery to explore clients' response to visualizations.*

THE TRANSITION TO THE MIDDLE
STAGE OF THERAPY

Two aspects of therapy, an established therapeutic contract and the nature of the client(s)-therapist relationship, determine when shame-prone clients are able to proceed to the middle stage of therapy.

The Therapeutic Contract

The state of the therapeutic contract is a viable measure for knowing if therapy has shifted to the middle stage. An established contract includes an explicit agreement about what the client and therapist will work on, including shame-prone issues, that clients will attend therapy regularly, and that they will not leave therapy without discussing it with their therapist and therapy team, preferably face to face.

Nature of Client(s)-Therapist Relationship

Another indication of transition is that the therapists' ability to be "with" the clients is so well established that clients can express their feelings to their therapists. This means that clients and therapists can have verbal disagreements, offer each other honest and frank information and feedback, and still remain convinced that neither will abandon the other.

The nature of the relationship therapists establish with shame-prone clients is crucial to their treatment. Therapists' ability to be accountable in providing for clients' intimacy and dependency needs sets the stage for the rest of treatment.

CHAPTER 13

Treating Shame-Prone Systems: Middle Stage

S URPRISES, MURKY WATERS, progress, disappointments, acceleration, backsliding, unexpected treasures, harsh realities, flashes of inspiration, and sluggishness are but a few of the challenges therapists and clients face in the middle stage of therapy. In discussing this stage of therapy, Whitfield (1987) used verbs that capture the prevailing themes: learning, practicing, clarifying, sharing, beginning, trusting, experiencing, talking about, and loving. In comparison, the verbs for the early stage are identifying, realizing, recognizing, questioning, and defining love.

PITFALLS FOR THERAPISTS

Since most of the working through of shame occurs in the middle stage, it can be especially demanding on therapists' energies and emotional reserve. Continuing involvement in a consultation group and a team approach help a great deal. Following are some pitfalls that therapists should avoid during the middle stage.

Ignoring Clients' Intimacy and/or
Dependency Needs

As clients move into the middle stage of therapy, they are very vulnerable. Having identified and recognized some of their issues but still living with most of the pain, they may cover their pain, shame, and needs with pseudo-health or bizarre acting-out. At the same time, they may expect that more of their intimacy and/or dependency needs will be met in the therapist-client relationship than is possible. Or, clients' manipulations may become more sophisticated and persistent as they recognize their shame. These confusing messages from clients combined with therapist fatigue resulting from the intensity required to be "with" their clients can lead to complacency. Therapists go through the motions "on automatic."

Being Arrogant About Their Ability
to Meet Clients' Needs

Therapists who believe that they can meet all the intimacy and dependency needs of their clients may be inappropriate with clients. It is usually in the middle stage of therapy that sexual contacts and emotional affairs occur between therapists and clients. Sometimes the arrogance of the therapist is versed in the belief, "I can teach this client very quickly how to be intimate without any danger to either of us."

Insensitivity to Interventions That Do
Something "to" or "for" Clients Inappropriately

Some clients come to therapy wearing blatant signs, "Help me! You are my only hope!" They then proceed to do everything they can to seduce the therapist into taking care of them. Other clients wear signs of suspicion, doubt, or apparent indifference. They communicate, "You can't help me! I'm here, but keep your distance." Another type of client seems to have it all together, seems willing to listen and cooperate. On the inside these clients are as frightened as the others. Therapists may work through some of the defenses early on, but defenses and fear heighten as the uncovering of shame intensifies in the middle stage of therapy.

Whatever games clients play to protect themselves, therapists need to be on guard. Though not intended, therapeutic processes can be further shaming to shame-prone clients. Many are schooled in victim and martyr roles and expect the therapist to do something "to" them. In contrast, other clients want everything done "for" them. The seduction of such helpless clients hooks many therapists who are by nature and training desirous of giving support and being concerned. Yet, when therapists are caught in constantly doing things "to" or "for" clients, little progress is made. Therapists constantly need to be aware of signals that clients are feeling shame.

GUIDELINES FOR THERAPISTS

Set Reasonable Limits for Behavior in and
Outside of Sessions

Limits for in-session and out-of-session behavior require therapists to plan ahead and consider the kind of circumstances that are difficult for shame-prone clients. Setting limits in therapy is a dependency issue that at times interacts with both accountability and intimacy issues. One can think of clients' responses to the therapists' limit-setting as developmental stages. For example, in the early stages of therapy, clients may compliantly accept limits or ignore them. Such behavior is similar in nature to that of young children, who obey rules most of the time but also purposely ignore them at times. Later in therapy, clients may be more rebellious about limits and rules, and they may test therapists to see if they will hold to the limits. This behavior is more like that of adolescents. Even later, as clients and therapists move into more healthy, interdependent relationships, clients set their own limits and respect the other person's.

> *Observe and Monitor Tendencies to Do Things*
> *"to" or "for" Your Clients That May Be Interpreted*
> *as Rejecting Them or as Verification of*
> *Their Unworthiness*

Therapists often act as the authority, believing that they know what is best for their clients. However, shame-prone clients expect that authority figures will eventually do something "to" them, e.g., punish them, abandon them, evaluate them negatively, take away their privileges. At other times therapists may do something "for" their clients, e.g., providing answers rather than requiring clients to explore, letting clients off the hook or rescuing them in some way. These behaviors are not therapeutic for shame-prone clients because they reinforce shaming feelings and beliefs.

CLIENT-THERAPIST RELATIONSHIPS

As the therapeutic relationship develops and shame-prone clients find the therapist to be trustworthy and helpful, they may become very demanding. As they feel understood for perhaps the first time in their lives, unmet needs rush forth. In such states, clients often send the following messages to therapists:

- "Be the warm loving father and/or mother that I never had."
- "Let me depend on you as I was never allowed."
- "Be my lover with all the understanding and compassion shown me in therapy sessions."
- "Be my confessor and help me set my life straight with God. Show me the love and acceptance that I never received from my (rabbi, priest, or minister).
- "Tell me how you handle these things in your life."
- "Be my siblings who have never been there for me."

- "Be my friend, always there for me."
- "I will do anything to please you—just tell me what."

Frequent telephone calls, backed by fabricated reasons for calling, can become commonplace, or clients may just call to talk and get support without regard for their inappropriate timing. During the middle stage, clients may use seduction and manipulation that have served them in their daily lives to get the therapist to meet their intimacy and dependency needs.

A dialogue from the case introduced in Chapter 1 serves as one example of how to respect the client and work with intimacy issues. This occurred in the middle stage of therapy.

Therapist: Marilyn, I notice that when I move toward you or even lean in your direction, you pull back and appear to be frightened. I want you to know that the chair that you are sitting in and the space around it is your territory. I do not intend to move closer to you than I am. I will not touch you or move into your space without your permission. I will always ask, and you have a right to say no. Leaning toward you does move me slightly toward you, but I am still in my space and intend to stay there. How are you responding to what I am saying?

Startled, Marilyn dropped her eyes to her hands in her lap and, after some time, lifted them to gaze at me.

Marilyn: I am frightened when you lean toward me. In my head I don't think you will hurt me, but you are bigger than I am and sometimes you move quickly.

I sat quietly, waiting for more information. Marilyn squirmed in her chair, dropped her head so her hair hid her face, and twisted her hands. In a quiet but reassuring voice, I responded.

Therapist: Do you know what is happening to you, Marilyn? (no response) Think about some of the things we have talked about in here. I think that you know and I am interested in what you are thinking.
Marilyn: (without raising her head and in a small voice) I am feeling ashamed and scared.
Therapist: Thank you for trusting me enough to share that. Please look at me so that we can see one another. Thank you for listening to me right now. Is this a good time to talk about what is happening to you and connect it to some of the other things we have done?
Marilyn: I don't know, I'm scared, but I would like to try.
Therapist: Do you know what happened to make you feel ashamed?

Marilyn: Something you said about me. . . .
Therapist: That certainly is a possibility. Would it be all right to explore what I said and how I said it?

As we explored what had been said, Marilyn identified that she felt fear when I said that she was entitled to her own space and that she could say no to intrusions into that space. Marilyn had not been abused sexually as a child, but her boundaries and space were often invaded. Her parents walked into her room at any time and they constantly read her mail and listened to her telephone calls. Her parents provided no boundary around their own relationship, confiding the most intimate details to Marilyn, asking for support and advice.

Although this was not the first time these issues had been dealt with, another element had been added. In reminding Marilyn what her rights were, I implied that the same rules also applied to my space. I hypothesized that Marilyn's responses meant something different from similar behavior in their first session. Then Marilyn did not want me to know that she was "bad." Yet she wanted to feel better and not be depressed. Later, in the middle stage of therapy and based on observations of Marilyn's behavior in our relationship, I thought she might be shamed by her feelings of wanting me to be closer to her. My leaning toward her may have triggered a need to be close to me and to be held by me, perhaps reminding her of sexual fantasies about me. In my interaction with her, I laid the groundwork for later work on Marilyn's intimacy issues with me. At the same time, I set limits for myself in a way that was acceptable to my client at this point in therapy.

ASSESSMENT GOALS

Preliminary assessment is completed in the first stage of therapy. However, in addition to being an ongoing process, assessment can also serve as intervention. Therapists and therapy teams have three assessment goals for the middle stage of therapy.

1. *Assess additional members of the family system as they enter therapy.*

As therapy unfolds, therapists can become more involved with various members of the nuclear family, the family of origin, and the extended family. For example, as more secrets are revealed, extended family members may be involved in order to work through various issues. Assessing these new members allows the therapist or therapy team to broaden their picture of the entire system in which the client functions.

2. *Follow leads in therapy that indicate the need for additional assessment information.*

This assessment focuses on clients and systems previously measured.
For example, in working with a shame-prone couple, the therapist had
difficulty breaking some of the collusions that seemed to maintain the
shame-prone couple identity. Each had made progress in releasing shame
feelings about his/her individual identity, but as soon as therapy focused
on resolving some of the couple issues, shame behaviors resurfaced. In a
team conference one person suggested doing more assessment of the couple to uncover the collusions. After a review of what was available, they
selected Bagarozzi and Anderson's (1989) Couple Relationship History and
History of the Presenting Problem to be used in conjoint sessions. Individual sessions were also held to complete Family Relationship Histories and
Family Myth Assessments. Based on Bagarozzi and Anderson's belief that
each spouse's personal mythology dovetails to form the couple mythology,
this combination of couple and individual data was designed to assist the
therapist in identifying central themes containing the collusions. The assessment data supported a hypothesis that the couple identity was shame-
prone.

3. *Perform second administrations of previous measures to determine if
outcome goals are being reached.*

Therapists and clients need to take the time to evaluate how therapy is
progressing on a regular basis. This type of evaluation serves a metacom-
munication function, helping both clients and therapists clarify their relationship, identify areas of growth and strength that might otherwise go
unnoticed, and change patterns and procedures in response to feedback.
The checklists in Chapter 8 (Tables 8.1 and 8.5) can be used to measure
progress from the beginning of therapy. Likewise, formal standardized
measures can be readministered and compared to the initial assessments to
determine progress. Other assessments related directly to the presenting
problems for each case may also be used.

THERAPEUTIC GOALS FOR THE CLIENT

Continue to Build on Early Goals

All of the clients' therapeutic goals for the early stage of therapy should
be built upon in the middle stage of therapy. To work through the shame-
prone issues, clients need to *continue the uncovering process* to expose
secrets, myths, and wishes that are part of their shame patterns. As clients

make progress or get stuck in the therapy process, *supportive relationships* become very important. Connecting with the *inner child* continues to be an important goal as clients work to get more in touch with their feelings and spontaneity. *Support groups* are as important in this stage of therapy as in the previous one. Finally, clients need to continue to explore and acknowledge their *spirituality* so that it is a healing force in their lives.

Demonstrate Healthy Identity

Because the major goal of therapy with shame-prone clients is achieving wholeness, it is important that therapists explicitly inform clients that they are helping them to develop a healthy identity. As part of that process, clients need to practice and demonstrate healthy identity in their interpersonal relationships. During some sessions therapists can reverse roles with the client and model verbal statements and even internal dialogue that represents healthy identity. The client can then rehearse similar behaviors in reenactments with the therapist. All of this can be followed up with homework assignments to demonstrate aspects of healthy identity in other relationships.

PROCESS GOALS FOR THERAPISTS

Two of the goals begun in the early stage of therapy—establishing the therapeutic contract and working client patterns of denial—need to be constantly reviewed and revised in the middle stage of therapy. The following additional process goals are also appropriate.

Set Limits

Many shame-prone issues for clients will surface in client-therapist relationships. As they surface, clients quite naturally transfer some of issues they have with their parents to their therapists. Understanding the affirmation triangle helps therapists to identity clients' interpersonal issues. To manage the feelings and behaviors of clients attached to the transference, therapists need to set limits while at the same time staying "with" their clients. The limits may include limiting clients' talking to therapists and prescribing certain behaviors in sessions. They are also related to boundaries. For example, therapists have to establish limits regarding sexual behaviors, touching, holding, etc. Therapists may also have to insist that clients be on time for appointments and that they attend regularly. All of these limits are necessary to facilitate the movement of clients through stages of dependency, e.g., from total dependency through counterdependency to independence to interdependence.

The least shaming way to remind clients what limits have been established is for therapists to verbalize their observations, e.g., "I notice that you are trying to get me to do something. Are you aware of that?" The therapist can then follow with a statement similar to the following, "You don't have to test the limits we have set. We still have a relationship even with the limits in place, and that won't change until we both agree that you are ready."

Integrate Therapy Modalities

As therapy progresses, the complexity and involvement of people increase. Each case requires an integration of the different modalities: e.g., individual; couple, parent-child, and nuclear family relationships; extended families; and groups. For instance, consider the case of a 57-year-old woman who was released from the hospital after a suicide attempt and entered into therapy with a therapist in private practice. She was identified as shame-prone in the early stage of therapy, which lasted for seven sessions—two with her alone, one with her husband alone, two with them as a couple, and two with their adult children (one separately and one with their parents). At that time, the therapist and the therapy team diagnosed both wife and husband as being shame-prone, but they also diagnosed the couple and the family as being shame-prone. Individually, the wife was diagnosed as shame-prone on both intimacy and dependency and the husband as shame-prone on intimacy.

In the middle stage of therapy, the therapists had the challenge of creating strategies that could serve all of these modalities. A number of the following questions were raised by the team and answered as the case proceeded.

- Should they both be involved in individual therapy before trying to do couple therapy? Or can couple and individual therapy take place concurrently?
- Do the adult children need to be seen separately because of the possibility that they might be shame-prone? If they need to be seen individually, do their nuclear families also need to be assessed for shame?
- What support groups are available for the husband and wife? Should either or both of them be in group therapy? If so, when? Where? What kind?

Once these questions were answered and the decisions set in motion other questions arose.

- Who on the team does what therapy?
- Who will track case progress and therapists' and clients' needs?

Answering these questions is the responsibility of the therapy team. Therapists who do not have the luxury of having a team as a resource can raise these questions with consultation groups.

Include Spouse, Nuclear Family, Family of Origin, and Extended Family in Therapy

All shame-prone clients, some more that others, have unresolved issues with their families of origins. The family-of-origin work begun in the early stage of therapy should be built upon in the middle stage. Working the patterns of unmet needs/interpersonal issues/emotion on the treatment map leads clients to deal with their families of origin. In this work, therapists search for themes of shame in every subsystem and system, e.g., the marriage, parent-child relationships, grandparent-grandchildren relationships, nuclear family-extended family relationships. Ethnicity issues (McGoldrick, Pearce, & Giordano, 1982) and gender issues (Lewis & Sussman, 1986; McGoldrick, Anderson, & Walsh, 1989) may be related to shame and should be included in overall treatment planning.

Some shame-prone multigenerational issues can be identified and worked through within a particular modality, such as individual or couple therapy (Boszormenyi-Nagy & Ulrich, 1981; Framo, 1981; Whitaker & Keith, 1981). As therapy progresses, the strategies for change include making decisions about what parts of the family to bring together, when, and with what interventions to uncover and release shame.

Work Through All Patterns on the Treatment Map

Working through the six dysfunctional patterns of unmet needs/interpersonal issues/emotions identified on the treatment map is not always done sequentially. The patterns are all related to each other and have recursive properties, meaning that each pattern influences and is influenced by the other patterns (Becvar & Becvar, 1988). Focus and intervention on a specific pattern affect all the other patterns. No pattern is completely finished until all are complete. Finding the right combination of issues to work first for specific cases proves challenging and definitely involves a discovery process. How to work the patterns is covered below in the intervention and therapeutic strategies section.

Test Clients' Reality

The purpose of homework assignments during the middle stage of therapy is to test clients' reality. This out-of-session testing is an integral and important part of shame-prone therapy. For example, the therapist noticed that Peter was able to maintain eye contact with him for longer periods of time and did not duck his head when he felt shame in the session. In discussing these observations, Peter reported that he was maintaining better eye contact and keeping his head up in his relationships at work. The therapist and Peter developed a way of checking this assumption. Peter had earlier asked a trusted colleague at work to be part of his support network. Peter felt that he could ask that same colleague to observe those two patterns (eye contact and head down) for a week when Peter was interacting with him and others.

Sometimes the reality check involves clients' visiting parents and observing if their shame reactions, specifically chosen beforehand, are different. Clients may also be challenged to perform some specific behavior that they have not been able to do before without feeling shamed, e.g., giving feedback to someone, telling someone they love them, asking for help on a specific task.

Deal With Inner Child, Adolescent
and Young Adult Issues

The objective in the early stage of therapy is for clients to acknowledge and contact the client's inner child. This process continues into the middle stage with interventions designed to nurture and give credibility to the feelings and spontaneity of that inner child. As therapy progresses, the inner child may have to work through adolescent and young adult issues with respective hurts and losses. If therapists are working with young children to free and heal the wounded inner child, the process goal is to prepare the child to enjoy age-related activities. When working with adults the task is different. The outcome goal is to integrate the free, creative, fun-loving inner child with the whole, healthy adult.

The wounded and frightened inner child may have blocked some of the adolescent peer bonding that is developmental for most children. It is also possible that clients may have missed much of the individual and group dating of young adults because they were too shamed to try. Therapists can maintain this developmental focus in working with emotions by focusing on issues related to the inner child as well as those related to the adolescent and young adult. The goal for the middle stage of therapy is to heal the inner core of the person at all ages and developmental stages. When this is accomplished, the fun-loving, creative inner child will be one with the healthy adult.

Work With Issues of Spirituality

In writing about aspects of self-worth, Wegscheider-Cruse (1985) pictured a person as a system with spirituality at the center. Spirituality is made up of the mind, the unconscious, and intuition (Fossum & Mason, 1986). Therapists must address aspects of individuals' and families' lives that block intuition and inspiration. This emphasis on spirituality does not place a therapist in any type of religious role. Rather, the role is one of fostering the creative, intuitive, and feeling parts of clients in ways that empower them.

INTERVENTION AND THERAPEUTIC STRATEGIES

Working the Treatment Map

The treatment map charts the way by keeping therapists focused on shame-prone issues. The complexity of the map will diminish the more therapists use it. Supervisors will also find it useful for understanding the progress of a case and for spotting where therapists are stuck.

In Chapter 12 we introduced the first three steps for working the patterns on the treatment map: (1) identify an unmet need, an issue on the diagonal, or an affect based on what a client presents, (2) move clients to express affect and experience the unmet need, and (3) confront games and beliefs. In the middle stage we continue working these steps and add five others. With each step therapists need to use specific interventions that target feelings, thoughts and beliefs, behavior, and images and visualization. In addition, ethnic and gender issues may be related to each pattern and should be fully explored.

The fourth step has four parts to it. *The therapist is to identify and verbalize with the client(s):*

- *shame-prone issue(s) on the diagonal;*
- *unmet need(s);*
- *internal and behavioral responses, including emotion;*
- *places, situations, and relationships where the issues, needs, and responses manifest in the client's life.*

A couple came to therapy stating that they loved each other but seemed to have continual conflict. The wife, Adele, had recently attended a university class on the family and learned about the possible effects of family-of-origin issues on couple relationships. As they talked about the possibility of family-of-origin issues being at the root of their problems, something clicked for her and later for her husband, Sol. Although they had been in therapy a number of times and made valuable changes, many of the same patterns disrupted their relationship. They determined this time to find a therapist who worked with family-of-origin issues.

After working the first three steps with the couple over several sessions, the therapist turned to Adele and said, "I have some observations I wish to share with you. I am very interested in your reactions. It appears to me that you have experienced rejection in many parts of your life, beginning with your father. You perceived that he rejected you because there was something wrong with you. Now rejection and insufficiency seem to be an issue that motivates some of your behavior toward Sol. Although you yearn to be held, to cuddle, to share your innermost feelings, you often angrily reject him before he can reject you. He rarely understands the anger you carry, nor do you. Yet you tell me that he does not reject you."

As the wife nodded her head in recognition and agreement, the therapist turned to Sol and said, "The major issue for you seems to be fear of abandonment. Through the events of your mother's major illness connected to the birth of your sister three years younger than you, you felt abandoned and shamed by your needs. After all, your mother was ill and the baby needed her more than you did, although you were only three. In this way your need to be close to your mother shamed you. In your mind your mother's death when you were a teenager confirmed your worthlessness. Possibly your anger and shame, combined with the fear of his potential death, has blocked the more positive relationship you desire with your father. Notice how this same fear motivates you to demand your wife's attention and solicit repeated promises that she will never leave you. With you in the role of martyr and with Adele as the tyrant, you send thousands of misunderstood messages to each other. You are such a nice guy, placating, and doing things to please her so that she will not leave you. On the other hand, Adele often believes that she is fighting with a wimp."

The therapist then made the following statement to the couple: "The combination of these two issues—Adele's issues of rejection and Sol's issues of abandonment—with the accompanying feeling of shame makes it very difficult for you two to sustain the intimacy that you both so desperately want."

The clients evidenced relief and acceptance of this lengthy formulation. The therapist then led them into a discussion of how these issues interacted in their marriage to inhibit the way they felt toward each other. Within Sol and Adele were wounded inner children who needed attention in the therapy sessions. The therapist also intervened to help them release some of their anger and fear. As these interventions unfolded in their own drama, the therapist continued to point out how the clients were shamed because they had needs that others did not meet or could not meet because of circumstances. The needs of intimacy, productivity, and dependency were addressed directly.

Step five utilizes the work done in step four to further uncover and release shame. In this step, therapists assist clients to *examine the continuity between the present and the historical as the bridge to the pain and losses connected to the family of origin, the extended family, and past significant relationships.*

As clients are invited to examine how their current behavior, issues, and feelings are connected to the past, emphasis is on recognizing the continuity between the past and present rather than trying to place blame. For some clients interventions and interpretations may be necessary to make the connection. Experiential interventions in sessions, and perhaps in a four- or five-day intensive workshop, address the reservoirs of pain and the losses clients have maintained and run from over the years. Being with a larger supportive group working on some of the same issues creates a climate of vulnerability that allows well defended clients to sense the pain of others. Then their pain surfaces and can be worked through.

Specific relationships and family systems and subsystems, present and past, should be incorporated into therapy. Some key people may be dead or otherwise unavailable but can still be brought into therapy through empty chair techniques. Rituals for forgiving, releasing, and mourning family-of-origin relationships assist clients to uncover and release more shame (Imber-Black, Roberts, & Whiting, 1988).

Step five directly addresses individuals' needs to make sense and order of the world in which they live. In the shaming systems in which they have lived, their world often seems confusing and crazy. Continuing with the case mentioned earlier, Sol was born into a loving family with two older brothers. With the illness brought on by pregnancy and birth of a sibling, his mother and father became less available to him. His world made no sense to him, and he carried this confusion and pain into his adult world. When the current events, beliefs, feelings, and attitudes were bridged to the family of origin, extended family, and past significant relationships, his world begin to make sense to him.

The grieving process begins but is not completed. As clients get in touch with grief and attempt to deal with their losses, they trigger the emotions of nonspecific rage, anger, humiliation, fear, and terror. The losses of self, of childhood, of positive loving relationships, of opportunities are overwhelming at the conscious and unconscious level. All of these losses reflect their shame, their unworthiness. The emptiness and terror are overwhelming as clients approach the core issues of their worthiness and of their ability to survive on their own. At this step, it sometimes feels to therapists and clients that they are going backwards in therapy. Therapists who recognize the enormity of what clients are dealing with can provide direction, stability, and hope.

Interventions that address the release of pain, the surrender of victim and martyr roles, and an acceptance of losses dominate this step. Body work, visualizations, hypnosis, inner child, and cognitive structure interventions are essential. Support networks and groups are necessary to provide some structure and stability as clients begin to accept that they have the right to make their own choices and that they are capable of being stable and free.

In step six, therapists support clients in *assessing the cognitive and affective costs of continuing in the present way and the meanings and benefits of the old conflict (the secondary gains).*

Step six examines what clients do to maintain present shame beliefs, feelings, and behaviors and what the costs are. It promotes explicit choice-making as dysfunctional choices are examined and discarded. In examining the belief, affect, and behavioral costs invested in their shame, clients answer the following questions:

- "If I continue as I am, what do I believe about myself?"
- "If I continue as I am, what feeling will I continue to experience?"
- "If I continue as I am, how will I behave?"

To get at system costs the questions are worded as "we" instead of "I." Answers may be similar to the following:

- "I am bad."
- "I can't do anything right."
- "I am often scared and angry."
- "We are so distant and unfeeling toward each other."
- "I can't maintain meaningful relationships."
- "We fight and are mean to each other."
- "I am always waiting for you to do something to me."

This step has healing aspects. Recognizing secondary gains is what motivates clients to stop some behavior or feeling. Since clients usually have not thought in terms of what they get out of continuing dysfunctional behavior, they often have difficulty with this concept. The therapeutic goal is to have clients recognize secondary gains and accept their responsibility for the choices they have made in maintaining old behaviors, feelings, and beliefs. Interventions that stimulate visualization and imagery (e.g., guided imagery, hypnosis, dreams, other-handed writing and drawing, metaphorical stories, fairy tales, body work) can be used to put clients in touch with the secondary gains.

Sol and Adele's therapist had them close their eyes and focus on things they had not created in their relationship but wanted. They were then told to think of a symbol that represented what they did not get. When they signaled that they were finished, the therapist had them open their eyes and share their journey and symbol with each other. Adele's symbol was a bird with a wing that would not heal. Her job was to mend the wing so that it could fly off with its mate. Everytime the wing would be almost strong enough, a giant hand would reach out and break the other wing. Adele would immediately splint the broken wing and soothe the bird.

Sol's symbol was a giant Rubik's cube. He was on the inside with a computer, reading directions on how to manipulate the cube so that all of the colors on the outside would match. If he could do this, he would leave the inside with a reservoir of wisdom to create all that he and Adele wanted. However, he never got out. As he attempted to manipulate the cube he was filled with immobilizing terror.

When the therapist asked them if they were willing to give the symbols to each other, or to him, they declined. Sol said he just needed a little more time and perhaps some help with the terror. With more time, he was sure that he could give his symbol away. Adele said that the bird had almost flown the last time. She was sure that she could do something to teach the bird to protect itself from the hand.

When the therapist asked them to relate their symbols to their relationship, they were startled. They were instructed to determine if the symbols represented their relationship in the past, present, and future. Their answers were related to secondary gains. Their unwillingness to give their symbols away illustrated to them that their behavior served some purpose. Each in his/her own way was trying to fix the marriage, and each thought he/she had the right way to do it. By pursuing the same behavior, they did not have to admit failure as long as they were still trying to fix it. Adele thought outside forces stopped her, which allowed her to maintain her victim role. Sol simply could not become "wise enough" to figure out what was wrong and how to fix it. By maintaining this position, he could keep his role as benevolent but confused martyr.

It seemed less shameful to keep trying than to admit defeat, but neither one trusted that the other could fix it. Once these issues and their costs were identified, they could, through redecision therapy, make choices that would serve them. They were then invited, if they wished, to ceremoniously burn their symbols and spread the ashes to the wind.

For the second part of this intervention, the therapist asked Sol and Adele to close their eyes again and picture their relationship. This time they were to imagine that they were explorers with the very latest equipment for detecting hidden positive qualities in relationships. They were to explore their relationship as they never had before. As soon as they discovered a new positive quality in their relationship, they were to signal, keep their eyes closed, and enjoy examining that positive quality. They were instructed to enjoy pleasant memories and feelings associated with this quality. Then they were told to choose a symbol for this positive aspect of their relationship and implant it somewhere in or on their body. The implanting was to be done with ceremony and respect.

Interventions that draw from intuition are fertile ground for affirmations from therapists and others in the session. Therapists can teach clients to recognize how wise, creative, funny, etc. they are when they allow themselves to be connected to their intuition. Therapists can reframe intuition as a part of clients that has always been there, protecting them, cleverly laying and executing plans for them to survive in their world.

Working step seven empowers and affirms clients as they move closer to healthy identities. They are capable of completing this step if they have worked through all of the patterns on the treatment map for themselves, nuclear families, and key relationships from their extended families, and other significant shaming relationships. Accountability and responsibility are shifted completely to clients, with therapists playing supportive roles. In step seven clients *examine alternative patterns of beliefs, feelings, and behaviors that do not have the same costs as those identified in the preceding step.* Therapists should have clients write a list of the patterns they want to practice. Feelings, beliefs, and behaviors patterns for individuals as well as systems (e.g., couple relationships, families, extended families, and other significant and ongoing relationships) should be included. Once the list is made, therapists and clients should discuss together the costs of implementing these patterns. Resistance to completing any part of this step indicates unfinished work. Identify the unmet need(s), issue(s), and emotion and work the necessary steps to release the shame. On the other hand, feelings of shame may be transitory rather than internalized. Therapists can emphasize the difference between internalized and transient shame and help clients to label their feelings properly.

For therapists, this step allows a thorough review of the work done in therapy. It usually cannot be completed in one session. As clients begin to make their lists, they may become overwhelmed and fall into relapses. This is a time for interventions that empower clients. Affirmations and healing rituals (Imber-Black, Roberts, & Whiting, 1988), guided imagery, stories with metaphors of personal power, enlightened autobiographies, changing internal dialogue, and focus on the inner child and spirituality are appropriate interventions for this step.

Step eight focuses on learning new behaviors and testing reality. As with the last step, clients are expected to be responsible and accountable for the process and their behavior. Therapists journey "with" clients as they *stabilize and reinforce new patterns by rehearsing and learning new skills and patterns in sessions. The patterns are reality-checked outside of sessions.* The new patterns targeted in step seven are rehearsed and practiced in sessions. Clients working individually should do parts of this step in a group setting with supervision. Couples and families are encouraged to get additional feedback. Support groups and other supportive relationships can be informed of the goals and encouraged to give feedback. Interventions that focus on clients' strengths will provide opportunities to practice their skills.

A therapist worked with an eighth grade girl, Andrea, who felt shamed by her mother and her older sisters, 16 and 17. Andrea had done well in school until this grade. Now she was inattentive, tardy, late and sloppy with her work, and prone to crying. She revealed to the therapist that she believed her mother and her two older sisters did not love her anymore and did not want to be with her. Sometimes they stopped talking when she came in the room.

The counselor met with Andrea's mother and sisters. They said that nothing they said or did could convince Andrea that they loved her. They stopped talking when she came into the room if they thought they were discussing things she could not understand. These "things" were "girl talk" as they called it, about dating and sex. Andrea wanted to listen and learn.

The counselor and her supervisor categorized Andrea as experiencing transitory shame but having a hard time letting her feelings of shame go. Her feelings of shame were related to issues in her stage of development. The onset of puberty and wanting to be recognized and accepted as "one of the girls" in her own family were met with insensitivity by her mother and sisters, who loved her as the little girl they knew. Andrea's needs to be intimate with them as a group and accepted as unique and valued were unmet. She was shamed by her needs not being met and believed that she had done something bad or that she was unworthy of being included. This was translated to mean that she was unlovable to everyone.

Although Andrea was certainly not shame-prone and her family was not dysfunctional, her "stuckness" came from the shame she felt. The assignment the counselor gave her is one that is appropriate for clients when they get to the eighth step. It involved rehearsal, prescriptions, an assignment outside of therapy, and contact with significant relationships as a test of Andrea's reality.

1. The therapist asked Andrea to make a list of her strengths and read them to her. The definition of a strength was anything about her that served her in a positive way some of the time. Focusing on process first, the therapist talked with Andrea about her resistance to looking at herself in a positive light, how difficult it was to write a personal strength, and how much more difficult it was for her to read the list out loud. She drew much of this information from Andrea before commenting on it.

2. Andrea made a list of people who she thought knew her well. This included her father, mother, younger brother, her grandmother, and a girlfriend.
3. Andrea was asked if she was willing to conduct an experiment about her strengths. The therapist indicated that there was nothing in the experiment that she could not do, that it would take courage to do it, and that she would learn some very interesting things about herself. She hesitantly agreed.
4. Andrea was to go to her mother, her father, her grandmother, and her little brother and ask them to tell her what they thought her strengths were. She was to write them down and bring them back to the therapist.
5. The therapist indicated that she would teach Andrea to ask for the information and that they would rehearse it until she felt comfortable. They rehearsed the following:
    a. Asking in a straightforward way for the other person's participation in an assignment Andrea had to fulfill.
    b. Establishing a time to do it.
    c. Beginning with a request for the person to tell Andrea what he/she perceived as her strengths. She was to give the person the definition of what a strength was.
    d. Andrea was to accept whatever was given. She could not indicate in any way that she did not agree with the person. She was also to keep in mind how hard it was for her to write her list and not be disappointed if the list people gave her was short. The therapist told her to be prepared to tell the other persons the strengths she observed in them if they asked. (Three of the four people interviewed did ask.)

After rehearsing with the therapist, who role played each person she was to approach, Andrea left with her assignment. She was very animated when she came back to therapy. To her surprise, all four of the people interviewed knew her well and saw many strengths that she had not thought to include on her list. Each one told her that they loved her and liked to be with her. Her reality check with significant others was so different from the shameful feelings she had that she had to reconsider. Her energy in the session was so high that the therapist could tell that she had made a major shift in her feelings and beliefs.

Interventions

Targeting Feeling Patterns.   Freeing the blocked and repressed feelings of shame-prone individuals and systems is the task for this stage of therapy.

Treatment goals for feelings are listed below and followed by possible interventions:

- *Experience a wide range of feelings.*
- *Release shameful feelings.*
- *Increase clients' ability and willingness to express feelings.*
- *Complete the grieving process.*
- *Continue assisting couples, families, and subsystems of families to get in touch with their collective anger, sadness, depression, or fear.*
- *Participate in four- to five-day intensive experiential workshop focused on family reconstruction.*

Interventions such as sand trays, cuddly cloth animals, movies, music, pounding, pushing against pillows, reenactments of past experiences, transference with the therapist or group members, sculpting, psychodrama, and family reconstruction, hypnosis, guided imagery for forgiveness to assist in the process of grieving (Bradshaw, 1988; Bozarth-Campbell, 1982; Feinauer, 1984; Stroup, Harper, Steele, & Hoopes, 1984; Wegscheider-Cruse, 1989) assist clients in identifying, releasing, and expressing their feelings.

Targeting Belief and Cognition Patterns. Cognitive therapy (Beck, 1988; Beck, Rush, Shaw, & Emery, 1979; Meichenbaum, 1985) is a viable way to intervene in shame-prone beliefs. Cognitive therapy focuses on individuals' negative and distorted thought processes. Interventions can also have an interpersonal focus on alternative explanations for why others do what they do (Beck, 1988; Emery, Hollon, & Bedrosian, 1982). Concepts of how people perceive, misperceive, and fail to perceive each other, as well as the ways they communicate, miscommunicate, and fail to communicate, hold many clues to shame-prone beliefs and behaviors. In many shaming systems individuals were taught to ignore and deny the reality of what they were perceiving and what was communicated to them.

The major goal in therapy for shame-prone individuals and systems is to revise the shame-prone beliefs (e.g., "I am bad," "We are bad," "I can't do anything right!" "We always get the short end of things." "No one can love me." "If I touch the pain I feel I will die."). Therapists and clients can use checklists to assess clients' resistance to changing beliefs. Then interventions can be introduced to modify the beliefs, thereby reducing the resistance (see Beck, 1988, pp. 153–154 for checklist of "Beliefs about Change" with headings of "defeatist beliefs," "self-justifying beliefs," "reciprocity arguments," and "the problem is my partner").

The goals for interventions in this area are:

- *Continue work begun on genograms and histories.*

This includes family-of-origin work, nuclear family history, couple or relationship history, and productivity history.

- *Assess the change perceptual orientation of individuals and systems.*
- *Teach couples, families, and family subsystems a beginning awareness of a collective shame-prone identity.*
- *Change current couple, family, and family-of-origin shame-prone identities.*

Whether the focus is on feelings or beliefs, when family systems begin to understand that as a group they have collective feelings and a group identity, they begin to understand the collective pain.

- *Change internal dialogue so that negative talk changes to positive.*

Beck (1988) uses a nine-step procedure for changing personal distortions: (1) link emotional reactions with automatic thoughts; (2) use imagination to identify thoughts; (3) practice identifying automatic thoughts; (4) use replay techniques; (5) question automatic thoughts; (6) use rational responses; (7) test predictions; (8) reframe; and (9) label distortions (pp. 199–210).

- *Change the beliefs about how intimacy, dependency, and accountability needs are met by others.*
- *Assist clients in demonstrating personal empowerment.*
- *Integrate disowned parts.*

Many people have split off parts of themselves so that these parts are not integrated into the whole identity of the person (Akhtar & Byrne, 1983). Shame-prone people often split off the "good me" parts because of shaming voices from inside and outside. Dream work (Mahrer, 1990; Mindell, 1987), parts party (Satir & Baldwin, 1983; Wegscheider-Cruse, 1985), and voice dialogue (Stone & Winkleman, 1986) are useful.

- *Assist clients in identifying and hearing their own and others' faulty beliefs about shame-prone identities.*
- *Break the attachment of feelings and beliefs to release them.*

This can be done through guided imagery, empty chair, and cognitive therapy techniques.

- *Break individuals' and family systems' silence about secrets and secret lives.*
- *Investigate and identify individual and family faulty beliefs.*

Methods for accomplishing these goals include hypnosis, journal writing, other-handed writing and drawing, role playing, video feedback, pretending (Madanes, 1981), using the magic wand (Wegscheider-Cruse, 1989), and cognitive dream work (Freeman, 1982).

- *Change the symbolic meaning of beliefs, rules, myths, and rituals from shaming systems.*

Healing rituals can be substituted for dysfunctional rituals (c.f. Imber-Black, Roberts, & Whiting, 1988).

Targeting Behavior Patterns. One way to develop relevant, case-specific interventions is to refer to the behavior checklists for individuals and systems in Chapter 8.

- *Comment explicitly about nonverbal, verbal and interpersonal patterns to teach clients about their shame. Examine dysfunctional communications patterns. Assist clients in becoming aware of dysfunctional self-talk and how it affects interactions with others. Examine system patterns in couples, families and subsystems for patterns of interaction that are shaming.*
- *Assist clients in learning to be "with" people rather than expecting others to do things "to" them or "for" them.*
- *Assist clients to be accountable, intimate, and appropriately dependent, independent, and interdependent.*
- *Assist clients in learning to reality-test with others.*
- *Assess and identify addiction and codependency behaviors and cycles with clients.*

If clients are not in therapy for addiction or codependency and need to be, therapists should arrange for specific treatment. However, involvement in addiction treatment programs has to be carefully integrated with shame-prone treatment. Clients have enough abandonment and rejection issues without adding to them.

- *Identify and work to relieve compulsive behavior.*
- *Explore victimization issues, behaviors, and their costs, and practice alternative behaviors. Support change and explore the consequences of giving up old behavior.*
- *Break family rules and myths and formulate new rules.*

Therapists should be aware of the eight rules of shame-bound systems identified by Fossum and Mason:

1) *Control.* Be in control of all behavior and interaction.
2) *Perfection.* Always be "right."
3) *Blame.* If something doesn't happen as you planned, blame someone (self or other).
4) *Denial.* Deny feelings, especially the negative or vulnerable ones
   like anxiety, fear, loneliness, grief, rejection, need.
5) *Unreliability.* Don't expect reliability or constancy in relationships.
   Watch for the unpredictable.
6) *Incompleteness.* Don't bring transactions to completion or resolution.
7) *No talk.* Don't talk openly and directly about shameful, abusive, or
   compulsive behavior.
8) *Disqualification.* When disrespectful, shameful, abusive, or compulsive behavior occurs, disqualify it, deny it, or disguise it. (Fossom & Mason, p. 86).

• *Restructure personal and system boundaries.*

This can be done by imagery, use of space, structural family therapy interventions (Umbarger, 1983), and reenactment.

• *Identify codependent behaviors and alliances and exchange them for*
  functional behaviors.
• *Realign alliances to support marriage and parenting.*
• *Practice communication skills.*
• *If appropriate encourage and support individuals and systems in work-*
  ing a 12-step program.

Many tools are available for understanding and applying the 12 steps (Bradshaw, 1988; Grateful Members, 1977; Sheperd, 1988). If therapists are not
in the addiction field or recovering, they are rarely trained or experienced
in understanding and integrating the 12 steps with therapy. All addicts and
codependents live and/or lived in shaming systems.

• *Examine systems, e.g., couples, families and subsystems, for patterns*
  of interaction that are shaming.

Targeting Visualization, Metaphors, and Affirmation Patterns.

• *Assist individuals and systems in identifying the differences between*
  negative and positive affirmations.
• *Change the negative inner voice to a positive one.*
• *Affirm personal worth for individuals, couples and families.*

One way of changing the negative inner voice to a positive one is through the use of affirmations. The task is to create an alternate voice that replaces the old tapes inherited from past experiences (Bradshaw, 1988; Wilde, 1987). Substituting a new understanding and a new frame of reference for old ingrained patterns of thinking can be done with affirmations. As affirmations reach and impress the unconscious, long forgotten or repressed traumas begin to surface (Borysenko, 1987). Positive affirmations, when used correctly and persistently, modify negative thinking and behavior and positively affirm personal worth.

Affirmations are based on what an individual wants and are often couched in "I am" statements. To shame-prone clients and systems in the early stage of therapy, affirmation work may seem like a con game, although clients shamed only on intimacy or dependency issues may be ready to do this work. For many, affirmations and visualizations may not be useful until the middle stage.

Affirmations for every day (Benson, 1989), audiotapes, and experiential activities (e.g., the Affirmation Chant and the Affirmation Circle, Wegscheider-Cruse, 1989 are examples of interventions that are available). Affirmations for couples and families can be written and practiced. The negative self-talk of system, couched in "we" terms, also impresses the identity of each member of the system.

- *Use fantasies, stories, guided imagery, and metaphors to break myths and secrets that bind in the shame.*

Cultures through the ages are replete with stories, fantasies, visualizations, fables, epic poems, and fairy tales that have been used to entertain, teach, and heal. When any of these story sources are presented with the intent to teach or help people and when listeners identify with some part of the story, it becomes metaphoric for them (Mills & Crowley, 1986). In fact, people make sense of what others present to them by the use of metaphors. Therapists often naturally and unconsciously use therapeutic metaphors as they tell stories. Formal metaphors can be developed that meet clients in their model of the world and provide the possibility of solutions. Gordon (1978) describes how to develop metaphors, deliver them, and utilize them in therapy. Metaphors that include shame pieces and provide opportunities to release feelings and behaviors can be very helpful in working through the shame-prone patterns identified on the treatment map.

- *Use hypnosis to uncover feelings and events.*

Those therapists who have training in using hypnosis will find that it is a very useful tool for uncovering shame in some clients; however it is not the panacea for all clients. For examples of using hypnosis with families, see Araoz and Negley-Parker (1988) and Ritterman (1983).

• *Work with inner child issues and pain.*

Whitfield (1987, p. 59) identified four steps for working with the inner child:

1. Have clients discover and practice being real self or child within.
2. Identify clients' ongoing physical, mental-emotional, and spiritual needs. Help clients practice getting these needs met with safe and supportive people.
3. Help clients identify, reexperience, and grieve the pain of un-grieved losses or traumas in the presence of safe and supportive people.
4. Help the client identify and work through core issues.

TRANSITION TO THE LAST STAGE OF THERAPY

Signs of recovery in individuals and systems are indications of the need to prepare for termination. Grieving, symptom reduction, a change in the therapist-client relationship, and less hiding of shame are positive signs that clients have moved from internalizing shame to healthy shame and guilt.

Evidence that clients have changed beliefs from a "poor me" style to acceptance of losses in their lives is an indication that they are ready to move to the termination phase of therapy. If clients have moved successfully through the middle stage of therapy, the symptoms presented in the beginning stage should show improvement. Reassessment through use of the individual and systems behavior checklist, anecdotal client information about out-of-session behavior, improved in-session behavior, and repeated measures on standardized questionnaires provide information on symptoms. During the middle stage of therapy the therapist-client relationship changes from one of dependence to independence. Both clients and therapists should be in agreement that this is what has happened. When clients no longer sense the need to cover their shame, this is a good indication that they are ready for termination. Clients who successfully move through the middle stage of therapy uncover shame more easily and can transform it into healthy guilt.

CHAPTER 14

Shame-Prone Clients: Late Stage of Therapy

THE LATE STAGE OF therapy focuses on termination, which is set in motion when the goals of therapy have been met, when clients for various reasons decide to leave therapy before the goals are complete (e.g., finances, moving, want to try it on their own for a while, flight into health after a few changes), and when other circumstances make leaving therapy necessary (calamities, death in the family, or therapist moves, retires, dies, or leaves practice for other reasons). Regardless of the situation, therapists should be aware of typical feelings of shame and interpersonal issues from the treatment map that are related to termination.

Events and relationships left uncompleted are scattered throughout dysfunctional, shame-prone families. Goodbyes have not been said in relationships; the dead have not been mourned; interpersonal contracts have been broken and never talked about; withholds, cutoffs, abuses, broken dreams, unmet needs, broken promises, hurts, pain, numbness litter the interactional battlefields of these homes. Handling termination issues in an appropriate way provides shame-prone clients with a model for bringing closure to events and relationships.

ASSESSMENT GOALS

A final outcome evaluation of shame-proneness and specific measures of symptoms related to individuals' and families' presenting problems is an essential part of the late stage of therapy. Direct observations of clients' emotional, cognitive, and behavioral patterns, interactional patterns in relationships and systems, and checklist and standardized measures of shame-proneness provide valuable data for decisions about what clients need to work on even after they finish formal therapy.

THERAPEUTIC GOALS FOR
THE CLIENTS

For clients, leaving therapy raises many issues. The excitement of know-ing that changes have taken place and that life holds markedly different opportunities, rewards, surprises, and challenges is alluring to them. On the other hand, the thought of separating from the known routine and support of therapy and losing the regular contact with their therapists is frightening. Clients go in and out of shame and guilt as termination ap-proaches. They feel shamed because they have needs that are threatened by leaving therapy. It reminds them of the old losses and abandonments. Some feel guilty because they known they have received so much, yet they want more. When clients can express these feelings rather than cover them up, they can successfully work through the transition at termination. Basi-cally, therapists help clients recognize that the shame is transitory and the guilt healthy.

Learn to Live with Wholeness

Wholeness for each client and family system has many meanings, some of them very specific to the goals of clients. For example, one woman said she knew that one indication of wholeness for her would be when she could enforce her intimacy boundaries. To clients who have worked their way through the relevant patterns on the treatment map, wholeness has a number of general meanings. Wholeness means:

- having their psychological needs met, and when they are not met, utilizing coping skills to deal with the disappointment (Allred & Smith, 1989);
- knowing that they are not "bad," and that mistakes are learning opportunities;
- experiencing and expressing a wide range of feelings;
- being accountable and responsible for oneself and for one's roles in family and other relationships;
- valuing oneself for talents and abilities;
- using positive affirmations in relationship to self and others;
- being intimate and dependent in healthy ways;
- knowing that shame and guilt are teachers in one's life, rather than a way of life;
- being able to ask for and accept support from others and to give support to others;
- practicing and growing, but rarely reaching perfection;

- being at peace with one's spirituality, with its unique meaning and influence;
- loving self and others, and accepting love.

Before leaving therapy, clients need to learn realistic expectations for living with wholeness. In some ways the responses of clients and the people around them to dropping shame-prone identities are similar to responses to a person who has lost a lot of weight. People who are used to the old appearance, behaviors, and attitudes may not know who this changed person is. People are shocked when a shame-prone person who used to be elusive, quiet, and demeaning to self, or one who was abrasive and angry, is suddenly present, attentive, interactive, and somewhat assertive. Some want the old behaviors back, because they knew how to interact with that person or because those patterns fit their needs in some way. Others may applaud the changes but not know how to be with the person because the relationship is different.

Clients attempting to live with wholeness need to continue to practice new behaviors and seek feedback both in and out of therapy sessions. Therapists should encourage them to develop their own unique list of what it means to be whole and observe and track how congruent they are with the stated criteria.

Develop Specific Plans
for Support After Termination

Shame-prone clients' pre-therapy world included very little support. Preparation for leaving therapy should emphasize the normalcy of having support and the need to create the most positive support networks possible. Plans may include continuing in support groups started during therapy, beginning a new support group, enhancing present supportive relationships, starting an education or training track, changing jobs to leave a shaming work system, leaving dysfunctional relationships, and planning time for oneself.

If clients have been participating in a 12-step program that has run somewhat parallel to therapy, the last three of the 12 steps can help clients integrate and convert the 12-step program into an ongoing process of wholeness and support. The last three steps are:

- Continue to take personal inventory and when wrong, promptly admitted it.
- Seek through prayer and meditation to improve conscious contact with God, as understood by the client, praying only for knowledge of His will for us and the power to carry that out.

• Having had spiritual awakening as the result of these steps, try to carry this message to others, and to practice these principles in all affairs.

Address All Issues of Termination

Shame-prone clients have very little confidence or hope when they begin therapy. Many of them have been to other therapists and "failed." Some have been hospitalized for mental illness and others have been treated for multiple addictions. Being shame-prone, they have believed that their "badness" prevented them from receiving help and relief for their pain and that they got what they deserved. As termination nears clients may feel some of the old feelings of humiliation connected to loss and fear of abandonment. However, this time the feelings are connected to their relationship with the therapist. With the help of the therapist these issues can be addressed directly.

PROCESS GOALS FOR THERAPISTS

The process goals focus on preparation for and completion of termination. Therapists emphasize the recognition of resurfacing shame patterns and assist clients to see the relevance of the patterns as part of this last phase of therapy.

Integrate Therapy Modalities

Because clients have usually participated in individual, couple, family, and group therapy, they need to terminate therapy with more than one therapist. Usually all terminations do not occur at the same time. If they did, the transition would be too abrupt for shame-prone clients. The therapy team and primary therapist(s) should consult and plan termination for each of the different types of therapy.

The following case illustrates the complexity of various therapist(s)-client relationships. Kerry and Geret began therapy looking for help with their four children. Therapy first focused on working with the family to reduce the chaos. The family was diagnosed as shame-prone and chaotically enmeshed and all family members were diagnosed as shame-prone. Treatment included therapy with individuals, the couple, the family, and some extended family members; drug addiction treatment for the 18-year-old son; a group for children of dysfunctional families for the children; a codependency group for the wife; a separate 12-step program focused on workaholism for the husband; and a five-day residential family reconstruction workshop that included the family and Geret's parents. All four members of a therapy team had primary responsibility for different modalities of treatment and, consequently, for termination.

Address Issues of Termination

The most common issues for shame-prone clients—rejection and abandonment, and fear of failure to maintain progress—need to be addressed directly and in multiple ways. Therapists know by experience that clients make progress and terminate. They also know that they return to therapy. Preparation for termination begins in the early stages of therapy with therapists' planting the seed of hope for recovery. An example from the case in Chapter 1 in the early stage of therapy demonstrates this concept. In reference to her previous attempts to alleviate her depression, Marilyn made the following statement in the second session.

Marilyn: Sometimes I think I am destined to be depressed all my life. Nothing seems to work. (ironically) It is my destiny. Why should therapy be any different from other things in my life!

Therapist: I hear what you are saying. Perhaps if you can be patient and hold in your mind the possibility that the outcome here can be a little different, chances are that it will be.

Marilyn: (suspiciously, with dropped head and shoulders) What do you mean? Are you saying I'm depressed because I think wrong?

Therapist: Absolutely not! I'm saying that you have worked hard, you seem determined, and that if you hold onto the possibility, maybe together we can create a different outcome. We won't know until we finish, but I do know it is possible.

The therapist then moved to some other topic, knowing that he had planted a seed that would need replanting, time, and careful nurturing.

Rituals that allow and encourage individuals and systems to rid themselves of old patterns and to grieve the loss of those old patterns prepare clients to end therapy, as do empowering ceremonies. For instance, a group of shame-prone women had been working on their issues in group therapy. Four of the women were ready to leave the group. In addition to doing some in-session goodbye work, the therapists prescribed a ritual outside the group. To prepare for the ritual, the four women were to make a list of behaviors, feelings, attitudes, thoughts, and negative relationships that they had worked on while in the group. Then they shared the items with the group and received additional input. The second part of the assignment was to share with the group what they thought, felt, and believed about themselves at that very moment.

The ritual instructions were for them as a group to go to some secluded spot, preferably outside, where they could have privacy. They were told to conduct a funeral service for those parts that were now dead to them. No one else was to be there. Each person in turn was to perform all her parts of the ritual, which would take two to three hours. The others were to serve as mourners. The service was to include a eulogy to the parts, mentioning their history and how they had served the person (e.g., survival, protective games, manipulations, hiding pain). The eulogy was to be followed by other short talks or poems that focused on the freedom experienced in saying goodbye to the departed parts. The service was to include appropriate music (a cassette player was permissible) and burial or cremation. After each had completed her service, they were to conclude by creating and participating in an original song and dance of joy.

Whatever the stage of therapy, references to its ending by therapists, by significant people in clients' lives, and by clients themselves, may be interpreted as abandonment and rejection. Although these issues may be appropriately addressed as they surface in the early and middle stages of therapy, the therapist's guaranteed presence prevents clients from directly addressing the abandonment issue until time for termination. In moving toward wholeness in the later stages of therapy, shame-prone clients must work through fears of isolation and aloneness as they assume responsibility and accountability for the direction and outcomes of their lives. Grieving their lost childhood and the nonretrievable losses from certain past relationships is a recent and ongoing process. Now they must lose the relationship with a therapist in which they have been respected, accepted, and nurtured. Fear of therapist abandonment and worry about surviving without therapy lie beneath most efforts to complete termination. As clients know that they are near completion, they need direct assurance that the therapist is still "with" them and that they can form significant relationships outside of therapy.

These issues of rejection and abandonment should be handled directly in the therapeutic relationship. The reality of being with the therapist less often and eventually not at all establishes a context for healthy interaction, with a full range of feelings experienced and expressed by clients. The therapist's participation in these issues and feelings is very therapeutic. It may well be the first time a client has successfully worked through an event that involved loss and change in a relationship and experienced it as a normal flow of life.

Test Patterns on the Treatment Map for Completion

By the time clients are ready for termination, they are familiar with the unmet needs/shame-prone issues/emotion patterns. Showing clients the treatment map (Table 10.1), the affirmation triangle (Figure 2.1), and assessment checklists may help them solidify what they have learned. As therapists and clients review together, they might prepare specific checklists that identify feelings, thoughts, and behaviors that have been changed and those that still cause problems. The therapy team participates in this review, bringing in information from a number of treatment modalities. The group also identifies and examines patterns that have for the most part been eliminated. These lists can be completed for both individuals and systems and provide a reminder of their journey in therapy to the present with its variety and richness.

Test Clients' Reality

Clients' reality includes their perception of who they are, what they choose to do or not do, what they think, and how they feel. Therapists encourage them to recognize shame and guilt feelings that occur outside the therapy sessions and to note what they do with them. They are also challenged to try new behaviors in situations that are risky to them. This can be done alone or in groups of two or more.

Because of their fear of leaving therapy, some clients unconsciously fail in these challenges. These failures are examined for work that still needs to be done, but therapists also encourage clients to look at a new game they have created, e.g., "I can stay in therapy if I want to. You can't get rid of me this easily."

The personalized checklists created in the review discussed earlier can also be used by clients to check their reality. For example, in the early stage of therapy Geret had many unresolved issues with his father and experienced fear and anger just thinking of him. He also felt very guilty and shamed because he had repeated some of his father's patterns of neglect with his son. As part of a reality check just prior terminating therapy, he invited his father to go on a one-day fishing trip with him and his son. The three of them left with trepidation but had a valuable and pleasant experience. This experiment bolstered Geret's confidence to carry through with termination.

Prepare Clients for a Return to Therapy

The issue of returning to therapy should be addressed directly. Wanting to come back but feeling shamed by their wants is a typical response. Therapists need to address any shame reactions that clients have, e.g., thinking that the therapist doesn't believe they can make it on their own. In addition to explicitly discussing the issues and clients' responses, therapists may tell metaphorical stories that describe the therapy process, its formal termination, and its evolution into "real life." These stories can be tailored to the culture and sophistication of the clients (Gordon, 1978). For termination the stories can include such ideas as:

1. Learning is never finished, but the context changes.
2. The new context becomes the new teacher.
3. Because of gains made in therapy, clients are better equipped each time the context changes.
4. The therapist is available for a quick repairs or resolution of new symptoms.
5. Reunions can be happy and productive.

Therapists should give explicit directions to help clients identify signals indicating that they should return for more therapy. Clients often find that they do not need to return, but knowing that it is possible is reassuring. The therapy team can also establish events that give clients an opportunity to return and connect without having to request therapy. Volunteer groups, reunion nights, pot luck suppers, special projects for needy groups (yard and housework for the elderly, serving the homeless), and classes on topics such as parenting or preparing for a second marriage allow for homecomings and also let clients know that they are valued.

CHAPTER 15

The Case of Joe:
I'm Crazy But Only My
Family Knows It

JOE, A 40-YEAR-OLD married man, entered therapy because he was depressed. Perceived as successful, productive, and very responsible by his boss and colleagues at work, Joe had been able to move into an executive position with a rapidly growing company. He reported that he was a very different person at work than he was in any other setting. At home he was verbally and emotionally abusive with his children and withdrawn from his wife. Joe participated very little in the discipline of the children and rarely took any responsibility for household tasks or maintenance. Having given up on trying to change him, his wife, Mary, shielded him from the children and did anything he asked or that she could anticipate to make him happy.

After several sessions of therapy, he confessed that he had been entertaining a daily fantasy that all members of his immediate family would be killed in freak car accident. The therapist was surprised to see how much detail Joe had built into the fantasy. He had imagined exactly how the accident would occur, how and who would come to inform him, how extended family members and friends of the family would react, details including attending the viewing of the bodies, songs, speakers at the funerals, and what he would do following the tragedy. He reported that this fantasy gave him relief and allowed him to get to sleep. It had become a nightly ritual. He confessed that he hated everyone in his extended family and wished that they would all leave him alone.

Joe had seen psychiatrists and several other psychotherapists during his life. He had decided to try therapy one more time on the advice of a friend. The antidepressants that he had been on at different times numbered at least eight, but when he came for therapy he had stopped taking any medications. He disgustedly reported that they hadn't helped.

Joe was the oldest grandson in his extended family. He thought he had done all the things his family wanted him to do—achieving in school, being courteous and compliant, attending college, marrying and fathering children, and landing a well paying job. But he quickly added that his family didn't care about him beyond that. Just as long as he didn't do anything to rock the boat or to embarrass them, they left him alone. He claimed not to need them even though his pain leaked through his deception.

He loved his wife and children, but he couldn't understand how they could put up with much more of his unpredictable behavior. Joe thought that they had suffered enough because of him. He blurted out, "I'm crazy, but my wife and kids are the only ones who know it because at home is where it shows up the most." After a few sessions of therapy, he speculated that his family might be better off if he just committed suicide. He wouldn't carry it out in any "gory" way, but having a car accident might be the answer. When the therapist inquired further, Joe said he was "too much of a chicken to even do that."

The description of Joe's therapy in this chapter illustrates the team approach, the use of formal and informal assessment, the use of the treatment map, and interventions that target areas of feelings, beliefs, behavior, and affirmation and imagery. Therapists who do not practice in settings where a team might be available should form consultation groups and modify the following approach.

EARLY STAGE OF THERAPY

Dr. Block, Joe's therapist, worked in an agency where they practiced a team therapy concept for difficult cases. If a client was diagnosed as shame-prone, all therapists who worked directly with the case became the team, with the first therapist involved in charge of the case. The team met on a weekly basis for as long as deemed necessary in the early and middle stages of therapy, and then shifted to a biweekly meeting. If therapists and services were involved from outside the agency, someone on the team was assigned to network with them and integrate information with what the agency team was doing. Interns in the agency were also assigned to the team. Sometimes they were assigned to observe through the one-way window and track clients' shame-prone behavior.

The primary tasks of the early stage of therapy were:

- to establish a therapeutic relationship with Joe and establish expectations for therapy;
- to determine the severity and nature of his depression as the presenting problem and to assess him, his marriage, and his family for proneness to shame;

- to make decisions based on the assessment for other therapy modalities and when they would begin for Joe and his family;
- to begin the therapeutic process.

This early stage for Joe lasted for six sessions over a four-week period.

Therapeutic Relationship

The therapist's relationship with Joe began with the initial telephone contact. The receptionist happened to be away from her desk, and Dr. Block picked up the telephone. She immediately sensed Joe's ambivalence about making a therapy appointment. While he desperately wanted help, he wasn't sure he could open himself up to anyone's "scrutinizing eye." Dr. Block commented that it is difficult for most people to make the first appointment for therapy and complimented Joe for his courage. Joe assumed that he was being criticized and began to defend his reasons for calling. Dr. Block listened, commented that those seemed like good reasons, and thanked him for calling. An appointment was made.

In the initial session, Joe appeared extremely anxious. He never made direct eye contact with Dr. Block, and he remained suspicious and defensive about even the mildest questions. At one point, Dr. Block indicated that maybe it would be easier if she didn't ask questions and just let Joe talk. He responded, "I'm not good enough for you to keep searching, huh? Some therapist you are!" Dr. Block calmly replied, "Joe, I will stay with you as long as it takes and with whatever it takes, me asking questions or just listening to you." Although the long periods of silence and suspicious stance toward questions continued, Dr. Block refused to give up.

Finding out that Joe was a first child, and relying on what she knew about first children, Dr. Block suspected that he needed approval. She told Joe that his cautiousness was a good thing. She stated that she wished every client would enter therapy with the same kind of suspicion. Recognizing that persons in the first systemic position appreciate explicit information, Dr. Block provided Joe with fairly detailed explanations about why a cautious and somewhat skeptical approach to therapy was a good thing. In later sessions, Joe reported that he thought she was "conning" him during this first session. He just couldn't believe that anyone could think his way of acting was a good thing.

Dr. Block told him that she recognized that he had no reason to automatically trust her. She validated that as a good thing. In time, she said, she would earn his trust and he would earn hers. Joe felt relieved when she said he didn't have to trust her. All of his other therapists had made an issue of his lack of trust the very first session. This new therapist was now telling him that it was okay not to trust her. In fact, he didn't ever have to trust her if she didn't earn his trust.

In that initial session, Dr. Block was also careful to give Joe information about her expectations and the structure of therapy. She told him that the length of therapy sessions might be somewhat different from what he had previously experienced. They would meet for two-hour sessions instead of the usual 50 minutes. When Joe assumed that longer sessions meant he was a tough case, Dr. Block responded with humor in her voice, saying, "I like you Joe, and 50 minutes just isn't enough time to be with somebody you like." She could sense immediately that her remark had shamed Joe. He just sat in silence staring at the floor. Dr. Block realized that she had not been careful enough with her humor. Joe had not evidenced much humor during the session, and her remarks could certainly be construed as having sexual connotations even though she did not mean them to be.

Recognizing the importance of restoring the interpersonal relationship, Dr. Block disclosed her own feelings. She was embarrassed that her remark had evoked Joe's reaction. She was sorry and asked that he might be forgiving and willing to let her be less than perfect. Although Joe could not do much more that first session than nod his head, the fact that this therapist talked about her own feelings in relation to him made its mark.

Toward the end of the initial session, Dr. Block explained that most cases in their clinic were handled by a team of therapists. While pointing out that she would be Joe's individual therapist, she explained that other therapists might become involved. She also explained that at some point the therapy would involve Joe's wife and children in couple and family sessions. How this would occur would depend on what she and Joe worked out together.

Dr. Block worked hard in the early stage of therapy to establish a trusting relationship with Joe. She wanted to communicate to him that she would be "with" him through whatever the therapy process or his life brought about. She wanted him to know that in therapy sessions he could be however he was. He didn't have to muster all his energy to be the successful corporate executive. He could be bad. He could be silent, angry, whatever. She simply wanted to affirm his right to be however he felt.

In other sessions during the early stage of therapy, Dr. Block continued to validate and positively affirm Joe in whatever ways she could. She used empathic statements to identify what he might be feeling. She encouraged him to express whatever emotion came up. She praised him for feeling and for respecting her enough to share anything, no matter how small. She continued to remind Joe that therapy was like a mutual contract. They needed to reach a point in their relationship where they could express what they were thinking and feeling without fear of being abandoned by the other. Part of her expectation was that Joe would agree to attend therapy sessions and not just "fade away" if therapy became uncomfortable. As part of the contract, he would agree to talk to her face to face before he ever decided to leave therapy. She wanted that kind of relationship with him and expected that he would return the courtesy to her.

Assessment of Joe, His Marriage, and Family

Because Joe's reason for coming to therapy was his depression, Dr. Block had him complete the Beck Depression Inventory (Beck et al., 1979) to screen the severity of his depression. During the interview, she also gathered information regarding sleeping and eating habits, ability to function at work and socially, suicidal thinking and plans, and somatic complaints. After determining that Joe was severely depressed but not suicidal at that point, Dr. Block recommended that he receive a physical exam and be evaluated for medication by the psychiatrist who was part of the clinic's therapy team. She assured him that the psychiatrist recognized the need to individualize antidepressant medications and would continue to follow up until things were in order. Joe was somewhat surprised by this because in the past he had usually received a prescription for the medication without a request that he return. When he had come for a follow-up visit to check his medication, the doctors had asked him a few questions about how he was doing and told him to continue the medication. Dr. Block was able to convince Joe to try medication one more time because of her reassurance that the psychiatrist would stay "with" Joe. Because they worked as a team, she would insist on it. Joe was placed on an antidepressant after his visit to the psychiatrist.

During the second session Joe came 20 minutes early so that he could complete the *Internalized Shame Scale* (Cook, 1989, Table 8.1). The results indicated that Joe experienced high degrees of shame. After the second session, Dr. Block used the Assessment Checklist for Identifying a Shame-Prone Individual (Table 8.2) to identify and record which of the symptoms Joe exhibited.

Dr. Block had noticed in the first and second sessions that Joe expressed predominantly anger. As she tried to get him to express other emotions, he seemed blocked. His anger seemed inappropriate for most of the contexts in which it occurred. Little things set him off, like remarks made by people calling in to a talk show he listened to on the radio. Once he had gotten so angry that he smashed the radio. His anger was frightening to him, his wife, and his children.

Joe also reported that God would never forgive him for all he had done to his wife and children. When Dr. Block asked what specifically he had done, he was vague and evasive. She commented on how hard it must be to keep from being discovered and reinforced his right to be however he wanted to be in sessions with her.

In the first session, Dr. Block had discovered many of Joe's cognitive patterns. He was negative about himself and others. He always anticipated that things would be worse than they turned out to be. Everything had to be black and white for him. Either he was perfect or he was absolutely no good. He was angry with his family of origin for what he called "setting him up to be perfect" and then never giving him any leeway. He reported that neighbors and acquaintances thought he was a jerk. He also thought that people were down on him at work, even though all evidence seemed to support the idea that people at work valued him very much. His outward appearance and behavior were designed to cover his feelings and beliefs toward others. In later sessions his wife reported that their neighbors and friends felt he was thoughtful and easy to talk with, though a little distant at times.

Joe's nonverbal behavior in sessions was another indication of his shame. He never made eye contact. Most of the time he just stared at the floor. He liked to slump in the chair with his hands covering his eyes.

The pattern of interpersonal relationships in Joe's life seemed to fit the symptoms on the checklist. He responded with contempt and anger when others tried to get close to him. He was highly suspicious of others, especially people who treated him well. He told Dr. Block that he took careful notes of conversations with people he did not trust so that he could use them as evidence to "nuke" them.

When asked about his sexual experiences, Joe became very sullen. He told Dr. Block that he didn't want to talk about them. When she said that he didn't have to, he turned on her in an angry fury. "You're a no good therapist," he said, "You'll let me get away with anything." Dr. Block simply told him that she would continue to see him as long as it took. Joe then divulged that he enjoyed hustling women because it provided a way for him to hurt them. He had developed a pattern of soliciting prostitutes and hurting them, not severely but enough to create pain during the sexual encounter. When Dr. Block asked if he ever sexualized his anger toward his wife in similar ways, he refused to talk. To restore the interpersonal bridge, Dr. Block commented on how difficult it was to talk about these things. She shared her own feelings of caution and embarrassment as she asked him these very personal questions. Joe seemed surprised that a therapist could have such feelings.

Toward the end of the second session, Dr. Block began to construct a genogram of Joe's family of origin (see Figure 15.1). In preparation for the third session, Dr. Block informed Joe that she wanted him to bring his wife to the next two sessions. His wife's help would be invaluable in the construction of his genogram, and Dr. Block wanted to assess the state of their marriage.

Joe's genogram was very revealing. His parents had divorced when he was three years old. Although his father had maintained some contact after

FIGURE 15.1
Genogram of Joe's Family

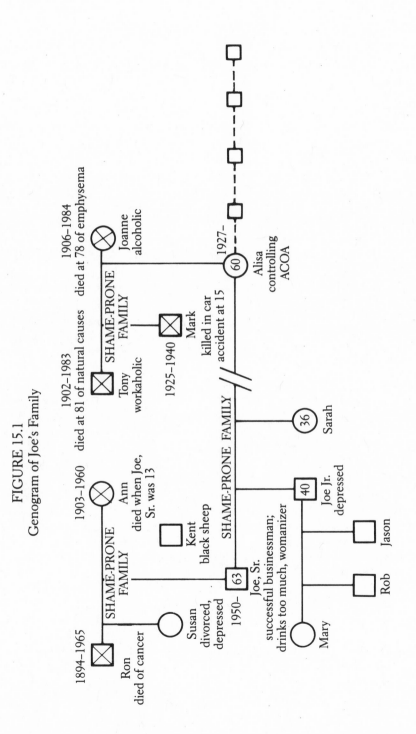

the divorce, it usually led to fighting between his parents. He and his father had restored some contact as Joe grew to adulthood. He described his mother as a controlling woman who interfered in everybody's business. His father was a successful businessman who drank too much and "womanized." His mother, Alisa, was the second child in her own family, and his father, Joe Sr., was the second child in his family.

Joe reported that things had been difficult when he was a child because his parents were divorced. He felt caught in the middle of a war that wasn't his, although he was the one who received the most wounds. As Joe grew older, his mother always had to know where he was and what he was doing. Feeling that she was too intrusive, he became more secretive. He resented the men whom she dated during his adolescent years. She loved to tell his father about them, and that infuriated Joe as well. He thought his mother's boyfriends were abusive and manipulative. They stole money from his mom, and she knew it and allowed it. He resented the sexual relationships he thought they had with her. Yet, as much as Joe felt disgust toward his mother, he also felt very responsible for her and did not want her to hurt so much. He wished he could fix her pain. He felt just as responsible for his father's pain. Why were they so unhappy and what could he have done to prevent the awful tragedy in their marriage and in their individual lives?

Joe had one sister, Sarah, four years younger than he was. She was born after his father and mother were divorced. He reported that their relationship was pretty good when they were younger. He took care of her because his mother didn't do a very good job. As they had both gotten older, they fought a lot about the kinds of guys she dated. Joe didn't approve of them and tried to run many of them off. He even got into a physical fight with one of her boyfriends.

Sarah was not married so she often visited Joe's family. Much as she did when they were young, she seemed to sense his pain and confusion. He reported that she worried too much about him, and she always hassled him by asking too many questions about his life and how he was doing. Sometimes he wanted to hide from her and never see her again.

Joe's maternal grandparents tried to help after his father and mother were divorced, but Joe's mom argued all the time with her mother, Grandma Joanne. Joanne was an alcoholic although she tried to keep it a secret. Grandpa Tony had protected Joanne by hiding her drinking from the family and the community. Alisa, Joe's mom, didn't really know how much her mother was drinking until she dropped by unannounced one morning. Her mother was passed out on the bathroom floor. Tony, Alisa's father, coped with his wife's drinking by investing himself in work. He tried to do everything for everybody, and Joe thought his grandfather often got "ripped off" by others.

Joe didn't know very much about his grandparents on the paternal side.

His father's mother, Ann, had died in an accident when his father was 13. His father's father, Ron, had died of cancer when Joe was 18. His father had one older sister, Susan, who was divorced and depressed. Kent, the younger brother, was the family black sheep and had not been heard from for over 40 years. No one knew whether he was dead or alive. Joe had not had much contact with his father's family. Joe's results on FACES III indicated that he perceived his family of origin to be chaotically disengaged, which is one of the types with high potential for fostering proneness to shame.

The results of the standardized tests and observational and interview data convinced Dr. Block that not only was Joe totally shame-prone but his family of origin was shaming as well. After seeing Mary and Joe with their children in the fourth session, Dr. Block had Mary complete the Internalized Shame Scale and had Joe and Mary complete Faces III for their immediate family. Dr. Block and two interns assigned to the therapy team completed the Assessment Checklist for Identifying a Shame-Prone Individual (Table 8.2) for Mary and each of the children, and one for the family system, Assessment Checklist for Identifying Shaming Systems (Table 8.6).

Dr. Block presented her assessment conclusions about the family to the therapy team. She thought Mary was shamed on intimacy issues and that their marriage had a shame-prone identity. As a couple and family, they felt bad and looked bad. She did not have conclusive information on the children, but had observed shame-prone behaviors when the children were in session. Yet in the workplace Joe appeared to be a capable, totally functional person. Because he shunned other people, only his family knew the shadow of shame within him.

Examples of Interventions Used in Early Stage of Therapy

Believing that Joe's symptoms of depression and his shame-proneness were related, Dr. Block decided to test this supposition by working the patterns on the treatment map. For the early stage of therapy, Dr. Block had three goals for using the treatment map (Table 10.1):

1. Based on what Joe had presented, identify an unmet need, an issue on the diagonal, or an affect that would provide a way to enter Joe's shame world.
2. Assist Joe to express his feelings and experience the unmet need and issue attached to the affect.
3. Confront Joe's games and beliefs that defended the pain and shame he felt.

In choosing where to enter Joe's shame, Dr. Block noted that Joe exhibited primarily anger. According to the treatment map and in spite of how successful Joe appeared, his anger suggested that he had the unmet need of being recognized and accepted for the things he "produced" and had probably experienced repeated rejections in shaming ways. Identification of this pattern (Table 10.3) completed the first step in working the map.

As Dr. Block focused on rejections that had occurred during Joe's life, he began to open up. He had always been very sensitive to others' expectations of him to get things done. He was supposed to achieve in school; his father always expected him to be better than the other kids. Yet he thought he was never good enough. His position in the family system made him more vulnerable to his father's unrealistic expectations and harsh demands. His mother expected him to take care of her and his younger sister because there was no father in the house. She called him her "little man of the house." Yet, as he watched boyfriend after boyfriend parade through his house, he felt a total sense of failure in "being the man of the house."

In order for Joe to feel that he was productive, he needed positive affirmation from one or both his parents, not just for the end product of good grades but as an acknowledgment of how hard he tried, of all of his attempts to do what they expected. Not being able to articulate this need and feeling rejected for his efforts, Joe experienced mounting anger and frustration. In therapy, as Joe began to acknowledge the source of his anger and identify issues of rejection, he more readily talked about his anger, rather than just being angry. By investigating the rejection issues and the shame that accompanied them, Dr. Block helped Joe to express his feelings and experience the unmet need and issue attached to the affect. With Joe she completed the second step of working the treatment map. Because it was the early stage of therapy, she didn't expect him to completely work through that pattern, nor any of the other patterns, but she was pleased to see him beginning the work.

The third step in working the map was to confront Joe's game of "To hell with you. I won't let you get close to me." She had experienced this message from the very first contact with him. During the third session, when Joe told her that he didn't care about anything, she reframed his statement as "I don't dare care because it would hurt too much if I did." Although somewhat shamed by the statement, it shocked him enough to break through his carefully built defense. For the next 20 minutes, he became totally "little." He put his hands over his eyes, started sobbing, pulled his feet up in the chair, and began rocking in synchrony with the sobbing. Dr. Block pulled her chair close to his and stayed with him, experiencing his "littleness" with him. When he was able to hear her, Dr. Block thanked him for listening to her and to himself and validated his capacity to feel. She affirmed his right to feel the emotions he was feeling and told him how proud she was of him at that moment. It appeared that Joe was beginning to uncover some of his shame and get in touch with his wounded inner child.

During this early stage of therapy, Dr. Block arranged for Joe to join a men's therapy group run by two other therapists at their clinic. The therapy team suggested that the therapists explore with Joe his sexual behavior and determine if he had sexual addiction cycles. This group was designed to give him support in and out of sessions while examining some of his issues in a group of men who were doing the same thing. She also recommended that he and his wife begin couples therapy with her and a male co-therapist. She let both he and his wife know that at some point in time they would also need to bring their sons to family sessions. She was careful to reassure Joe that the couple, family, and group involvement would in no way detract from his individual therapy.

MIDDLE STAGE OF THERAPY

The middle stage of therapy with Joe, his wife, his family, extended family, and group support lasted for a period of 14 months. During that time Dr. Block continued to meet with Joe in individual sessions; Dr. Rigby, a marriage and family therapist joined with her as they met with Joe and his wife on a regular basis and with their boys in occasional family sessions. When Mary and the boys needed some individual sessions, Dr. Rigby saw them. Joe continued with the men's therapy group at the clinic, and his wife attended a 12-step group for codependency. During the tenth month of therapy, Joe and Mary attended an intensive five-day family reconstruction workshop at the advice of Dr. Block. She and the therapy team were familiar with the workshop and were able to integrate Joe's and Mary's experiences with their ongoing therapy.

Therapist-Client(s) Relationship

The number of client-therapist relationships increased as Joe and his family were involved in therapy. All these relationships were vital to the outcome of therapy, but only Joe's client-therapist relationship is described here.

One of the tasks of the therapist during the middle stage is to move clients through various developmental stages of dependency. During the early stage of therapy, Joe learned that Dr. Block was willing to own her shame and provide a model for Joe to learn to appreciate and express his feelings. As their relationship developed, Joe became more and more dependent on Dr. Block. At times he even fantasized that she could be his mother and take care of him totally. Her message that he could be any way he felt in her office had begun to sink in. This type of dependency was not something that Dr. Block could support as the outcome of therapy. However, she recognized it as a necessary stage that Joe had to go through to reach the end goal of being able to function on his own and be whole. Dr. Block was capable of taking care of Joe and allowing him to be dependent on her, but she also wanted Joe to develop a sense of his own power. She recognized that she would have to set appropriate limits for Joe, just as a parent does with children at different developmental stages.

Dr. Block explained to Joe what was happening and what would occur in their relationship as therapy progressed. She told Joe that he was like a child in some ways. Because his need for dependency had not been met in his own family of origin, he found the acceptance of his dependency in the early sessions of therapy very comforting and satisfying. At times it probably even felt to him that he could never get enough of being cared for in this way. He was like a little child who wanted to be totally taken care of. Dr. Block informed Joe that she would never abandon him, that she would be responsible for him. He could depend on her. This meant that as various issues came up for him in therapy she would support him as he worked through the pain and confusion. In allowing him to be dependent, she would also be responsible to him and to herself. Being responsible to him meant helping him learn to be independent, and being responsible to herself meant setting limits explicitly and clearly.

She explained that the nature of dependency in their relationship would also change as therapy progressed and he became more accountable. They could both recognize that changes in dependency would be an indication that Joe was improving. She predicted that at some point in therapy he would become counterdependent, meaning that he would rebel against her and her authority. Although he would be angry and they might even fight about things he thought she wanted him to do, this transition into a different type of dependency relationship would be a positive sign. Later, their relationship would change even more, and he would seek to be totally independent of her, just as older adolescents strive to become separate and free of dependency on their families. As they moved toward the end of therapy, she explained, they would establish a more interdependent relationship. At that point he would be whole and ready to leave therapy. Joe didn't understand all that she was telling him, but he was very interested in the information.

Joe learned to trust Dr. Block more and more. He remembered that she had said early in therapy that he had no reason to trust her but she would earn her trust, and he would earn hers. What he discovered was that she meant it when she told him he could be any way he felt in therapy. He even tested it a few times. One day he came to therapy drunk. It took all the control that Dr. Block had to keep from inappropriately doing something "to" Joe. She was very angry at him, and she told him so. But in the next breath, she also told him that he couldn't use drinking to drive her away. She reframed it as an intimacy issue and told Joe that, if he felt they were getting too close, he could bring it up directly, and she would listen. However, if he thought drinking was a way to handle it, it wasn't going to work to drive her away. Even though she did not totally believe that intimacy regulation was the reason for Joe coming drunk, the reframe was a way to get at some of Joe's issues with intimacy. Dr. Block also told Joe that, although many in his family of origin had used alcohol to medicate their pain, she expected him to deal more directly with his issues. She would stay with him until she was sure that he was dealing directly with his pain.

Needless to say, that was the only time Joe ever came to a session drunk. He had tested her willingness to be accountable in providing appropriate dependency and intimacy in their relationship. Her willingness to set limits for him and for herself and to deal with intimacy matters directly appeared consistent and genuine to Joe. She seemed willing to stick with him through thick and thin, through his rage, anger/hurt, humiliation, fear, terror, and grief. Yet she wasn't willing to compromise her own boundaries and values to do so. That is the quality of the "interpersonal bridge" (Kaufman, 1989) that is healing to shame-prone clients.

Steps for Working Through Patterns
on the Treatment Map

The first three steps for working through the patterns on the treatment map were begun in the early stage of therapy. Certainly, there were still times when Joe became rageful or angry/hurt in the middle stage of therapy. When Joe moved into couple and family therapy with Dr. Rigby, he used the same game of "I don't care" and Dr. Rigby confronted him in the same way. Because Dr. Rigby and Dr. Block were co-therapists, they were able to coordinate working the map in individual sessions and couple and family sessions. The co-therapists for the mens' therapy group were also kept informed, so that the issues could be addressed, when appropriate, in the group.

The *fourth step* for working the treatment map takes major emphasis in the middle stage of therapy. Dr. Block and her team were to assist Joe and his family to identify and verbalize their shame-prone issue(s) on the diagonal, their unmet need(s) with their internal and behavioral responses, and emotions attached to the issues. Although these were cognitive processes, the only way Joe, Mary, and their boys could "identify" and "verbalize" was to experience the shame and abscessed pain attached to each pattern. Working this step for all of the individuals, the couple, and family system took time, patience, and much support.

The second part of this step involved identifying places, situations, and relationships where the issues, needs, and responses were manifested in Joe's and his family's lives. It is impossible to cover all of the details for this step, but enough examples are given to demonstrate procedures for accomplishing the goals. Therapists can use their own style of therapy to reach these goals and design strategies for specific clients.

Because Joe had many issues of rejection associated with unmet productivity needs and anger/hurt, Dr. Block continued work with that pattern. Whenever Joe started his angry tirades, Dr. Block reframed his anger as hurt. When he appeared angry, she would ask him to talk about the hurt; then she would ask him to express the hurt. During one session she used the Gestalt empty chair technique, making one empty chair Joe's hurt and the other Joe's anger. She then had Joe switch from chair to chair, being his hurt and his anger as they talked to each other. As Joe switched several times, he eventually ended up in his "hurt chair" sobbing.

As emotions of anger/hurt came up, Dr. Block explicitly connected those emotions to the interpersonal issue of rejection. She provided more information to Joe than she might normally give to clients because she knew he was the first child in his family, and first children need lots of information. She also taught Joe about his need for productivity. She explored the several contexts in which Joe's need to be productive was operating—his family of origin, his relationships with his wife and children, his work relationships, and others. Joe seemed very relieved to discover that Dr. Block could understand his processes. Throughout the educational and information-giving parts of sessions, Dr. Block was careful to always check with Joe to see what he was feeling and thinking. They identified his cynicism in response to not getting productivity needs met. His "I don't care" attitude soon lost its effectiveness as Dr. Block consistently reframed it as "not daring to care."

The experiential parts of the therapy in all modalities created activities for Joe to reexperience his pain and release it. Joe was eventually able to admit that his reclusiveness and shutting out of others were attempts to not be hurt anymore, to not be rejected again, and to not allow anyone to evaluate whether he and his products were good enough.

All of these attempts to explicitly identify the unmet needs, interpersonal issues, emotions, internal and behavioral responses, and contexts in which the pattern occurred were attempts by Dr. Block to work the fourth step in relation to the productivity/rejection/anger-hurt pattern. She was very much aware that they would reenact the same steps with each of the other patterns before therapy was finished.

They entered the *fifth step*, bridging the current to the past, when Dr. Block asked Joe to explore with her how this productivity/rejection/anger-hurt pattern has operated in his family of origin. In one session, Joe took the role of his father and reenacted an early childhood situation, with Dr. Block playing Joe's role. When they were finished, they each shared feelings they had experienced. Because Dr. Block had role played Joe's position, she was able to express many of the feelings Joe experienced in that situation but had felt at the time showed that he was "bad" and "crazy." Hearing and seeing her express them was a deeply moving experience. It allowed him to think that maybe he wasn't "crazy," since someone else in his role could also have those feelings.

In another session, they explored how Joe's mother contributed to his unmet need for productivity. As a result of these sessions, Joe agreed that he would be willing to schedule an extended family therapy session with both Dr. Rigby and Dr. Block present.

The *sixth step* involved getting Joe to explore cognitive, affective, and behavioral costs of maintaining his current behavioral responses to not getting his needs met. For Joe, this involved exploring what it cost him to maintain his reclusiveness, his cynicism, his anger and hurt, and his issues of rejection. Many of these costs had been alluded to as therapy had progressed. Now they would be addressed directly. Dr. Block worked steps six and seven at the same time.

For *step seven*, Joe and his therapist were to examine alternative patterns of beliefs, feelings, and behaviors that would not have the same costs as those identified in the preceding step. To work steps six and seven, Dr. Block used a reframing technique (Bandler & Grinder, 1982) that allowed Joe to go into a semi-trance state to work internally on costs of his dysfunctional behavior. Reframing also facilitates awareness of what people get out of continuing the maladaptive behavior in terms of secondary gains. The following dialogue illustrates how Dr. Block used the technique to get Joe in touch with not only what he got out of continuing the productivity/rejection/anger-hurt pattern but also what it was costing him.

Dr. Block: (after taking the time to have Joe close his eyes, deepen his breathing, and relax) Joe, go inside yourself. Find a place that seems peaceful and serene to you. When you find that place, imagine that it is magical—that somehow it can give you answers to many of the things you are confused about. In a moment you are going to ask this part of you if it is willing to communicate with you. It may take some time for you to get an answer. First, let's establish what a yes and a no response from that place will be. If the answer is yes, you will feel a tingling in the fingers of your right hand; if the answer is no, you will feel that those fingers are heavy, as though they are filled with water and weigh you down. Now ask that part of you if it is willing to communicate with you. When you have an answer, let me know.

Joe: I think I have an answer. He said yes.

Dr. Block: Good Joe. Now go back inside and thank that part of you for

being willing to communicate to you. Ask it if it is willing to give you
answers to some questions you are confused about.

Joe: The answer is yes. (The therapist already knew what the answer would
be because of the ideomotor signs in Joe's fingers.)

Dr. Block: Good, Joe. You are doing well. Now ask that part of you if it will
communicate with you about how cynical, reclusive, and rejecting
you become when others don't notice your contribution, your products, and your attempts.

Joe: The answer is yes. It's quite a list.

Dr. Block: Good. Now go back inside and thank that part for being willing
to communicate with you. Ask if it is willing to reveal to you all the
good things that happen to you because of that behavior, the pattern
of anger, hurt, rejection, not caring in response to not getting your
need to be productive met.

(There is silence for several minutes.)

Joe: I think I have a whole bunch of answers.

Dr. Block: Good, write that list in your mind so that you can remember it.
Now be sure to thank that part for giving you some answers.

Joe: Okay.

Dr. Block: Now ask that part of you to show what prices you pay to keep
the pattern going. First ask it to show you how it affects your relationship with others. Ask it to play it for you in different movie scenes.

Joe: (after several minutes in tears, but still with eyes closed) I can see.

Dr. Block: Thank the part for being so honest with you. Now ask it to show
you how continuing in the pattern of behavior affects how you feel
and think about yourself.

Joe: (again, after some silence) I have a list.

Dr. Block: Good. Be sure to thank the part. Now remember the list of good
things you get from keeping the pattern going. Go back and ask the
part to explore with you other ways of behaving that might help you
keep the good things happening but avoid the costs to you in relationships and the ways you feel and think about yourself.

Joe: (after a long period of silence) I have some.

Dr. Block: Good, Joe. Now ask the part if it is willing to let you choose one
of these other behaviors instead of continuing in the other pattern
that costs you so much.

Joe: The answer is yes.

Dr. Block: Now thank the part for its help and willingness to be so open
with you. Also imagine that the part thanks you, Joe, for being so
willing to ask these questions. When you are ready, please open your
eyes.

Of course, there are many other ways that therapists could work steps
six and seven with the patterns on the treatment map, but the reframing

technique above illustrates what needs to happen in terms of assessing interpersonal costs and clients' internal thoughts and feelings about themselves.

For *step eight*, Joe and Dr. Block stabilized and reinforced new patterns by rehearsing and learning new skills in sessions and testing them in other settings. Much in contrast to the first five steps, Joe exhibited responsible and accountable behavior. Gradually he developed new patterns of beliefs, feelings, and interpersonal interactions.

After they finished steps six and seven, Joe began exhibiting much less anger in therapy and in other relationships as well. This release of anger moved him into other emotions and issues on the map. At one point Joe really connected with his feelings of humiliation. As that happened Dr. Block began exploring his issues of worthlessness and his unmet dependency needs. With each new pattern that arose, Dr. Block continued to work the seven steps, ending by exploring alternative ways of behaving, rehearsing them in therapy sessions, and then assigning Joe to try out the new behaviors outside of the sessions. At first, Joe's marriage, family, and the support group served as the contexts in which Joe could try out the behavior. Then he moved into other settings.

At times Joe slipped back into previous patterns, but Dr. Block understood that such oscillations are a normal part of working through the map. Eventually Joe reached the point where he could begin grieving for all the losses, the unmet needs, the parents who were emotionally and psychologically unavailable to him, his family's inability to meet dependency and intimacy needs, his broken dreams, etc. At that point Dr. Block very explicitly connected his feelings of grief to the interpersonal issues of loss and his unmet need to have choices about how those things occurred in his life.

At times the therapy sessions included funeral rituals for some of Joe's losses. In one session, both he and his wife gave eulogy speeches to the dependency and intimacy that never existed in Joe's family. They cried together and they grieved together. For the first time they were able to really share with each other. It was ironic that the loss in Joe's family of origin was the very issue around which sharing and intimacy entered their marriage.

Couple, Family, and Therapy Sessions

The therapy that Drs. Block and Rigby did with Joe and Mary also focused on the patterns in the treatment map and on the dysfunctional beliefs and interaction patterns in their relationship. In one session Dr. Rigby made the pattern of collusion between the two of them very explicit and identified the unexpressed beliefs they both had about each other and about their relationship. As Joe worked through the pattern of productivity/ rejection/anger-hurt in individual sessions, this same pattern was worked for them as a couple. Neither of them felt that they had been able to be productive as a couple. They had failed to meet their goals and dreams in a large part because they had not been able to really share with each other.

In the marriage, the most observable problem seemed to be Joe's abusive behavior. Dr. Rigby was quite concerned initially for Mary's safety. He used a decision chart to determine whether or not they needed to be separated for a period of time to guarantee her safety (Rosenbaum & O'Leary, 1986). He and Dr. Block decided that they could safely stay together if Joe worked in individual therapy on anger control.

Using the treatment map, Dr. Rigby determined that the way to enter their shame as a couple was through the dependency/worthlessness/ humiliation pattern, since the outward behavioral response to the unmet need of dependency is abuse and being a victim. Mary was working two specific patterns in individual therapy—intimacy/insufficiency/rage, and sense and order/abandonment/fear. Joe had done some work in his therapy group on the pattern of sense and order/abandonment/fear, with Drs. Block and Rigby integrating the steps for them.

Using the seven steps for working the map, the therapists began to work through the pattern with them as a couple. As they worked on this issue as a couple, Dr. Rigby raised the issue of sexuality and their sexual relationship. Joe began to realize how angry he was with women and how he expressed much of his anger through inappropriate sexual manipulation.

At that point Dr. Rigby flipped to the first pattern on the treatment map, intimacy/insufficiency/rage, and connected Joe's feelings to the issues of being insufficient in situations that should have met his intimacy needs. After Joe reexperienced the pain of continually being rejected by both his mother and father when he tried to be close to them physically and emotionally, he was able to make some cognitive connections. He recognized how quickly he could flip from issues of insufficiency in intimacy contexts to issues of worthlessness in dependency contexts. Both intimacy and dependency dynamics were related to the way he interacted sexually. He realized how confusing his messages were to his wife, and how much of his behavior was motivated by his fear that she would eventually reject and abandon him.

Mary learned her part in this and dealt with her own pain. She would do anything to placate Joe because her fears were similar to his. She worried that someday he would leave her, and she was frightened.

Several family sessions were held with the couple and their two sons, Rob, 12 years old, and Jason, 10. In those sessions the therapist worked hard to open up lines of communication and establish patterns of sense and order. How the parents established rules and enforced them was a major topic. No one seemed to know. Boundaries were worked on as family members negotiated how to enter each others' personal space—actual physical space such as bedrooms as well as emotional and psychological space.

Sessions focused on getting the family to experience a greater range of emotions than just anger. The feeling-barometer game was learned and practiced in the family sessions. The rule for this game was that at any time when they were together someone could ask for a feeling-barometer check. Family members would, to the best of their ability, tell what they were feeling. The therapist modeled positively affirming behavior, thanking them for sharing their feelings and emphasizing that there were no "bad" feelings. Being included in the game, the therapist also modeled honesty and a range of feelings.

The family reenacted various conflicts and then tried alternative ways of behaving. Family sculpting was frequently used to assess how family members saw each other and how dependency and intimacy dynamics changed from time to time.

As therapy progressed, Joe stopped taking out his anger on his wife and children, and they began to behave in new ways as well. Toward the end of the middle stage, as Joe began to grieve, other family members also became much more aware of their own losses. The therapy team felt that it was important for the children to be able to observe at least part of Joe's grieving process. They were invited to participate in some of the funeral rituals, the forgiveness rituals, and the eventual celebration of wholeness ritual.

Joe was quite reluctant to participate in an extended family session when Dr. Block first proposed it. He was scared not only of his relatives but also of what he might do that could hurt them. They spent a great deal of time rehearsing, both in Joe's individual sessions and in couple and family sessions with the children, what would go on in the extended family session. They role played Joe's asking his father and mother and his sister Sarah to attend therapy with him. Dr. Rigby suggested ways that his wife and children could support him in extending the invitations. Joe's parents and sister agreed to come to therapy; it took some convincing to get Joe's father and mother to come to the same session, but Sarah helped talk them into it.

After introductions were completed, Dr. Rigby explained to Joe's parents and sister why they had been invited to the session. Dr. Block explained what her and Dr. Rigby's roles would be—that of facilitating exchange between family members and helping Joe and others really talk to each other. They explained that Joe had several unanswered questions about his early childhood. He wanted more information about that, and he also had some things to share with them.

Joe started the discussion by talking about what he hoped would happen as a result of this session and perhaps others with them. He told them about how he wished things could be different between them now. He had wished they could be different for him as a child. That couldn't happen, but perhaps he was in a place where he could have a different relationship with each of them now.

With the nudging of Drs. Block and Rigby and the help of his wife and boys, Joe told his parents and sister what he had learned about his need to be productive. He talked about how much he felt pushed as he grew up. He had tried to reach their expectations, but nothing he did ever seemed good enough.

Joe's father interrupted at that point to tell Joe that he had always been good enough for him. Dr. Rigby intervened to ask Joe's father if it was possible that his desires and concern for Joe were different from what his behavior often communicated to Joe. Dr. Block asked Joe's father if he was willing to find out from Joe what he had experienced.

Joe's parents were quite shocked to discover how badly Joe felt about his ability to please them. As they pointed to how successful he had been at work, Joe's wife asked them to listen to what Joe really had to say. The session ended with all agreeing that they had learned something new, even though the experience had been painful. They all agreed to return for several more sessions.

The last extended family session involved each member's asking for forgiveness from others. When it was Joe's father's turn, Dr. Rigby asked him if he would be willing to get down on one knee in front of Joe and ask for his forgiveness. Dr. Rigby helped Joe's father while Dr. Block helped Joe. When his dad asked Joe to forgive him, Joe burst into tears and literally collapsed into his father's arms. Dr. Rigby helped Joe's father hold Joe and rock him. It eventually culminated in an extended family holding in which everyone held each other, with Joe in the center. They ended the session talking about how their relationships were different and how they wanted them to continue to be as time went on.

Tracking Joe's Depression

One of the assessment goals in the middle stage of therapy was to monitor Joe's depression on a regular basis. There were times when Joe's symptoms got worse during the course of therapy. Particularly when Joe hit the pattern on the treatment map of uniqueness/emptiness/terror, he became worse. He had been doing fairly well prior to that time. This intense period of loneliness and terror lasted about one month and required a great deal of support from the therapy team, from the therapy group, and from Joe's family. In many ways it was the various support networks' ability to meet Joe's needs for intimacy and dependency that made a difference in how Joe did after the intense period was over.

As Joe moved into the pattern of choices/loss/grief, he became much less depressed. He was getting more in touch with his ability to make a difference and control his own life. He learned that he could redecide, make new choices, and be fully responsible for the results. Dr. Block re-administered the Beck Depression Inventory several times during Joe's therapy. As he moved into the final stage of therapy, his depression lifted and stayed that way. His medication was also discontinued.

FINAL STAGE OF THERAPY

The final stage of therapy for Joe and his immediate family lasted several months, but only five sessions were held during that time. Only two individual sessions were held with Joe, and they were one month apart. One couple and two family sessions were held to finalize couple and family business. Joe continued in his therapy group for some time after individual, couple, and family sessions were finished. Because Joe's father had started his own therapy at the clinic, Joe became involved in some of the family sessions with his father. Mary continued with her 12-step group and became a sponsor for a new member.

Learning to Live with Wholeness

At first, Joe had difficulty trusting how good he was doing and how well he was feeling. He experienced so many new feelings that he never knew he had. When asked to talk about different emotions, he could, rather than just being angry all the time. Even though his emotions fluctuated, he felt much more peace and joy.

Part of living with wholeness was accepting the child within him, the playful, creative, at times needy child. The work he had completed in this area had healed and freed this part of him, but he knew that other pieces would surface. He and Mary were having fun being children together, allowing some of the cuddling and touching needs to be met without becoming sexual. Getting on the floor and roughhousing with the boys with lots of laughter, hugging, and testing of muscles was fun for Joe. He had never experienced this kind of freedom before and he loved it.

Part of being whole for Joe was exploring his spirituality. Spending time outdoors, watching the stars, and feeling the wonder inspired by animals and plants gave him a sense of peace and a desire to acknowledge something greater than himself. These feelings contrasted sharply with the old feelings of having to go to church, feeling guilty and shamed because he didn't know how to please God any better than his parents.

However, with all this newness, Joe was also scared. He recognized that he needed to continue to relate to new friends he had developed, but he wasn't confident that he could trust the changes he had made, especially knowing that he wouldn't have the support of therapists so regularly.

The therapy team responded to these issues by suggesting to Joe that the time between sessions be extended. That way he could experiment with new behaviors and still have the benefit of returning to therapy sessions, both individually and with his wife and family. The team also suggested to Joe that he stay in the therapy group for a longer period of time. That way he would have the men's help as he "tried out" his new life. It was also suggested that he get involved in the scouting program with his boys. They were delighted when their father agreed to do so.

Changing Relationship with Therapy Team

When Joe began to realize that therapy was not going to last forever, he became angry at everybody. Inside he felt sad. Drs. Block and Rigby and the other members of the team had become so close to him. They had provided a place where he felt safe. He had learned to find himself with them, and he had learned that what was deep inside him wasn't "bad." In fact, he was beginning to believe that there was some good inside of him. Now leaving therapy meant that he would once again have to give up something very meaningful and precious. Mary and the boys had similar issues.

To help them with these issues, the team decided to develop a ritual with Joe, his family, and the entire treatment team. The ritual would help symbolize all the good that was part of the family's case and their relationships with the various therapists. The team decided that each therapist would make something that would symbolize how he or she felt about the relationship with Joe, Mary, Rob, and Jason. Team members would present these symbols to the family members, one by one, at an appropriate time during the ritual. They would give each person explicit permission to always keep a part of the team with him/her. Each could incorporate it into himself/herself to be an enduring part as long as she/he wished.

One by one, the therapists entered the room, placed a hand on Joe's shoulder and, looking into his eyes, asked him if he was willing to incorporate and always remember the gifts they offered him. Then they handed him something and named a specific gift that they had given him in therapy, e.g., the sharing of tears, a tough confrontation, patience, holding him—all gifts of love. They asked Joe if they could keep the gifts he had given them, and they enumerated them. For example, Dr. Block gave him a red rose and said this was to remind him of the love she had given him over the months. But it was also to remind him of the love he had for himself and his family. She thanked him for what she learned from his courage as he faced one painful episode after another. The therapists proceeded on to Mary, Rob, and Jason.

This beautiful ritual touched them all and healed the parting somewhat. The family was invited, when they were ready and if they wished, to come to the monthly open meetings held at the clinic, open to former clients and friends of the agency who wished to help with some community projects. The family seemed delighted to have the opportunity to do so.

Teaching Joe How to Identify If He Needed to Return to Therapy

The therapy team used the checklist for identifying individual shame, the checklist for identifying shaming systems, the Internalized Shame Scale, and the items on the Beck Depression Inventory to explicitly teach Joe and Mary about symptoms related to shame, depression, and family functioning. They also taught them about the difference between healthy guilt and shame. As a couple, they were assigned to review their own individual status and the state of their family on several occasions during that first year following therapy.

Using these checklists and inventories also helped Joe and his family see their progress during therapy. Their levels of current functioning were identified and compared to how they were before therapy started. The team congratulated them on their hard work, and they were told that they should return to the clinic if any of the symptoms on the checklists or inventories returned and lasted longer than ten days. The process for how to contact Dr. Block and Dr. Rigby was made explicit.

Believing in Joe

Approximately one year after therapy had ended, Joe called Dr. Block one day and asked if he and his wife could meet with the entire therapy team. When they showed up for the appointment, their outward appearance startled the team. Both of them had lost weight and appeared vibrant and happy. They reported that they had joined a local health spa and took much better care of themselves than they had in the past.

Joe started the session by telling the team why he had asked to meet with them. He wanted to thank them again for all they had done. When Dr. Block asked him if he could share what he thought had made the most difference in his therapy, Joe said, with tears in his eyes, "You believed in me and my family even when I wasn't capable of believing in myself or in them." This was a happy occasion for all as they shared other events that had transpired in their lives.

References

Akhtar, S., & Byrne, J. P. (1983). The concept of splitting and its clinical relevance. *American Journal of Psychiatry, 140,* 812–825.

Allred, K. D., & Smith, T. W. (1989). The hardy personality: Cognitive and physiological responses to evaluative threat. *Journal of Personality and Social Psychology, 56,* 257–266.

Alonso, A., & Rutan, J. S. (1988a). Shame and guilt in psychotherapy supervision. *Psychotherapy, 25,* 576–581.

Alonso, A., & Rutan, J. S. (1988b). The experience of shame and the restoration of self-respect in group therapy. *International Journal of Group Psychotherapy, 38,* 3–14.

Anderson, S. L. (1987). *Cognitive and affective interactional analysis of varied sibling position marital dyads using the systems approach to sibling position.* Unpublished dissertation, Brigham Young University, Provo, UT.

Aponte, H., & VanDeusen, J. M. (1981). Structural family therapy. In A. S. Gurman & D. P. Kniskern (Eds.). *Handbook of family therapy.* New York: Brunner/Mazel.

Araoz, D. L., & Negley-Parker, E. (1988). *The new hypnosis in family therapy.* New York: Brunner/Mazel.

Arnkoff, D. B. (1981). Flexibility in practicing cognitive therapy. In G. Emery, S. D. Hollon, & R. C. Bedrosian (Eds.), *New directions in cognitive therapy* (pp. 203–223). New York: Guilford.

Auerswald, E. H. (1987). Epistemological confusion in family therapy and research. *Family Process, 26,* 317–330.

Averill, J. R. (1982). *Anger and aggression: An essay on emotion.* New York: Springer-Verlag.

Bagarozzi, D. A., & Anderson, S. A. (1989). *Personal, marital, and family myths.* New York: W. W. Norton.

Bandler, R., & Grinder, J. (1975). *The structure of magic, I.* Palo Alto, CA: Science and Behavior Books.

Bandler, R., & Grinder, J. (1982). *Reframing.* Moab, UT: Real People Press.

Beall, L. (1972). The Shame and Guilt Test. Unpublished test, available from L. Beall, The Wright Institute, 2728 Durant Avenue, Berkeley, CA 94704.

Beattie, M. (1989). *Beyond codependency and getting better all the time.* New York: Harper & Row.

Beck, A. T. (1988). *Love is never enough.* New York: Harper & Row.

Beck, A. T., Rush, J. A., Shaw, B. R., & Emery, G. (1979). *Cognitive therapy of depression.* New York: Guilford.

Becvar, D. S., & Becvar, R. J. (1988). *Family therapy: A systemic integration*. Boston, MA: Allyn & Bacon.

Beer, W. R. (1988). *Relative stranger: Studies of stepfamily processes*. Totowa, NJ: Rowman & Littlefield.

Bensman, J. (1979). *Between public and private: The lost boundaries of the self*. New York: Free Press.

Benson, R. (1989). *Souls rising: A book of reflections and affirmations on life, relationships, sexuality, and spirituality*. London, Ontario: P. S. A. Ventures.

Bigner, J. J. (1971). Sibling position and definitions of self. *Journal of Social Psychology, 84*, 307–308.

Birtchnell, J. (1988). Defining dependence. *British Journal of Medical Psychology, 61*, 111–123.

Borysenko, J. (1987). *Minding the body, mending the mind*. Reading, MA: Addison-Wesley.

Boss, P. (1980). Normative family stress; Family boundary changes across the life-span. *Family Coordinator, 29*, 445–450.

Boss, P. (1984). Family boundary ambiguity: A new variable in family stress theory. *Family Process, 23*, 535–546.

Boss, P. (1988). *Family stress management*. Newbury Park, CA: Sage.

Boss, P., & Sheppard, R. (1988). Family victimization and recovery. *Contemporary Family Therapy: An International Journal, 10*, 202–215.

Boszormenyi-Nagy, I., & Spark, G. (1984). *Invisible loyalties: Reciprocity in intergenerational family therapy*. New York: Brunner/Mazel.

Boszormenyi-Nagy, I., & Ulrich, D. N. (1981). Contextual family therapy. In A. S. Gurman & D. P. Kniskern (Eds.), *Handbook of family therapy* (pp. 159–186). New York: Brunner/Mazel.

Bowen, M. (1978). *Family therapy in clinical practice*. New York: Aronson.

Boyce, W. D. (1974). *The relationship of family interaction style and age to adolescent conformity and individuation*. Unpublished master's thesis, Brigham Young University, Provo, UT.

Boyce, W. D., & Jensen, L. C. (1978). *Moral reasoning: A psychological-philosophical integration*. Lincoln: University of Nebraska Press.

Bozarth-Campbell, A. (1982). *Life is goodbye, life is hello: Grieving well through all kinds of losses*. Minneapolis, MN: CompCare.

Bradley, B. (1982). *Where do I belong? A kid's guide to stepfamilies*. Reading, MA: Addison-Wesley.

Bradshaw, J. (1988). *Healing the shame that binds you*. Deerfield Beach, FL: Health Communications.

Bry, A. (1978). *Visualization: Directing the movies of your mind*. New York: Harper & Row.

Burgoyne, J. L., & Clark, D. (1984). *Making a go of it: A study of stepfamilies in Sheffield*. Boston, MA: Routledge & Kegan Paul.

Burns, R. C. (1982). *Self-growth in families: Kinetic family drawings (K-F-D), research and application*. New York: Brunner/Mazel.

Capacchione, L. (1988). *The power of the your other hand*. North Hollywood, CA: Newcastle.

Carnes, P. (1989). *Contrary to love: Helping the sexual addict*. Minneapolis, MN: Compcare.

Carter, E. A., & McGoldrick, M. (1989). *The changing family life cycle: A framework for family therapy*. New York: Allyn & Bacon.

Cashmore, E. (1985). *Having to—The world of one parent families*. Boston, MA: Allen & Unwin.

Cattell, R. B., & Scheier, I. H. (1960). *Handbook and test kit for the objective-analytic anxiety battery*. Champaign, IL: Institute for Personality and Ability Testing.

Churchill, J. (1977). *Cognitive style and birth order: The intellectual responses of first-borns and third-borns to two hypothetical dilemmas*. Unpublished dissertation, University of Minnesota, Minneapolis, MN.

Cohen, L. H. (1988). *Life events and psychological functioning: Theoretical and methodological issues*. Newbury Park, CA: Sage.

Coleman, E. (1982). Family intimacy and chemical abuse: The connection. *Journal of Psychoactive Drugs, 14*, 153–157.

Combs, G., & Freedman, J. (1990). *Symbol, story, and ceremony: Using metaphor in individual and family therapy*. New York: W. W. Norton.

Constantine, L. L. (1986). *Family paradigms: The practice of theory in family therapy*. New York: Guilford.

Cook, D. R. (1987a). Measuring shame: The internalized shame scale. *Alcoholism Treatment Quarterly, 4*, 197–215.

Cook, D. R. (1987b). Self-identified addictions and emotional disturbances in a sample of college students. *Psychology of Addictive Behaviors, 1*, 55–61.

Cook, D. R. (1988, August). *The measurement of shame: The Internalized Shame Scale*. Paper presented at APA Convention, Atlanta, Georgia.

Cook, D. R. (1989). *Internalized Shame Scale*. Menomonie, Wisconsin.

Cook, D. R. (1990). *Draft manual: Clinical use of internalized shame scale*. Menomonie, WI: University of Wisconsin-Stout.

Damon, W. (1988). *The moral child: Nurturing children's natural moral growth*. New York: Free Press.

Dastrup, S. (1986). *Interaction in marital combinations of identical position dyads: Based on a systems approach to sibling position*. Unpublished dissertation, Brigham Young University, Provo, UT.

Denning, M., & Phillips, O. (1987). *Creative visualization: The fulfillment of your desires*. St. Paul, MN: Llewelyn.

De Rivera, J. (1977). *A structural theory of the emotions*. New York: International Universities Press.

Derlega, W. J., & Chaiken, A. L. (1975). *Sharing intimacy: What we reveal to others and why*. Englewood Cliffs, NJ: Prentice-Hall.

Dilts, R. B. (1983). *Roots of neuro-linguistic programming*. Cupertino, CA: META.

DiOrio, R. A. (1986). *The healing power of affirmation*. Garden City, NY: Image Books.

Donohew, H. E., Sypher, E., & Higgins, R. (1988). *Communication, social cognition, and affect*. Hillsdale, NJ: Erlbaum.

Duhl, F. J. (1981). The use of the chronological chart in general systems family therapy. *Journal of Marital and Family Therapy, 7*, 361–369.

Edwards, D. G. (1976). Shame and pain and "Shut up or I'll really give you something to cry about." *Clinical Social Work Journal, 4*, 3–13.

Einstein, E., & Albert, L. (1986). *Strengthening stepfamilies*. Circle Pines, MN: American Guidance Service.

Eisenstadt, M. (1989). *Parental loss and achievement*. Madison, CT: International Universities Press.

Elbow, M. (1982). Children of violent marriages: The forgotten victims. *Social Casework, 63*, 465–471.

Elkin, M. (1984). *Families under the influence*. New York: W. W. Norton.

Elkins, D. P. (1978). *Teaching people to love themselves*. Rochester, NY: Growth Associates.

Emery, G., Hollon, S. D., & Bedrosian, R. C. (1982). *New directions in cognitive therapy*. New York: Guilford.

Epstein, E. S., & Loos, V. E. (1989). Some irreverent thoughts on the limits of family therapy: Toward a language based explanation of human systems. *Journal of Family Psychology, 2,* 405–421.

Epstein, N. B., Bishop, D. W., & Baldwin, L. M. (1982). McMaster model of family functioning: A view of the normal family. In F. Walsh (Ed.), *Normal family processes* (pp. 115–141). New York: Guilford.

Evans, S. (1987). Shame, boundaries, and dissociation in chemically dependent, abusive, and incestuous families. *Alcoholism Treatment Quarterly, 4,* 157–179.

Fairbairn, W. R. D. (1963). Synopsis of an object-relations theory of the personality. *International Journal of Psychoanalysis, 44,* 224–225.

Falicov, C. (1988). *Family transitions: Continuity and change over the life cycle.* New York: Guilford.

Feinauer, L. L. (1984). Multiple family therapy for single rape victims and their families. In M. H. Hoopes, B. L. Fisher, & S. H. Barlow (Eds.), *Structured family facilitation programs: Enrichment, education, and treatment* (pp. 101–124). Rockville, MD: Aspen.

Feldman, L. B. (1979). Marital conflict and marital intimacy: An integrative psycho-dynamic-behavioral-systemic model. *Family Process, 18,* 69–78.

Fischer, S. F. (1985). Identity of two: The phenomenology of shame in borderline development and treatment. *Psychotherapy, 22,* 101–109.

Fisher, B. (1987). The process of healing shame. *Alcoholism Treatment Quarterly, 4,* 25–38.

Fisher, B. F., Giblin, P. R., & Hoopes, M. H. (1982). Healthy family functioning: What therapists say and what families want. *Journal of Marriage and Family Therapy, 8,* 273–284.

Fisher, B. F., & Sprenkle, D. H. (1978). Therapists' perception of healthy family functioning. *International Journal of Family Counseling, 6,* 1–10.

Ford, F. (1983). Rules; The invisible family. *Family Process, 22,* 135–145.

Fossum, M. A., & Mason, M. J. (1986). *Facing shame: Families in recovery.* New York: W. W. Norton.

Framo, J. (1976). Family of origin as a therapeutic resource for adults in marital and family therapy: You can and should go home again. *Family Process, 15,* 193–210.

Framo, J. L. (1981). The integration of marital therapy with sessions with family of origin. In A. S. Gurman & D. P. Kniskern (Eds.), *Handbook of family therapy* (pp. 133–159). New York: Brunner/Mazel.

Freeman, A. (1982). Dreams and images in cognitive therapy. In G. Emery, S. D. Hollon, & R. C. Bedrosian (Eds.), *New directions in cognitive therapy* (pp. 224–238). New York: Guilford.

Freedman, L., & Strean, H. S. (1986). *Guilt: Letting go.* New York: Wiley.

Frey, J., Holley, J., & L'Abate, L. (1979). Intimacy is sharing hurt feelings: A comparison of three conflict resolution models. *Journal of Marital and Family Therapy, 5,* 35–41.

Friesen, V. I. (1979). On shame and the family. *Family Therapy, 6,* 39–58.

Gaylin, W. (1984). *The rage within: Anger in modern life.* New York: Simon & Schuster.

Gelles, R., & Cornell, C. P. (1985). *Intimate violence in families.* Beverly Hills, CA: Sage.

Glover, J. (1988). *The philosophy and psychology of personal identity.* London: Penguin.

Goodbread, J. H. (1987). *The dreambody toolkit: A practical introduction to the philosophy, goals and practice of process-oriented psychology.* Boston, MA: Routledge & Kegan Paul.

Goodrich, W. (1984). Symbiosis and individuation: The integrative process for residential treatment of adolescents. *Current Issues in Psychoanalytic Practice, 1,* 23–45.

Gordon, D. (1978). *Therapeutic metaphors.* Cupertino, CA: META.

Gottschalk, L. A., & Gleser, G. (1969). *The measurement of psychological states through the content analysis of verbal behavior.* Berkeley, CA: University of California Press.

Grateful Members (1977). *The twelve steps for everyone who really wants them.* Minneapolis, MN: CompCare.

Greenway, J. D., & Greenway, P. (1985). Dimensions of interaction in psychotherapeutic groups: Sensitivity to rejection and dependency. *Small Group Behavior, 16,* 245–264.

Grotevant, H. D., & Carlson, C. I. (1989). *Family assessment: A guide to methods and measures.* New York: Guilford.

Grotstein, J. B. (1981). *Splitting and projective identification.* New York: Aronson.

Guerin, P. J., & Pendagast, E. C. (1976). Evaluation of family system and genogram. In P. J. Guerin (Ed.), *Family therapy: Theory and practice* (pp. 450–466). New York: Gardner.

Haley, J. (1987). *Problem solving therapy* (2nd ed.). San Francisco, CA: Jossey-Bass.

Hammond, D. C., Hepworth, D. H., & Smith, V. G. (1980). *Improving therapeutic communication.* San Francisco, CA: Jossey-Bass.

Hanna, S. (1982). *An empirical test of birth order influences upon social interaction in second- and fourth-borns.* Unpublished dissertation, Brigham Young University, Provo, UT.

Hardman, R., Hoopes, M. H., & Harper, J. M. (1987). Verbal interaction styles of two marital combinations: Based on a model for four sibling positions. *The American Journal of Family Therapy, 15,* 131–144.

Harper, J. M., & Elliott, M. L. (1988). Can there be too much of a good thing? The relationships between desired level of intimacy and marital adjustment. *American Journal of Family Therapy, 16,* 351–360.

Hauser, S. (1988). *Developmental projectories and family process: Normal, psychiatrically disturbed and diabetic adolescents.* Paper presented at third annual summer institute, Family Research Consortium, NIMH project #1R01MH40357, Hilton Head, SC.

Heise, D. R. (1979). *Understanding events: Affect and the construction of social action.* New York: Cambridge University Press.

Hersh, R. H., Politto, P., & Reimer, J. (1979). *Promoting moral growth: From Piaget to Kohlberg.* New York: Longman.

Hoblitzelle, W. (1982). *Developing a measure of shame and guilt and the role of shame in depression.* Unpublished dissertation, Yale University, New Haven, CT.

Hoopes, M. H. (1974). Touch me! Touch me not! *Family Perspective, 9,* 47–56.

Hoopes, M. H. (1987). Multigenerational systems: Basic assumptions. *American Journal of Family Therapy, 15,* 195–205.

Hoopes, M. H., & Harper, J. M. (1987). *Birth order roles and sibling positions in individual, marital, and family therapy.* Rockville, MD: Aspen.

Horowitz, M. (1981). Self-righteous rage and the attribution of blame. *Archives of General Psychiatry, 38,* 133–138.

Hultberg, P. (1988). Shame: A hidden emotion. *Journal of Analytical Psychology, 33,* 109–126.

Hyde, M. O. (1981). *My friend has four parents.* New York: McGraw-Hill.

Imber-Black, E., Roberts, J., & Whiting, R. (1988). *Rituals in families and family therapy*. New York: W. W. Norton.

Izard, C. (1977). *Human emotions*. New York: Plenum.

Jacob, T. J. (1987). *Family interaction and psychopathology: Theories, methods, and findings*. New York: Plenum.

Jones, E. E., Cumming, J. D., & Horowitz, M. J. (1988). Another look at the nonspecific hypothesis of therapeutic effectiveness. *Journal of Consulting and Clinical Psychology, 56*, 48–55.

Kalish, R. A. (1981). *Death, grief, and caring relationships*. Monterey, CA: Brooks/ Cole.

Kaufman, G. (1985). *Shame: The power of caring*. Rochester, VT: Schenkman.

Kaufman, G. (1989). *Psychology of shame: Theory and treatment of shame based syndromes*. New York: Springer.

Kehle, M. (1987). *In the middle: What to do when your parents divorce*. Wheaton, IL: H. Shaw.

Kemper, T. D. (1987). How many emotions are there? Wedding the social and autonomic components. *American Journal of Sociology, 93*, 263–289.

Kerr, M. E., & Bowen, M. (1988). *Family evaluation: An approach based on Bowen theory*. New York: W. W. Norton.

Kohlberg, L. (1981). *The philosophy of moral development: Moral stages and the idea of justice*. San Francisco, CA: Harper & Row.

Kohlberg, L. (1984). *The psychology of moral development: The nature and validity of moral stages*. San Francisco, CA: Harper & Row.

Kohlberg, L., Levine, C., & Hewer, A. (1983). *Moral stages: A current formulation and a response to critics*. New York: Karger.

Korpi, D. R. (1977). Psychohistorical aspects of shame and guilt as functions of political ideology. (Doctoral dissertation, California School of Professional Psychology, San Francisco). *Dissertation Abstracts International, 38*, 2866B.

Kramer, J. R. (1985). *Family interfaces: Transgenerational patterns*. New York: Brunner/Mazel.

Kurtines, W. M., & Gewirtz, J. L. (1987). *Moral development through social interaction*. New York: Wiley.

Kurtz, E. (1981). *Shame and guilt: Characteristics of the dependency cycle*. Center City, MN: Hazelden.

LaGrand, L. E. (1988). *Changing patterns of human existence: Assumptions, beliefs, and coping with the stress of change*. Springfield, IL: Charles C Thomas.

Lankton, S. (1980). *Practical magic*. Cupertino, CA: META.

Lansky, M. R. (1980). On blame. *International Journal of Psychoanalytic Psychotherapy, 8*, 429–456.

Lansky, M. R. (1984). Violence, shame and the family. *International Journal of Family Psychiatry, 5*, 21–40.

Lansky, M. R. (1985). Preoccupation and pathologic distance regulations. *International Journal of Psychoanalytic Psychotherapy, 11*, 409–425.

Lansky, M. R. (1986). Shame in the family relations of borderline patients. In J. S. Grotstein, M. Solomon, & J. Lang (Eds.), *The borderline patient: Emerging concepts in diagnosis, psychodynamics, and treatment*. Hillsdale, NJ: Analytic Press.

Lansky, M. (1987). Shame and domestic violence. In D. L. Nathanson (Ed.), *The many faces of shame* (pp. 335–362). New York: Guilford.

Larranaga, I. (1987). *Sensing your hidden presence: Toward intimacy with God*. Garden City, NY: Image Books.

Lauer, D. K. (1961). An investigation of defensive reactions to shame. (Dissertation, University of Pennsylvania). *Dissertation Abstracts International, 22*, 1285.

Lavee, Y., McCubbin, H. I., & Olson, D. H. (1987). The effects of stressful life events and transitions on family functioning and well-being. *Journal of Marriage and the Family, 49,* 857–873.

Lawson, G. W., Ellis, D. C., & Rivers, P. C. (1984). *Essentials of chemical dependency counseling.* Rockville, MD: Aspen.

Lazarus, R. (1984). On the primacy of cognition. *American Psychologist, 39,* 124–129.

Lewis, H. B. (1958). Overdifferentiation and underindividuation of the self. *Psychoanalysis and the Psychoanalytic Review, 45,* 3–24.

Lewis, H. B. (1986). The role of shame in depression. In M. Rutter, C. Izard, & P. Read (Eds.), *Depression in young people: Developmental and clinical perspectives.* New York: Guilford.

Lewis, H. B. (1987). Shame and the narcissistic personality. In D. L. Nathanson (Ed.), *The many faces of shame* (pp. 93–132). New York: Guilford.

Lewis, J. M., Beavers, W. R., Gossett, J. T., & Phillips, V. A. (1976). *No single thread: Psychological health in family systems.* New York: Brunner/Mazel.

Lewis, R. A., & Sussman, M. B. (1986). *Men's changing roles in the family.* New York: Haworth.

Lidz, T., & Fleck, S. (1985). *Schizophrenia and the family* (2nd ed.). New York: International Universities Press.

Lindsay-Hartz, J. (1984). Contrasting experiences of shame and guilt. *American Behavioral Scientist, 27,* 689–704.

Lusterman, D. (1985). An ecosystemic approach to family-school problems. *American Journal of Family Therapy, 13,* 22–30.

Luthman, S. G., & Kirschenbaum, M. (1974). *The dynamic family.* Palo Alto, CA: Science & Behavior Books.

Lynd, H. M. (1958). *On shame and the search for identity.* New York: Harcourt, Brace.

Madanes, C. (1981). *Strategic family therapy.* San Francisco, CA: Jossey-Bass.

Mahrer, A. R. (1990). *Dream work in psychotherapy and self-change.* New York: W. W. Norton.

Maslow, A. H. (1970). *Motivation and personality* (2nd ed.). New York: Harper & Row.

Masterson, J. F. (1985). *The real self: A developmental, self and object relations approach.* New York: Brunner/Mazel.

Masterson, J. F., & Klein, R. (1989). *Psychotherapy of the disorders of self: The Masterson approach.* New York: Brunner/Mazel.

McCubbin, H. I., Cauble, A., & Patterson, J. (1982). *Family stress, coping, and social support.* Springfield, IL: Charles C Thomas.

McCubbin, H. I., & Patterson, J. (1982). Family adaptation to crisis. In H. I. McCubbin, A. Cauble, & J. Patterson (Eds.), *Family stress, coping, and social support.* Springfield, IL: Charles C Thomas.

McGoldrick, M., Anderson, C., & Walsh, F. (1989). *Women in families: A framework for family therapy.* New York: W. W. Norton.

McGoldrick, M., & Carter, E. A. (1982). The family life cycle. In F. Walsh (Ed.), *Normal family processes* (pp. 167–195). New York: Guilford.

McGoldrick, M., & Gerson, R. (1985). *Genograms in family assessment.* New York: W. W. Norton.

McGoldrick, M., Pearce, J. K., & Giordano, J. (1982). *Ethnicity and Family Therapy.* New York: Guilford.

Meichenbaum, D. (1985). *Stress inoculation training.* New York: Pergamon.

Metzner, R. (1985). Knots, ties, nets, and bonds in relationships. *Journal of Transpersonal Psychology, 17,* 41–45.

Miller, A. (1981). *The drama of the gifted child*. New York: Basic.

Miller, S. B. (1988). Humiliation and shame: Comparing two affect states as indicators of narcissistic stress. *Bulletin of the Menninger Clinic, 52*, 40–51.

Miller, S. J. (1986). Conceptualizing interpersonal relationships. *Generations, 10*, 6–9.

Mills, J. C., & Crowley, R. J. (1986). *Therapeutic metaphors for children and for the child within*. New York: Brunner/Mazel.

Mindell, A. (1987). *The dreambody in relationships*. New York: Routledge & Kegan Paul.

Minuchin, S., & Fishman, C. H. (1981). *Family therapy techniques*. Cambridge, MA: Harvard University Press.

Morrison, A. (1987). The eye turned inward: Shame and the self. In D. L. Nathanson (Ed.), *The many faces of shame* (pp. 271–291). New York: Guilford.

Mowatt, M. H. (1987). *Divorce counseling: A practical guide*. Lexington, MA: Lexington Books.

Naiditch, B. (1987). Rekindled spirit of a child: Intervention strategies for shame with elementary age children of alcoholics. *Alcoholism Treatment Quarterly, 4*, 57–69.

Nathanson, D. L. (Ed.) (1987a). *The many faces of shame*. New York: Guilford.

Nathanson, D. L. (1987b). A timetable for shame. In D. L. Nathanson (Ed.), *The many faces of shame* (pp. 1–63). New York: Guilford.

Nathanson, D. L. (1987c). Shaming systems in couples, families, and institutions. In D. L. Nathanson (Ed.), *The many faces of shame* (pp. 246–270). New York: Guilford.

Nelson, J. B. (1988). *The intimate connection: Male sexuality, masculine spirituality*. Philadelphia: Westminster Press.

Nelson, T. S. (1989). Book review: Birth order roles and sibling patterns in individual and family therapy. *Journal of Marital and Family Therapy, 15*, 435–438.

Olson, D. H., McCubbin, H. I., Barnes, H., Larsen, A., Muxen, M., & Wilson, M. (1983). *Families: What makes them work*. Beverly Hills, CA: Sage.

Olson, D. H., Portner, J., & Lavee, Y. (1985). *Family Adaptability and Cohesion Evaluation Scales III*. St. Paul, MN: University of Minnesota.

Olson, D. H., Sprenkle, D. H., & Russell, C. S. (1979). Circumplex model of marital and family systems: I. Cohesion and adaptability dimensions, family types, and clinical applications. *Family Process, 18*, 3–28.

Papp, P. (1983). *The process of change*. New York: Guilford.

Patent, A. M. (1984). *You can have it all: The art of winning the money game and living a life of joy*. Piermont, NY: Money Mastery Publishing.

Patent, A. M. (1989). *Death, taxes, and other illusions*. Piermont, NY: Celebration Publishing.

Patton, D., & Waring, E. M. (1984). The quality and quantity of marital intimacy in the marriage of psychiatric patients. *Journal of Sex and Marital Therapy, 10*, 201–206.

Pearlin, L. I., & Schooler, C. (1983). The structure of coping. In H. I. McCubbin, A. Cauble, & J. Patterson (Eds.), *Family stress, coping, and social support*. Springfield, IL: Charles C Thomas.

Peele, S., & Brodsky, A. (1975). *Love and addiction*. New York: Taplinger.

Pendagast, E. G., & Sherman, C. O. (1979). A guide to the genogram. *The Family, 5*, 101–112.

Perlman, M. (1958). An investigation of anxiety as related to guilt and shame. *Archives of Neurological Psychiatry, 80*, 752–759.

Phillipson, C., Bernard, M., & Strang, P. (1986). *Dependency and interdependency in old age.* London: Croom Helm, in Association with the British Society of Gerontology.

Pichert, J. W., & Elam, P. (1986). Guilt and shame in therapeutic relationships. *Patient Education and Counseling, 8,* 359–365.

Pillari, V. (1986). *Pathways to family myths.* New York: Brunner/Mazel.

Ponizovsky, A. M., & Rotenberg, V. S. (1987). Psychological mechanisms of dependent relations and the methods of their psychotherapeutic correction. *Psikologicheskii Zhurnal, 8,* 118–124.

Potter, E., & Ronald, T. (1987). Shame and guilt: Definitions, processes, and treatment issues with AODA clients. *Alcoholism Treatment Quarterly, 4,* 7–24.

Reimer, J., Paolitto, D. P., & Hersh, R. H. (1983). *Promoting moral growth: From Piaget to Kohlberg.* New York: Longman.

Reiss, D. (1981). *The family's construction of reality.* Cambridge, MA: Harvard University Press.

Ritterman, M. (1983). *Using hypnosis in family therapy.* San Francisco, CA: Jossey-Bass.

Roddy, P. P. (1984). *A closer look at children in single-parent families.* New York: ERIC Clearinghouse on Urban Education, Institute for Urban and Minority Education, Columbia University.

Rosenbaum, A., & O'Leary, K. D. (1986). The treatment of marital violence. In N. S. Jacobson, & A. S. Gurman (Eds.), *Clinical handbook of marital therapy* (pp. 385–406). New York: Guilford.

Russell, D. (1984). *Sexual exploitation.* Beverly Hills: Sage.

Ryan, P. (1981). *Single parent families.* Washington, DC: U.S. Department of Health and Human Services, Office of Human Development Services, Administration for Children, Youth, and Families. (DHHS publication no. (OHDS) 79-30247.)

Satir, V. (1972). *Peoplemaking.* Palo Alto, CA: Science and Behavior Books.

Satir, V., & Baldwin, M. (1983). *Satir step-by-step: A guide to creating change in families.* Palo Alto, CA: Science and Behavior Books.

Schaef, A. W. (1987). *When society becomes an addict.* San Francisco, CA: Harper & Row.

Schaefer, M. T., & Olson, D. H. (1981). Assessing intimacy: The PAIR Inventory. *Journal of Marital and Family Therapy, 7,* 47–60.

Scharff, D. E., & Scharff, J. S. (1987). *Object relations family therapy.* Northvale, NJ: Aronson.

Scheff, T. J. (1985). Universal expressive needs: A critique and a theory. *Symbolic-Interaction, 8,* 241–262.

Schneider, C. D. (1977). *Shame, exposure, and privacy.* Boston: Beacon Press.

Schulman, M., & Melker, E. (1985). *Bringing up a moral child: A new approach for teaching your child to be kind, just, and responsible.* Reading, MA: Addison-Wesley.

Semin, G. R. (1983). *The accountability of conduct: A social psychological analysis.* New York: Academic Press.

Severine, S. K., McNut, E. R., & Feder, S. L. (1987). Shame and the development of autonomy. *Journal of the American Academy of Psychoanalysis, 15,* 93–106.

Seymour, W. R. (1982). Counselor/therapist values and therapeutic style. In J. C. Hansen & L. L'Abate (Eds.), *Values, ethics, legalities and the family therapist.* Rockville, MD: Aspen.

Shane, P. (1980). Shame and learning. *American Journal of Orthopsychiatry, 50,* 348–355.

Sheperd, S. (1988). *Survival handbook.* Minneapolis, MN: CompCare Publishers.

ɔnerman, R., & Freedman, N. (1986). *Handbook of structured techniques in marriage and family therapy*. New York: Brunner/Mazel.

Shotter, J. (1984). *Social accountability and selfhood*. New York: Blackwell.

Sidoli, M. (1988). Shame and the shadow. *Journal of Analytical Psychology, 33,* 127–142.

Simos, B. G. (1979). *A time to grieve: Loss as a universal human experience*. New York: Family Service Association of America.

Slipp, S. (1984). *Object relations: A dynamic bridge between individual and family treatment*. New York: Aronson.

Slipp, S. (1988). *The technique and practice of object relations family therapy*. Northvale, NJ: Aronson.

Smith, R. (1972). The relative proneness to shame and guilt as an indicator of defensive style. (Unpublished doctoral dissertation, Northwestern University). *Dissertation Abstracts International, 33,* 2823B–2824B.

Stahmann, R. F., & Harper, J. M. (1983). Therapist-patient relationships in marital and family therapy. In M. J. Lambert (Ed.), *Psychotherapy and patient relationships* (pp. 190–230). Homewood, IL: Dow Jones-Irwin.

Stahmann, R. F., & Hiebert, W. J. (1987). *Premarital counseling: The professional's handbook* (2nd ed.). Lexington, MA: Lexington Books.

Stierlin, H. (1974a). Shame and guilt in family relations. *Archives of General Psychiatry, 30,* 381–389.

Stierlin, H. (1974b). *Separating parents and adolescents*. New York: Quadrangle.

Stone, H., & Winkelman, S. (1986). *Embracing ourselves*. Marina Del Ray, CA: Devors.

Stroup, M. R., Harper, J. M., Steele, W. R., & Hoopes, M. H. (1984). Helping stepfamilies get in step. In M. H. Hoopes, B. L. Fisher, & S. H. Barlow (Eds.), *Structured family facilitation programs: Enrichment, education, and treatment* (pp. 355–374). Rockville, MD: Aspen.

Thrane, G. (1979). Shame. *Journal of Theory of Social Behavior, 9,* 139–166.

Toman, W. (1976). *Family constellation*. New York: Springer.

Toman, W. (1988). *Family therapy and sibling position*. Northvale, NJ: Jason Aronson.

Tomm, K. (1987). Interventive interviewing: Part I. Strategizing as a fourth guideline for the therapist. *Family Process, 26,* pp. 3–14.

Tompkins, S. S. (1962). *Affect, imagery, and consciousness*, Vol. 1. New York: Springer.

Tompkins, S. S. (1963). *Affect, imagery and consciousness*, Vol. 2. New York: Springer.

Tompkins, S. S. (1982). Affect theory. In P. Ekman (Ed.), *Emotion in the human face* (pp. 353–395). Cambridge, England: Cambridge University Press.

Tompkins, S. S. (1984). Affect theory. In K. R. Scherer & P. Ekman (Eds.), *Approaches to emotion*. Hillsdale, NJ: Erlbaum.

Tompkins, S. S. (1987). Shame. In D. L. Nathanson (Ed.), *The many faces of shame* (pp. 133–163). New York: Guilford.

Umbarger, C. C. (1983). *Structural family therapy*. New York: Grune & Stratton.

Ursu, M. W. (1984). *An investigation of the construct validity of several measures of proneness to shame*. Unpublished dissertation, University of Minnesota, Minneapolis, MN.

Van Kaam, A. (1987). Addiction: Counterfeit of religious presence. *Studies in Formative Spirituality, 8,* 243–255.

Visher, E. B., & Visher, J. S. (1988). *Old loyalties, new ties: Therapeutic strategies with stepfamilies*. New York: Brunner/Mazel.

Vivekananda, K., & Nicholson, S. (1987). *Picking up the pieces: Helping young people cope with divorce and stepfamilies*. Boston: Allen & Unwin.

Von Bertalanffy, L. (1968). *General system theory*. New York: George Braziller.

Waring, E. M. (1981). Facilitating intimacy through self-disclosure. *American Journal of Family Therapy, 9*, 33–42.

Waring, E. M. (1988). *Enhancing marital intimacy through facilitating cognitive self-disclosure*. New York: Brunner/Mazel.

Weenolsen, P. (1988). *Transcendence of loss over the life span*. New York: Hemisphere.

Wegscheider-Cruse, S. (1985). *Choicemaking for codependents, adult children, and spirituality seekers*. Deerfield Beach, FL: Health Communications.

Wegscheider-Cruse, S. (1989). *Training manual for experiential therapy*. Rapid City, SD: Nurturing Networks.

Wegscheider-Cruse, S., & Cruse, J. R. (1989). *The co-dependency trap*. Rapid City, SD: Nurturing Networks.

Weigel, D. E. (1974). The association of parent/child-rearing practices with children's reports of shame and guilt (Dissertation, Michigan State University). *Dissertation Abstracts International, 361B*, 462.

Whitaker, C. A., & Keith, M. D. (1981). Symbolic-experiential family therapy. In A. S. Gurman & D. P. Kniskern (Eds.), *Handbook of family therapy* (pp. 187–225). New York: Brunner/Mazel.

Whitfield, C. L. (1987). *Healing the child within*. Deerfield Beach, FL: Health Communications.

Wicker, F. W., Payne, G. D., & Morgan, R. D. (1983). Participant descriptions of guilt and shame. *Motivation and Emotion, 7*, 25–39.

Wilde, S. (1987). *Affirmations*. Taos, NM: White Dove International.

Williamson, D. S. (1981). Personal authority via termination of the intergenerational hierarchical boundary: A new stage in the family. *Journal of Marital and Family Therapy, 7*, 441–452.

Williamson, D. S. (1982a). Personal authority via termination of the intergenerational hierarchical boundary: Part II—the consultation process and the therapeutic method. *Journal of Marital and Family Therapy, 8*, 23–38.

Williamson, D. S. (1982b). Personal authority via termination of the intergenerational hierarchical boundary: Personal authority defined, and the power of play in the change process. *Journal of Marital and Family Therapy, 8*, 309–321.

Windmiller, M., Lambert, N., & Turiel, E. (1980). *Moral development and socialization*. Boston: Allyn & Bacon.

Woititz, J. G. (1985). *Struggle for intimacy*. Minneapolis, MN: Compcare.

Wolin, S. J., & Bennett, L. A. (1984). Family rituals. *Family Process, 23*, 401–420.

Wolin, S. J., Bennett, L. A., & Jacobs, J. S. (1988). Assessing family rituals in alcoholic families. In E. Imber-Black, J. Roberts, & R. Whiting (Eds.), *Rituals in families and family therapy* (pp. 230–256). New York: W. W. Norton.

Wright, F. (1987). Men, shame, and antisocial behavior: A psychodynamic perspective. *Group, 11*, 238–246.

Wurmser, L. (1981). *The mask of shame*. Baltimore: Johns Hopkins University Press.

Wurmser, L. (1987). Shame: The veiled companion of narcissism. In D. L. Nathanson (Ed.), *The many faces of shame* (pp. 64–92). New York: Guilford.

Zinner, J. (1974). The implications of projective identification for marital interaction. In H. Grunebaum & J. Christ (Eds.), *Contemporary marriage* (pp. 293–308). Boston: Little, Brown.

Zuk, G. R., & Zuk, C. V. (1987). Parental blaming and acquisition of guilt: A developmental task of childhood. *Contemporary Family Therapy: An International Journal, 9*, 221–228.

Name Index

Subject Index